社会契约论
·双语版·

[法]卢 梭◎著　戴光年◎译

（鄂）新登字08号

图书在版编目(CIP)数据

社会契约论：双语版/ (法) 卢梭(Rousseau,J.J.) 著；
戴光年译. —武汉：武汉出版社,2012.4（2015.2重印）
ISBN 978-7-5430-6736-3

Ⅰ.①社… Ⅱ.①卢…②戴… Ⅲ.①英语－汉语－
对照读物②政治哲学－法国－近代 Ⅳ.①H319.4：D

中国版本图书馆CIP数据核字(2012)第032926号

社会契约论：双语版

著　　者：[法]卢　梭 著　戴光年　译
策划编辑：李异鸣
特约编辑：周乔蒙
责任编辑：万洪涛
封面设计：上尚设计
出　　版：武汉出版社
社　　址：武汉市江汉区新华下路103号　　邮　编：430015
电　　话：(027)85606403　85600625
http://www.whcbs.com　　　E-mail:zbs@whcbs.com
印　　刷：北京市文林印务有限公司　　经　销：新华书店
开　　本：787mm×1092mm　　1/16
印　　张：17.75　　字　数：260千字
版　　次：2012年4月第1版　　2015年2月第2次印刷
定　　价：22.00元

版权所有·侵权必究
如有质量问题，由承印厂负责调换。

译序

  文明时代的一切思想在不断向前发展，即使是对人类最有益的最杰出的著作，在经过一段时期之后，可能也会由于更新的发现而减少它原来的价值。但有些却不会，时间的推移非但不会减少它的光彩，反而会历久弥新，不断焕发新的生命力。无疑，本书就是这样一部伟大的著作。

  这本产生于18世纪的政治理论书籍从它诞生之初便不断被编者出版，被人们热读，直到今天，它的内容还在不断被引用着和争论着。这本叫做《社会契约论》的不足十万字的薄薄小书，有如此魅力长留于世，何以然？

  本书的作者让·雅克·卢梭（1712-1778）生于瑞士日内瓦，但他大部分时间都在法国活动。卢梭思想活跃、多才多艺，在自然科学、文学、音乐、哲学、教育等领域都有很深的造诣。他是18世纪法国大革命的思想先驱，启蒙运动最卓越的代表人物之一。代表作主要有：政治性著述《论人类不平等的起源和基础》和《社会契约论》，教育专著《爱弥儿》，自传体文学作品《忏悔录》。卢梭经历坎坷，一生几乎都处于颠沛流离之中，还因为其著作触犯权威而屡遭驱逐和通缉，并遭到很多人的谴责唾弃，但死后却受人膜拜。正如尼采所说："我的时代还没来到，有些人是为后世而生的。"古往今来，有识之士都在探讨如何建立一种合乎人类本性的最理想的社会组织形式。无疑，这本书对这种探索提供了一种新的途径。

  《社会契约论》于1762年4月出版，它开篇便提出"人是生而自由的，却又无

社会契约论
The Social Contract

时不处在枷锁之中。"指明了人类对自由、平等的永恒追求，一问世便在欧洲社会引起了巨大的震动。这本书的中心思想是：人是生来自由和平等的，国家是自由协议的产物；一切主权和立法权都属于人民的集合体，政府只是这个集合体事务的执行者，并不拥有主权；一旦政府滥权，人民就有资格推翻它。

卢梭在书中为我们描摹出了理想之国的样子，这种理想之国却是一个很难实现的梦想，但这并不影响这部书的伟大，正如卢梭在文中所说的："难道明知道不平等是不可避免的，就不采取措施加以控制了吗？"的确，难道我们明知建立一个完全自由与平等的理想国度不可能，难道就停止对它的探索吗？

关于对社会契约思想的探讨，卢梭不是第一个，也不是最后一个，然而他恰恰生于一个伟大的时代。在他死后的第11年，法国大革命爆发，这本《社会契约论》便被作为革命者们所奉行的宝典。法国大革命的领袖罗伯斯庇尔对卢梭更是推崇备至，曾在卢梭生前专程登门拜访，向其讨教，在卢梭死后还献上了橡树叶的花冠。今天，在法国国民议会的大厅中，卢梭的半身像与美国开国领袖华盛顿及富兰克林的像相面而立，他所倡导的民主与自由更是深深地扎根于人们的思想之中。

卢梭不但是一个伟大的思想家，更是一个浪漫主义文学家。在这本书中，通篇都能感受到他那种抑制不住的热情在时时感染着读者，这或许也是这本书盛行不衰的原因之一吧。

二百多年过去了，在民主与自由的理念早已深入人心的今天，我们惊喜地发现，这本书依然可以作为指引众人前行的灯塔，因为民主与自由是任何文明的时代和任何文明的国度都无法避免的话题。我们有必要把这本小册子拿出来重读一遍，让民主与自由的种子在我们的心中长成参天大树。

能对这样一本伟大的作品重新加以编译，编者在深感荣幸的同时，也满怀惶恐与不安，但既做之，则安之，我们将以最大的努力来回报作者及先贤。对于书中的疏漏与不足，也恳请诸位读者不吝批评与指教。

最后引用托尔斯泰评价卢梭的话作为本篇的结束语："卢梭是不老的。"

是的，真理万岁。

目录

前言

第一卷 / 003

第一章　本卷要旨 / 005

第二章　论最初形态的社会 / 006

第三章　论最强者的权力 / 008

第四章　论奴隶制度 / 009

第五章　论必须追溯最初的契约 / 014

第六章　论社会契约 / 015

第七章　论主权体 / 017

第八章　论公民社会 / 019

第九章　论财产权 / 020

社会契约论
The Social Contract

第二卷 / 023

第一章　论主权是不可转让的 / 027

第二章　论主权是不可分割的 / 028

第三章　论公意是否会犯错 / 030

第四章　论主权权力的限度 / 032

第五章　论生死权 / 035

第六章　论法律 / 036

第七章　论立法者 / 039

第八章　论人民 / 043

第九章　论人民（续）/ 044

第十章　论人民（再续）/ 046

第十一章　论种种不同的法律体系 / 049

第十二章　法律的分类 / 051

第三卷 / 053

第一章　政府总论 / 057

第二章　论不同政府形式的构成原则 / 062

第三章　论政府的分类 / 064

第四章　论民主制度 / 065

第五章　论贵族制 / 067

第六章　论君主制 / 069

第七章　论混合形式的政府 / 074

第八章　论任何一种政府形式都不能适用于所有国家 / 075

第九章　论一个好政府的标志 / 079

第十章　论政府的滥用权力和它衰退的倾向 / 081

第十一章　论政治体的灭亡 / 083

第十二章　论如何维持主权权威 / 084

第十三章　论如何维持主权权威（续）/ 085

第十四章　论如何维持主权权威（再续）/ 087

第十五章　论议员或代表 / 088

第十六章　论政府的建立不是一项契约 / 091

第十七章　论政府的建立 / 092

第十八章　论防止政府篡权的方法 / 093

第四卷 / 097

第一章　论公意是不可摧毁的 / 099

第二章　论投票权 / 101

第三章　论选举 / 104

第四章　论罗马的人民大会 / 106

第五章　论保民官制 / 115

第六章　论独裁制 / 117

第七章　论监察官制 / 119

第八章　论公民宗教 / 121

第九章　结语 / 131

社会契约论
The Social Contract

PREFATORY NOTE / 133

BOOK ONE / 135

CHAPTER 1 Subject of the First Book / 137

CHAPTER 2 Primitive Societies / 138

CHAPTER 3 The Right of the Strongest / 140

CHAPTER 4 Slavery / 141

CHAPTER 5 That It Is Always Necessary to Go Back to a First Convention / 145

CHAPTER 6 The Social Pact / 146

CHAPTER 7 The Sovereign / 149

CHAPTER 8 The Civil State / 151

CHAPTER 9 Real Property / 152

BOOK TWO / 157

CHAPTER 1 That Sovereignty is Inalienable / 159

CHAPTER 2 That Sovereignty is Indivisible / 160

CHAPTER 3 Whether the General Will Can Err / 162

CHAPTER 4 The Limits of the Sovereign Power / 164

CHAPTER 5 The Right of Life and Death / 168

CHAPTER 6 The Law / 170

CHAPTER 7 The Legislator / 173

CHAPTER 8 The People / 177

CHAPTER 9 The People(continued) / 179

CHAPTER 10 The People(continued) / 181

CHAPTER 11 The Different of Legislation / 184

CHAPTER 12 Division of the Laws / 186

BOOK THREE / 188

CHAPTER 1 Government in General / 191

CHAPTER 2 The Principle which Constitutes the Different Forms of Government / 197

CHAPTER 3 Classification of Governments / 199

CHAPTER 4 Democracy / 201

CHAPTER 5 Aristocracy / 203

CHAPTER 6 Monarchy / 205

CHAPTER 7 Mixed Governments / 210

CHAPTER 8 That Every Form of Government Is Not Fit for Every Country / 211

CHAPTER 9 The Marks of a Good Government / 216

CHAPTER 10 The Abuse of the Government and Its Tendency to Degenerate / 219

CHAPTER 11 The Dissolution of the Body Politic / 222

CHAPTER 12 How the Sovereign Authority Is Maintained / 223

CHAPTER 13 How the Sovereign Authority Is Maintained (continued) / 224

CHAPTER 14 How the Sovereign Authority Is Maintained (continued) / 226

CHAPTER 15 Deputies or Representatives / 227

CHAPTER 16 That the Institution of the Government Is Not a Contract / 230

CHAPTER 17 The Institution of the Government / 231

CHAPTER 18 Means of Preventing Usurpations of the Government / 233

社会契约论
The Social Contract

BOOK FOUR / 237

CHAPTER 1   That the General Will Is Indestructible / 239

CHAPTER 2   Voting / 241

CHAPTER 3   Elections / 244

CHAPTER 4   The Roman Comitia / 246

CHAPTER 5   The Tribuneship / 256

CHAPTER 6   The Dictatorship / 258

CHAPTER 7   The Censorship / 261

CHAPTER 8   Civil Religion / 263

CHAPTER 9   Conclusion / 273

 # 前 言

这篇短论是我多年前想试图完成却没有完成的一部长篇著述中的一部分,由于当时没能充分认识到自身能力,这部长篇著述我已经放弃很多年了。在已经完成的部分中,本文是最有意义的,也是我认为最值得奉献给公众的,其余部分已尽悉毁去。

社会契约论
The Social Contract

　　我写作本文意在探讨：从人类本身的实际情况着眼，结合法律的可能性，在公民社会秩序中是否存在某种合法又确切的政权准则。在探讨中，我会尽力将权利所许可的和利益所要求的结合起来，以使正义和利益两者并存。

　　在尚未证明我论题的重要性之前，我已经开始了我的研究。有人也许会问我：你如此热衷于对政治问题的论述，你是一位君主或立法者吗？我会回答：我不是。但这正是我做这件事的原因，如果我是君主或立法者，我将不会把这么多时间浪费在讨论上，我所做的，会是采取行动或保持沉默。

　　生为一个自由国度中的公民和这个政权下的一员，我明白我的声音对公共事务的影响是极其微弱的，但我既然拥有投票权，我就应该承担起这一项微小权力赋予我的责任。我所能感到欣慰的是，每当我对政府进行思索，我总会在其中找到新的理由，使我更加热爱我们的国家。

第一巻
BOOK ONE

With regard to the right of conquest, it has no other foundation than the law of the strongest. If war does not confer on the victor the right of slaying the vanquished, this right, which he does not possess, cannot be the foundation of a right to enslave them. If we have a right to slay an enemy only when it is impossible to enslave him, the right to enslave him is not derived from the right to kill him, it is, therefore, an iniquitous bargain to make him purchase his life over which the victor has no right, at the cost of his liberty. In establishing the right of life and death upon the right of slavery, and the right of slavery upon the right of life and death, is it not manifest that one falls into a vicious circle?

Jean-Jacques Rousseau

第一卷
BOOK ONE

第一章
本卷要旨

人是生而自由的,却又无时不处在枷锁之中。人类向来认为自己是万物的主宰,但事实上,他们比其他任何事物所受的奴役都要多。这种情况是如何发生的呢?我无法解释。我所能解释的是,这种情况是如何被合法化的。

如果只是考虑强力和由强力施加的影响,我会说:"如果人民被强迫去服从,并且服从了,这样做很对;同样,如果人民可以打破这种桎梏,并且打破了,这样做更对。因为，人民正是依据当初夺走自己自由的方式来重新夺回自己自由的，所以他们完全有权利来重新获得这种自由。如果说这种方式不正当，那只能说当初夺走人民自由的方式也不正当。"社会秩序就是这样一种神圣的权力，它为其他权利提供了存在的依据。然而，这项神圣权力并非天然存在，而是建立在约定的基础之上，弄清这些约定是什么就是问题所在，但在探讨该问题之前，我必须首先论证我上述提到的观点。

第二章
论最初形态的社会

在一切社会形态中，最古老而又唯一自然的社会便是家庭，然而在这种关系中，只有在孩子需要父亲养育时，才会依附于父亲，一旦这种需要停止，其中的天然依附关系便结束了。孩子从缘于依附关系而产生的顺从关系中解脱出来，而父亲也从对孩子的养育负担中解脱出来，这时，两者都平等地恢复了独立状态。之后，如果他们还想继续保持原来的关系，这只是出于双方的自愿，就不再是自然的了。这时的家庭就只是靠约定来维持了。

可见，这种人类所共有的独立与自由，乃是人类自然天性发展的结果。人性的首要法则就是要维护自身的生存；人性的首要关怀就是要关注与其自身生存有关的事物。一旦一个人成长到具有理性的年龄，且能够决定适合自己的生存方式时，他就成为了自己的主人。

如此，我们可以把家庭比作政治社会的原始模型：社会的首领相当于父亲，社会中的人民相当于孩子；每个人都生而自由、平等，只有当为了自己利益时才会牺牲自己的自由。家庭和政治社会唯一的不同是：家庭中的父亲是为了爱才竭

第一卷
BOOK ONE

力去抚养自己的儿女，而在政治社会中，位高权重的首领当然不会对臣民有这种爱，他们通常是采取发号施令的方式来取而代之。

格劳秀斯【译注1】否认所有的人类政权是为了被统治者的利益才建立的，为此，他举了奴隶制作例子，他一贯的推理方式是采取已有的现实来作为判定权力的根据【原注1】。我们完全可以设想一种更合乎逻辑，而非更有利于专制君主的方式。

根据格劳秀斯的说法，究竟是全人类属于某一百个人，还是某一百个人属于全人类，这点尚属疑问；而在他的著作中，似乎是更倾向于第一种观点，这也正是霍布斯的看法。依据他们的这种观点，人类似乎可被当成一群群的牛羊；每一群都有自己的首领，而这些首领保护它们的目的正是为了吃掉它们。

就如牧羊人拥有比他自己放牧的羊群更优秀的品质，作为人群的放牧者，也就是人类的统领，也拥有比自己统领的人民更优异的品性。根据费洛的记载，罗马皇帝卡里古拉就是据此推理的，他得出如下结论：要么君主都是神灵，要么人民都是牧畜。

这位罗马皇帝的推论恰恰同霍布斯和格劳秀斯的推论不谋而合，实际上，亚里士多德早在他们之前也曾说过，人并不是生来平等的，一些人生而为奴隶，而另一些人却天生是统治者。

亚里士多德的这个说法是对的，但他却错将结果当成原因。出生于奴隶制统治下的人们，自然是生来做奴隶的，这毫无疑问。束缚在枷锁中的奴隶们失去了一切，甚至失去了摆脱枷锁获取自由的愿望；他们甚至变得喜爱自己的奴隶状态，正如尤利西斯们喜爱自己所处的卑劣环境一样【原注2】。然而，如果真的存在什么天然奴隶，那只能说是因为先出现了违背自然状态的奴隶制度。是强力创造了最初的奴隶，而懦弱使他们永远地成为了奴隶。

到现在为止我还没提到亚当王或诺亚皇帝，也就是那个把世界分成三大块的三个大君王的父亲，许多人甚至认为他们堪与萨士林的儿子做比较。作为这几位君主的后人，很有可能还是其中最正宗的支派，那么，我认为我亲爱的读者们应该对我的谦逊心存感激。因为考究起族谱来，何以知道我就不会是全人类最合法的国王呢？亚当是全世界最正当的国王，这点毫无疑问，这就如同鲁滨逊是他飘流到的那个荒岛上的唯一公民，他便是岛上的国王一样。这样的帝国有个极大的优势，就是君主完全可以安享王位，而不必担心叛乱、战争或篡位。

【原注1】"对公法的学术研究往往只是古人滥用权力的历史，对这些滥权的实例进行过详细的研究，会使人遭到误导，平添烦恼。"见阿冉松侯爵的《论法国及其邻国关系的利益》。
【原注2】参见普鲁塔克的一篇短论，题为《如果动物也使用理性》。
【译注1】格劳秀斯，17世纪荷兰著名政论家，他的研究范围相当广泛，涉及法学、政治学、文学、语言学、史学等，但使他享有盛名的是在法学方面，被人们同时尊称为"国际法之父"与"自然法之父"。主要著作有《论战争与和平法》（1625）、《海上自由论》（1609）等。

第三章
论最强者的权力

即使是最强大的人也不可能强大到永远奴役他人，除非他将强力转化为自己的权力，而将服从转化为别人的义务。由此"最强者的权力"便产生了，尽管这听起来颇具讽刺意味，实际上却已被确立为一项原则了。那么，我们是否还应该再重新详细解释一下这个名词呢？强力是一种物理性的力量，我看不出在它身上能产生什么道德。向强力低头，有时只是一种必要的做法，并非出于自愿，这顶多算是一种明智的行为而已。那么，在何种意义上，它变成一种道德上的义务了呢？

好吧，我们姑且假设这种所谓"最强者的权力"存在吧，但我认为这种假设的结果只能产生出一系列无法自圆其说的胡言乱语。因为一旦强力转化成权力，原因和结果便会颠倒，于是，当另一种强力战胜原来的强力时，这种新的强力就可以接替原来旧的强力所拥有的权力。如果人们的反叛行为得不到惩罚,那他的这种行为就成为合法的了。既然最强者永远正确,那唯一的问题就是如何成为最强者了。然而上述那种随着更强力的出现而消失的权力,又算什么权力呢?如果人们是因为强力才服从的,那就不存在根据义务而服从的说法了;如果施加在人们身上的强力停止了,那人们将没有其他服从的理由。可见,"权力"一词同强力并无关联,将它俩联系在一起纯属浪费时间。

"你应该服从权力。"如果将这句话解释为"你应该屈服于强力",毫无疑问这条命令是合理的,但它很多余;因为谁都明白"向强力屈服"这条规则不会被人违背。比如:一切权利都来自于上帝,这点我承认;可世间一切疾病也来自于上帝,难道说就应该禁止人们去求医问药了吗?如果我在森林边上遭遇强盗,他用强力威胁我把钱包交出,假如我能采用一种方式把钱包藏起来,难道我的良心还会迫使我把钱包交出来吗?因为按上面的说法,强盗手中的枪也是一种"权力"啊。

话说到此,我们已经很明确地看到,强力根本不能形成权力,只有合法的权力才能使人们履行服从的义务。这样一来,我们又被带回了最开始提出的那个问题上。

第四章
论奴隶制度

既然任何人都不拥有凌驾于他人的天然权力,而且强力也不会产生任何权力,那么人类的合法权威就是建立在契约的基础上了。

格劳秀斯说:"如果一个人可以转让自己的自由,成为另一个人的奴隶;那

社会契约论
The Social Contract

全体人民为什么不能转让自己的自由，成为国王的臣民？"在这段话中，尚存在一些不明确的字眼需要解释；我们就先拿"转让"一词来进行一下细致分析。通常，转让包括赠送或出售两个含义。如果一个人成为另一个人的奴隶，这绝不会是赠送，而是出售了自己，至少换回了生存权。但如果全体人民都把自己出售给国王，又能换回什么作为报偿呢？这个国王不但不会供养他的臣民，还会从臣民那里取得供养。何况，按拉伯雷的说法，国王所需的供养可不是那么一点点就能满足的。难道说臣民们以供养国王为条件，再将自己的自由双手奉上吗？那么我可看不出人民会从中获得什么好处。

或许有人说，专制君王会保证他治下的臣民的安全。就算这个说法是正确的吧，但如果这个专制君王同时是个野心家，所引起的与国外的战争不断，或者贪欲使他无休止地盘剥百姓，导致民不聊生，那这种后果岂不是比人民之间的争斗更严重数倍？那国内的安宁又有什么意义呢？如果人们要想获得国内和平必须以经历任何上述磨难为代价，人民能从中得到什么呢？住在牢狱里倒是很安全，就能说牢狱是一种很美好的选择吗？被囚禁在西克洛浦巨人族的洞穴里的希腊人处境也很安稳，但等待他们的却是一个个轮流被吞噬的命运。

如果说一个人愿意把自己奉送给别人而不求任何回报，这听起来无论如何都会让人感到不可思议。这种行为既不合常理，也没有任何意义，任何心智健全的正常人都不会这样做。倘若将这个道理推及一个国家，整个国家的人都这样做，那岂不成了疯子的国度？疯狂显然不能构成合理的权利。

就算一个人可以无偿奉送自己，但他却不能无偿奉送他的孩子。孩子身为人类，生来就是自由的；他们的自由属于自己，除了自己，任何人都没有权利处置这种自由。当然，在孩子们长大成人之前，他们的父亲是可以为他们确立一些原则的，但这只是为了孩子能够更好地生存和成长，并且要站在孩子的立场上；父亲绝不能无条件地剥夺孩子的自由，因为这是违反自然的，并且是在滥用父亲的职权。因此，一个独裁的政府想要取得合法的统治权，就必须使新一辈的国民

第一卷
BOOK ONE

自由地选择承认它还是反对它,这样才能合法,当然了,如果是这样,它就不能被称为独裁的政府了。

放弃自由就等于放弃了人性、放弃了自己作为人的权利,同时也放弃了自己的义务。对于一个放弃一切的人,是无法给予他任何补偿的;而事实上,这种放弃与人的本性相违背,因为倘若剥夺了一个人的意志自由,就相当于剥夺了这个人行为的道德性。任何一个条约,如果将缔约的双方规定为一方绝对统治另一方而另一方绝对服从,那这个条约是不合逻辑的,也是无效的。这个条约不就相当于:一个人拥有不必对任何事情承担责任的权力吗?这种没有互惠条款、而只有单方面履行责任的约定,不就很明白地显示了它的无效性吗?比如说,我的奴隶所有的一切都是属于我的,那他的权利就是我的权利,既然如此,他又凭借什么来反对我呢?如果说这是我拥有的一种反对我自己的权利,那听上去岂不是很滑稽?

格劳秀斯和另外一些人声称从战争中找到了这种奴役权利的另一个合理依据。他们认为,既然战胜的一方拥有杀死俘虏的权力,那战败的一方便以放弃自己的自由为代价来换取自己的生命。看起来,这种约定似乎要合理和合法得多,因为它对双方都有利。

但是,战胜者可以杀死战败者的所谓权力并非战争状态带来的结果。这一点可从最原始的时期说起:当人类生存在原始的独立状态,他们之间的交往并不确定,不足以形成一种稳定的和平状态或战争状态;因此,人与人之间并没有天生的仇敌关系。引发战争的,是物质拥有权的争夺,而不是单纯人与人之间的争吵。纯粹的人与人之间的关系是不可能引起战争的,战争只能源于物的拥有关系。那种一个人与另一个人的战争,不可能存在于没有固定财产权的自然状态中,也不可能存在于处于法律监督之下的社会状态中。

单个人之间的争斗、搏斗或冲突并不能构成任何一种战争状态;至于法兰西国王路易九世所颁布的允许个人之间可以存在战争的敕令,后来也被"上帝的和平"运动禁止了。那条敕令只不过是对政府职权的滥用，如果真的存在这样一种制度，也是非理性的，是与自然正义以及一切合理政体相违背的。

那么，战争就不是人与人的对抗关系，而是国家之间的对抗。在战争中，人与人之间是纯粹因为偶然才成为敌人的，因为他们并不是以个人的身份，甚至也不是以公民身份【原注1】，而是以士兵的身份加入；他们不是作为国家的成员，而是作为国家的捍卫者。总而言之，一个国家的敌人只能是另一个国家，而不是某些人，因为内在本质不相同的事物之间不能存在真正的关系。

上述原则符合自古以来所有时代的准则，也符合每个文明政权的惯常做法。宣战当然可以说是对臣民发出的警告，但更主要是对那个国家政权的警告。假如外来势力——不管是国王，单独的个人，抑或整个民族——对另一国家的臣民进行抢劫、杀害或拘禁，而没有首先向该国宣战，那他就不能被称作敌人，而只是强盗。即使在战争发生的过程中，一个正义的君主掠夺敌国领土上所有的财产，他却能尊重该国臣民个人的财产与人身尊严，也尊重自己的权利赖以为基础的那些原则。既然战争目的是征服敌对国，士兵们绝对有权力杀死这个国家拿着武器的守卫者，但一旦这些守卫者放下武器投降，他们就不再是敌人或敌方的工具，而又恢复普通人的身份，任何人都不再有权利杀死他们。有时会发生不伤害对方一兵一卒而能摧毁一个国家的情况。战争绝对不容许存在为了取得胜利而迫不得已造成的破坏之外的任何破坏。这些原则不是格劳秀斯独创的，也不是以诗人的权威为基础的，它们来源于事物的本质，建立在理性的基础之上。

至于征服者的权力，唯一的依据就是最强者的权力，假如战争并没有赋予征服者屠杀被征服者的权力，那么征服者奴役被征服者的权力也并不成立。一个人只有在无法将他的敌人变成他的奴隶的情况下，才可以把他的敌人杀死，所以奴役他人的权力并不能从杀死他人的权力中产生。由此，前面所说的被征服者用他们的自由来赎买自己的生存权，这原本就是一场不公平的交易，因为征服者并不拥有对被征服者生命的合法支配权。这样一来，无论是将奴役权建立在对他人生

第一卷
BOOK ONE

死权支配的基础上，或者对他人生死权的支配是建立在奴役权的基础上，这样的辩论很显然已经陷入了一个谬误的循环之中。

即使我们假设真的存在这种生杀予夺的权力，那我还是认为，战争中形成的奴隶或被征服的人民，对他们的征服者除了被迫服从之外，再没有任何其他的义务。征服者已经拿走了与被征服者生命同等价值的东西，那么征服者对于被征服者已无任何恩惠可言；与其杀死被征服者落个一无所得的结果，还不如剥削他们获得源源不断的利益。因此，除了最强者的权力之外，征服者对被征服者不再具有其他更多的权威。这样一来，征服者与被征服者的战争将持续进行着，他们之间的关系是战争的结果，战争权的持续使用就意味着根本不存在任何和平的条约。即使真的签署这样一个协定，也并不能终止战争状态，而只能是预示着战争状态的继续。

因此，无论从哪个角度来看这个问题，奴隶制中的权力都是无效的，这不仅因为它没有任何合理的根据，也因为它本身就是荒谬的，根本没有任何意义。"奴隶制"与"权力"两个词是相互矛盾的，它们相互排斥，无论是一个人相对于另一个人，一个人相对于一群人，都不能存在如此荒唐的论调：我和你在此立约，此条约要牺牲你的权利并且只对我个人有利，我是否遵守此约都完全听凭我个人意愿，但无论你愿意与否，你都必须遵守此约。

【原注1】罗马人在对战争权利的理解和尊重上比世界上其他任何民族都要强，他们对这个问题非常慎重，以至于如果一个公民没有明确表示他要反抗敌人或指名道姓反抗哪个敌人之前，他是不被允许自发参与战斗的。小卡图曾在波比里乌斯的军队里参加战斗，当波比里乌斯的军队改编后，老卡图给他写信说如果仍希望自己的儿子留在军中效力，就必须要重新进行一次战争宣誓，理由是第一次所做出的誓言已经无效，儿子不能再扛枪杀敌了。老卡图还写信给小卡图，警告他没有再次宣誓就不能参战。我知道有人会以克鲁修姆之围或罗马历史上的其他例子来反驳我，但是我所引用的是法律和惯例。罗马人比其他任何民族更遵纪守法，也没有哪个民族曾有过罗马人如此完善的法律。

第五章
论必须追溯最初的契约

即使我对我上述所反驳的所有观点都予以妥协，专制主义的拥护者们也不会安之若素。毕竟，征服一大批人和统治一个社会，两者之间存在着天壤之别。如果某个人不断地奴役他人，那么不管受他奴役的人的数量变得有多么庞大，这个人与奴役者之间的关系永远是主人与奴隶的关系，我丝毫看不出其中存在统治者与民族的关系。这些众多的人只是一群数量不断增加的聚集在一起的人，并非一个彼此相关的联合体，因为它的成员之间并不存在共同的价值观念，也不是一个政治团体。这个人即使把半个世界的人都奴役了，他依然是一个独立的个体，他的利益永远都是私利，同奴役者的利益完全相反。当这个人死后，他所奴役的这个帝国会因为缺乏内在的联系而土崩瓦解，就像一棵遭遇大火的橡树，最后只是剩下一堆灰烬。

格劳秀斯说过：人民可以将自己奉送给一位君主。根据格劳秀斯的观点，人民在将自己奉送出去之前首先是"人民"，"人民"这个说法本身就是一种社会约定，它的出现意味着公共意志的存在。所以，我们在探讨上述国王产生的过程之前，非常有必要先研究一下人民是如何形成的，因为后者必定是早于前者而产生的，这才是社会真正的基础所在。

确实，如果没有事先的契约，除非各位选举者的意愿都一致，否则，为什么少数人要服从多数人的意见？可以设想，如果有一百个人拥戴某位主人，而有十个人表示不同意，那为何这一百个人就可以代表这十个人投票呢？这种少数服从多数的表决制本身就是一种契约，这表明在选举进行之前就已经至少存在过一次全体一致同意的意见。

第一卷
BOOK ONE

第六章
论社会契约

我假设人类曾经发展到这样一种状况：在自然状态下，侵犯人类生存的阻碍力量过于强大，已经远远超出了人类维持生存的自我保护能力。在这种情况下，如果人类想要继续生存下去，就必须要改变当前的生活状况，否则人类将要遭到毁灭。

然而，人类是不能创造新的力量的，只能组合和利用现有的力量，那么人类为了保存自己别无他法，只能把他们分散在个体的力量联合成一种强大到足以抵抗任何阻力的力量，并且利用一个唯一的动机调动它，从而使它能够协调一致地行动。

这种合力只有通过分散的个体联合起来才能产生，这就产生了一个问题：一个人自己的力量和自由是他维持自己生存的首要条件，那么，他自己的力量和自由在与别人结合成一个整体的过程中，他如何才使自己不处于危险中并且又不至于忽视对自己的关照呢？这一难题引出了本章的主题，可用下述话来表述：

"怎样才能找到这样一种形式的联合：它在能够用全体成员所结成的集体力量保护其联合者的人身和财产权利的同时，又可使每个成员在联合过程中不用听从于其他的人，而是仅仅服从于自己的意愿，并且可以像以前一样拥有自己的自由。"这便是社会契约所要解决的根本问题。

这项契约的条款都是由人类的行为本质决定的，使得该条款如此精确，以至于哪怕最微小的更改都会使它变得失去原有含义；尽管它们可能从未被明确表述过，但它们无论在什么地方都是相同的，无论在什么地方都得到人们的一致认可；倘若人们违反了这种社会契约，他们会重新获得其原有的自然权利，同时失

社会契约论
The Social Contract

去了用天然自由换取的契约自由，并且重新获取他们的天然自由。

人人都认可的这些条约可被简要地表述为一句话：每个联合者都将自己的全部权利转让给整个共同体。这样，首先，只有每个人都将自己完全奉献出来，对于每个人的条件才能平等，其他人的负担就是自己的负担，为他人增加负担，对任何人都无利。其次，只要这种权利的转交是完全的、无条件的，整个集体将处于最佳状态，任何个体的成员将不再拥有私人的权利。只要有一个人还保留着他的某一项权利，在没有更高的权威在个人利益与公共利益进行裁决的情况下，这个人在某项事情上就开始成为自己的权威，久而久之，这种权力就会逐渐扩大。如此下去，人们又都会恢复到自然状态中去，人们的这种联合体便会面目全非或者干脆荡然无存。最后，每个个体都毫无保留地将自己奉献给联合体，就相当于没把自己交给任何人，每个成员都不拥有比其他人更多的权利。这样，每个人不但获得了与他所付出的同等价值的东西，还获得了来自更多力量的保护。

如果把社会契约中的非本质因素剔除，我们就可将社会契约归结为如下公式："在公共意志的最高指导下，我们每个人都将自身以及自己的一切权利转交出来，作为一个整体，我们每个人都成为不可分割的一部分。"

随后，这种联合行为就创造出了一个人为的集合体，使各位缔约者都不再成为单独的个人，这一团体是由众多成员组成；通过这种共同行为，这个团体成为一个统一体，它形成了统一的自我意识，拥有自己的生命和意志。这个由所有人联合而成的实体过去曾被叫做城市[原注1]，现在则被称为共和国或政体。当它处于被动状态时，被称为国家；当它处于主动状态时，被称为主权国家；与它的同类政体相比，它被称为强国。这种集合体的成员们有一个共同的名称叫"人民"；当他们处于共同的主权下，可被称为公民；当他们处于国家法律制度的管辖下时，可被称为臣民。不过，这几个词在具体使用时常被混淆，不加区别地混用，这并不是多严重的问题，我们只要能够区分出它们在使用时所要表达的具体含义就行了。

第一卷
BOOK ONE

【原注1】该词的真正含义在现代人中几乎完全消失了,大多数人误把城邦当做城市,把公民等同于市民。人们忘了,城邦是由房屋构成的,而只有市民才能构成城市。迦太基人曾为这一错误而付出了沉重的代价。我从听说过"cives"(公民)这个称号被用于任何君主统治下的臣民,即使是古代的马其顿人和现在的英国人也如此,尽管他们比其他任何国家都接近自由。只有法国人会随意使用这个词,因为他们并不清楚这个词的具体含义,这从他们的词典中就可以看出来。如果他们明白该词的确切含义又加以滥用,那他们就犯了谋篡罪了,他们只是把该词用作表示一种社会地位而不是法律上的权利。当博丹在说起我们的公民和市民时,他就犯了一个拙劣的错误将两者混为一谈。达朗贝先生没有犯同样的错误,在他的"日内瓦"条目中,明确地区分了我们城镇所拥有的四个等级的人(如果算上外国人,就是五个等级),而只有其中两个等级能组成共和国。据我所知,再没有其他法国作家了解"公民"这个词的真正含义。(注:达朗贝曾主持《百科全书》的编写,"日内瓦"是该书中的一个条目。)

第七章
论主权体

从以上公式中可以发现,这一联合行为包含了集体与个人的双向约定,每个人在缔结约定的时候(其实是在和自己缔约),会发现自己有着双重义务:作为主权体中的一员对其他成员的义务,作为国家的一员对国家的义务。民法中的那条原则不适用于上述情况,即每个人并不受与自己签订的契约的约束,因为自己对自己应负责任和对集体应负责任,这两者之间是存在巨大差异的。

由于每个人都要被置于两种关系中加以考虑,因此还需要指出的是,公共的决议可以使所有臣民服从主权体,但不能为主权体强加任何义务。如果主权体给自己设定了一条自己都不能违背的条约,这将会违背政治体的本性了。既然它只能作为单一的个体考虑,这种情况就类似于单个的人不能和自己达成限制自己的约定。这就表明了没有、也不可能有任何一种基本法来约束人民的共同体，即使是社会契约也不例外。这并不是说，在不破坏这一契约的情况下，这个政治共同体不能与其他政体订约，因为对于其他类似的共同体来说，这个共同体只是一个单一的存在、一个个体而已。

既然这一政治共同体或主权体的存在的基础是借助于社会契约的认可，那么它就绝不可能做出违背这一原始约定的行为，即使是与其他政体签署条约时也不例外，例如它不能转让自己的一部分，或者把自己置于其他政权的统治之下。对于共同体赖以存在的契约的破坏，将会消灭这个共同体本身，而这个被消灭了的主权体当然就做不了任何事情了。

一旦人们结成了这样一个共同体，对其中任何一个成员的侵犯必然意味着对整个共同体的侵犯，正可谓牵一发而动全身；而对整个共同体的侵犯也就是对其所有成员的侵犯了。义务和自身的利益使得缔约者彼此间能相互帮助，而同一个人也尽量从这种双重关系中获取他应得的种种利益。

既然主权体是由单独的个体构成的，那么主权体的利益同它的成员的利益一致，它就不可能去伤害成员的利益；因此主权体无须向臣民们做出任何保证，因为没有一个政治体会伤害自己的全体成员，之后我们也会看到，它也不可能伤害某个个别成员。主权体只要基于它是主权体这一简单的事实，它就永远是它应有的样子。

但是，臣民对于主权体的关系就没有这么简单了。尽管此间存在着诸多共同利益，但这些不足以使臣民自觉履行义务，除非找到一些恰当的办法来保障他们的忠诚。

因为但凡个体，必定有自己的个人意志，而这种个人意志与他作为公民所应有的一般意志有时会不同，甚至会相抵触。他的个人利益可能会完全不同于公共利益。个人绝对的、天然的独立性可能会使他认为自己对公共事业所做的奉献只是一种慈善行为，不这样做不会对他人造成伤害，这样做却给自己带来负担；而且他会把政治共同体的成员看成是虚幻的存在，而非真正的个人。这样，他就会只希望享受公民的权利，而不去履行公民应有的义务。这种想法具有极大的诱惑性，一旦在公民之间滋生蔓延，必然会带来整个政治共同体的毁灭。

因此，为了使社会契约不至于沦为空谈，这个契约本身总是暗含着一项约定，可以给契约以力量，那就是：任何人如果不遵从集体的意志，集体就应该强迫他服从，这并无他意，只是在强制他保持自由，因为这是使每个公民在献身于国家时，保证他摆脱一切人身依附的必要条件。也正是这一条件，使得政治机器得以运行，并赋予社会契约以合法化，如果没有这一约定，社会契约必然是荒唐的、残暴的，并且极易遭到滥用。

第八章
论公民社会

从自然人的国度过渡到了公民社会，人类本身也发生了显著的变化，在人的行为中，正义取代了本能成为人们的行为准则，并且人类开始具有了以前从未有过的道德品性。从这时起，责任感取代了生理的冲动，权利代替了贪欲，人们此前仅仅考虑自己的私利，而这时必须要依照另外一些原则来行动，并且必须要依靠自己的理性来进行。在公民社会中，尽管人类失去了自然状态下拥有的一些权利，但他得到的回报却远远大于付出；他的潜能得以开发，他的思想变得开阔，他的情操变得高尚，他的灵魂也得到了升华。如果这些新的能力不会被滥用从而使他堕落到比以前情况更糟的话，人类必然会对这种状态庆幸不已，因为从自然状态中走出来，人类从此摆脱了原始的狭隘、愚蠢的状态，一变而为充满智慧的人。

为了把这一过程说得更明白些，我们可以假设绘制一张人类社会得失平衡表，这样对所得和所失就可以轻易进行比较了。由于社会契约，人类所失去的是他天赋的自由和对任何东西都可占有的无限制的绝对权，而获得的是社会的自由和对他所占有财产的合法权利。为了避免在比较过程中出现错误，我们必须要明确区分天赋自由和社会自由，前者受限于个人体力，而后者受限于社会公意；还要区分占有权和所有权的区别，前者是建立在暴力或"最先占有权"基础上的，后者是建立在公众的法律认可基础上的。

我们不妨补充一点，即人类从公民社会中还获得了道德的自由，这种自由使人类成为自己真正的主人，因为如果人类只服从于自己的欲望便会成为欲望的奴隶，只有遵从为自己所制定的法律才是真正的自由。对这一主题我已经讨论过多，"自由"一词更多是哲学上的含义，并非我主题的组成部分。

第九章
论财产权

在公民社会形成的那一刻，这个社会共同体的每个成员将自己的一切——包括他的人身、他全部的力量和所有的财物——完完全全交付给共同体。但这并不意味着个人财物在转交给共同体时性质发生了变化，成了受主权体支配的财物，而是说，由于国家具有单独的个人所无法企及的巨大力量，所以公共的占有要比个人的占有具有更大的安全性，尽管公共的占有并不具有更多的合法性——至少在外国人看来是如此。因为就一个国家对于其成员而言，通过社会契约拥有着对个人财产权的绝对控制，从而成为其成员所有财物的主人；然而就一个国家对于其他国家而言，国家成为它财物的主人只是基于对财物的"最先占有权"的原则。

"最先占有者"的权利虽然比"最强者的权利"更为切实，但只有在财产权这一社会事实形成时，它才成为一种真正的权利。每个人都拥有对他所需物品予取予夺的天然权利，但这一积极行为在使一个人成为某种财产的所有者的同时也将自己同其他财产分离开来。他自己的那份财产一旦确立，他的财产就仅限于此了，就不能再对社会上的其他财产有所企及。如此一来，我们可清楚地看到在自然国度中，那脆弱的"最先占有权"如何在公民社会中得到了完全的尊重。这项权利使人们清楚地意识到与其说"哪些是属于别人的"，不如说"哪些是不属于自己的"。

按一般的原则，要确定对一块土地的最初占有的权利，必须要具备如下条件：首先，此片土地从未被任何人居住；第二，土地所有者对土地的占有数量不能超出他生存所需；第三，对土地的占用不能只是空洞的形式，而是必须要通过在这块土地上的劳动和开垦，因为这是在尚缺合法名义的情况下，能得到他人对所有权的尊重的唯一标志。

事实上，将"最先占有权"同生存和需要联系在一起，就已经把这种权利扩大到极限了。难道人们不应该为这种权利设置一个界限吗？是不是一旦某个人涉足一块土地，他就可以宣告这块土地为他所有？如果他暂时有能力将他人驱逐出这块土地，难道他就有权让他人永不再回来吗？当一个人或一个民族强取豪夺了大片领地，却不让他人涉足，这其实已经是一种应当受到惩罚的罪恶行为。因为大自然赋予每个人的权利都是平等的，他们却剥夺了其他人享有住所和食物的基本权利。当努涅兹·巴尔波站在海岸上以卡斯提王室的名义宣布拥有南太平洋和整个南美洲时，难道他就真的剥夺了当地居民的所有权并且让其他君王止步了吗？如果真可以这样，这种仪式必然会接二连三地不断重复。而那位天主教的国王甚至不必离开他的高贵寓所，翻翻书本就可以占有全世界，只要随后将那些已经为别的国王所占土地从他的帝国版图上减去就可以了。

我们可以很容易理解，个人的土地是如何被联合起来成为公共的领土，主权权利的范围也从臣民本身扩展到了臣民们所占有的土地，也就是说，主权权利不光包括人身权，也包括了财产权。这就使得土地所有者更加依赖国家，他们把自身的力量转变成了对国家忠诚的保证。但古代的君主们似乎并没认识到这等好处,他们仅仅是自称为波斯人的王、塞西亚人的王或者马其顿人的王,好像他们只是把自己看做这些人的统治者,而非整片国土的主人。现在的君主则聪明多了,他们号称自己为法兰西国王、西班牙国王或者英格兰国王等等。这样,通过控制土地,他们也成功地掌控了这些土地上的居民。

社会契约中关于转让的独特之处就在于,共同体在接受个人的财产时,并不是要剥夺其财产权,恰恰相反,是为了确保个人对财产的合法所有权,把占有权变成了真正的权利。既然每个所有者都被看做是公共财产的监护人,他的权利得到了国家其他成员的尊重,面对外国力量的侵害,他也能够受到集体力量的一致保护。因此,这种转让行为不仅有利于公众,更有利于个人,也就是说,个人在转让中又拿回他所奉献的一切。在以后我们阐述主权体和所有者对同一财产的权利有什么不同时,这种看似矛盾的说法能得到更好的解释。

可能也存在这种情况:人们在结为共同体时可能并没有占有任何东西,之后他们才去占据一块土地据以维持生存,他们对这块土地共同使用,也或者将其分割,在各成员间进行分配,分配的形式可以是平等的,也可以根据主权者规定的比例。不论这种分配是以何种方式进行,个人对土地的拥有权要永远从属于共同体对土地的权利;倘若没有这一点,社会的纽带将没有任何稳固性,主权的实施也不会有有效的权威和力量。

最后,我将用一小段话来结束对本章和本卷的论述,其可作为整个社会系统赖以生存的基础:社会契约远没有破坏自然的平等,相反,它把人类天生的身体上的不平等用道德的和法律的平等取而代之;从此,不管人与人之间在体力与智力上是如何不平等,人类通过社会契约和法律权利拥有了完全的平等[原注1]。

【原注1】在不好的政府的统治下,平等只是表面的和虚幻的,它只是使穷人安于贫困,使富人保持富有。事实上,法律总是有利于那些有产者,而不利于无产者。因此,只有当社会所有人都拥有一些财产而谁又不多占有时,社会状态对人类才是有利的。

第二巻
BOOK TWO

With regard to the rights of conquest it has no other foundation than the law of the strongest. If war does not confer on the victor the right of slaying the vanquished, this right, which he does not possess, cannot be the foundation of a right to enslave them. If we have a right to slay an enemy only when it is impossible to enslave him, the right to enslave him is not derived from the right to kill him, it is, therefore, an iniquitous bargain to make him purchase his life, over which the victor has no right, at the cost of his liberty. In establishing the right of life and death upon the right of slavery, and the right of slavery upon the right of life and death, is it not manifest that one falls into a vicious circle?

Jean-Jacques Rousseau

第二卷
BOOK TWO

第一章
论主权是不可转让的

前面所确立的原则所产生的最直接也是最重要的结果就是：公众意志只有按照创建国家的目的——即公共利益——来指导国家的各种力量。因为，如果个人利益的冲突使得建立公民社会成为必需，那么，正是这些个人利益之间的协调统一之处使得公民社会的建立成为可能。正是因为这些个人利益的相同点形成了社会联系的纽带，没有这些共同利益的交集，任何社会都不可能存在。因此，对社会的管理也必须要建立在这些共同利益的基础之上。

由此，我想说的是：主权是公众意志的行使，它永远不能被转让；而且主权体只是一个集体的存在形式，除了它自己，没有人可以代表它。权力可以被转移，意志却不可以。

个体意志与公众意志在某些点上达成一致不是不可能，但这些一致性却不具有规律性和持久性。个体意志由于它的天然本性总会具有不公正的倾向，而公众意志则更偏向平等。所以我们不能保证个体意志与公众意志会和谐一致，即使这种一致应该永远持续，并且果然出现了，那也不过是巧合而非机制如此。主权者的确可以说："现在我想要的恰恰就是这个人想要的，至少是他说他想要的。"但他不能说："这个人明天想要的也是我想要的。"因为如果一个人说希望自己的未来受束缚，这是荒唐可笑的，同时还因为任何人都不会赞同与自己利益相反的事情。如果一个民族的人民只是一味地做出服从的承诺，这个民族最终会为这种承诺所毁灭，人民也就不可称之为人民了；一旦有了一个主人，主权体便不复存在了，政治体也因此而分崩离析。

这并不是说在主权体有权行使否决的权利却没有行使的情况下，首领的政令不被公共意愿允许。此时，我们应该把整体的沉默视作人民的认同。关于这一点以后还会详述。

第二章
论主权是不可分割的

正如主权不可转让，基于同一原因，主权也是不可分割的。意志要么是公意【原注1】，要么不是；它要么是人民共同体的意志，要么只是其中一部分人的意

第二卷
BOOK TWO

志。在前一种情况下，这种公共意愿的宣言是主权行为，并构成法律；而后一种情况下，它只是一种个别意志或行政行为，顶多算一道政令而已。

然而，我们那些无法按主权原理来区分主权的政治理论家们，将主权按照对象来区分。他们将主权分为权力和意愿，即将其分为行政和立法，纳税权、司法权和战争权，内政权和外交权。我们的理论家们，时而将这些混为一谈，时而又把它们分裂开来。他们把主权体搞成一个东拼西凑出来的怪物，就好比是他们用这个人的眼睛、那个人的胳膊、另一个人的腿、再一个人的脚——用几个人的身体拼凑出一个新的人。据说，日本的一些江湖术士可以在众目睽睽之下将一个小孩子肢解，然后将身体的各个部位抛向空中，在孩子落地时，依旧活生生、完好无损。这或多或少有些类似于我们的政治理论家们玩的把戏，他们用那种完全可以当众表演的手法肢解了社会实体，又不知通过什么手法将它们重新组合起来。

造成这一错误的原因在于没有对主权形成正确的概念，把主权权威的表现误认为是主权权威的组成部分。例如，人们把宣布战争或者维护和平视为主权行为，其实不然，类似这样的行为都不是法律，它们只是法律的实施，是一种确定该如何解读法律的特殊行为，这一点在我确定了"法律"一词的含义之后，就会非常明了了。

如果用同样的方法来分析其他的主权划分，我们会发现，无论我们如何对主权进行划分，我们都是错误的，因为那些被认为是主权组成部分的权利，最终会被证明只是从属于主权，而且他们要以最高意志的存在为前提条件，这些权利只是最高意志的实施而已。

由于缺乏精确性，当这些政治理论家们在根据前述他们的那些理论来判断君王和人民的相应权利时，得出的结论总是极为模糊。在格劳秀斯第一本著作【译注1】的第三章和第四章中，读者们会很清楚地看到这位知识渊博的大师和他的翻译者巴贝拉克是如何陷入他们自己的诡辩中而无法自圆其说的，他们担心在书中说得太多或太少，从而不小心触犯到他们所想竭力赞美的那种利益。格劳秀斯因不满

社会契约论
The Social Contract

意于自己的祖国而流亡法国，为了讨好国王路易十三，他把自己的书献给了这位国王，书中他费尽心机地将人民的权利剥夺殆尽再想方设法将它们全都赋予了国王。而这本书又恰好迎合了巴贝拉克的口味，他将此书翻译之后献给了英格兰的国王乔治一世。但不幸的是，詹姆士二世的被放逐（巴贝拉克称此为"让位"）使这位译者不得不在书中采取了保留的态度，以致含糊其辞、吞吞吐吐，以避免把威廉三世暗指为一个篡位者。如果这两位作者能按照正确的原则，他们就不会那样为难了，所有的难题将会迎刃而解；但是，如果真要那样的话，他们必定带着莫大的悲哀，因为能接受他们的只是人民，真理从来不是使人谋取高官厚禄的康庄大道，人民是无法给予他们大使的头衔、教授的身份和丰厚的俸禄的。

【原注1】意志要成为公意，没必要总是全体一致，但是必须把全部票数都计算在内。任何形式的例外都会破坏它的普遍性。
【译注1】指《战争与和平法》。

第三章
论公意是否会犯错

　　从前面的论述可以推知：公众意志总是正确的，总是以大众共同的利益为中心。但这并不意味着人民所有的决议都是正确的。人们总是在追求对自己有利的事物，但很多时候人无法辨别哪些对他们有利。固然人民不会腐败，但他们有可能会受到蒙蔽，此时的人民就会接受一些不好的事物。
　　所有人的意志（众意）和公意之间经常存在很大区别，公意只考虑公共利益，而所有人的意志则考虑个人私利，其实是个别意志的总和。如果我们扣除所有人意志中意见不统一的部分，就形成了公意，它实际是个别利益的一种交集【原注1】。

第二卷
BOOK TWO

当人民对情况能充分了解并具有思考能力,人民之间没有进行相互串通,那么即使存在着数量众多的小差异,公意也可以从中产生,而且这种决定总是有益的。但如果人们在交往中开始形成小团体或派别,那么每个派别的意志对于其内部成员来说是公意,对于整个国家来说则成为了个别意志。这样一来,就形成了这样一种情况:不是有多少人就有多少投票者,而是有多少个团体就有多少投票者了。此时利益的冲突相对减弱了,但投票表决的结果却缺乏普遍性了。到最后,这些团体或派别中有某个规模大到可以压倒其他派别的意见而占据了主导地位,那投票的结果就不再是诸多差别的总和,而只存在一个差别了。这时就不存在什么公意了,那个主导观点只不过是一种个别意见罢了。

因此,要使公意得到清楚的表达,很重要的一点就是不要让国家中存在小集团,才能使每个公民都得以独立表达自己的观点【原注2】,这是绝对必要的,这是伟大的莱格古斯所发明的独特又高尚的体系。如果国家内已经存在了小集团,就应该像梭伦、努马、塞尔维乌斯所做的那样,大量增加这些组织的数量,越多越好,以此来防止它们之间的不均衡。要使公意能永远正确以及确保人民不犯错误,这些都是很有效的预防手段。

【原注1】阿冉松侯爵说:"每种利益都有它不同的原则,两种利益之间的协调是由于和第三种利益相对立而产生的。"他还可以再补充上:所有利益的协调是由于它和每种利益相对立形成的。如果没有不同利益的话,对于这种遇不上任何障碍的共同利益,我们几乎意识不到它的存在。一切都将运转自如,政治也就不再是一种艺术了。

【原注2】马基亚维利说:"分裂有时候对共和国是有害的,而有些时候则对国家是有利的;害处是由派系派别造成的,而没有派系派别时则对国家是有利的。因此,既然一个国家的创立者不可能杜绝敌对者的存在,他就应该建立完善的制度来预防派系的出现。"(见《佛罗伦萨史》,第七卷)

第四章
论主权权力的限度

如果把政治联合体或国家看成是一个法人，它的生命力便来自于其成员的团结，如果它的生存是首要法则，则它必须具有一种普遍的强制力量，以便为了整体的更高利益去引导或支配它的每个部分。这就如同大自然赋予了每个人控制自身各部分的绝对权力，社会契约也赋予政治体对其每个成员的绝对权力。如我前面所说，正是这种权力在公意指导之下，才拥有了主权这个名称。

但是，除了这种公共的人格之外，我们也必须考虑到构成公共人格的单独的个人，这些个人的生命和自由都是天然独立的，因此我们必须区别开公民和主权体各自的利益【原注1】，同时也要区别开公民作为臣民的责任和作为人的天然的权利。

我需要指出的是，根据社会契约，每个个体所转让的只是他部分的权利、财产和自由，这一部分对共同体来说至关重要；还必须要说明的是，唯有主权体才能判定究竟是哪一部分才具有这种重要性。

一旦主权体有所需要，公民就应当在他力所能及的情况下为国出力。但是主权体不能对臣民提出任何对主权体利益无用的要求；它甚至也不会有这样的意图，因为在理性的法律和自然的法则下，任何东西都不会无缘无故产生。

使我们和社会共同体联结起来的那些责任之所以是义不容辞的，只因它是互惠的，它们具有这样的本质，在履行这些责任时，每个人在为他人服务的同时其实也是在为自己服务。如果不是因为个人将"每个人"联系到自己，从而在为所有人投票时想着的是自己，公意如何总是正确的？人又如何以此而希求每个人都能得到幸福？这就证明了权利的平等和由它所产生的正义感都源自每个人对自身的优先考虑，这也是人的本性。这就证明了公意要想达到真正的普遍性，它不仅要在内容上，还要在对象上都应是普遍意志，它应当来自所有的个体以适用于所有的个体，当它倾向于某些特定的个体时，它就失去了自然公

第二卷
BOOK TWO

正性，因为这时我们判断的是一些很陌生的东西，已经没有任何真正的平等原则来指导我们了。

而一旦涉及某个特殊的事实或权利，而它又不在已有的共同契约的范围之内，争议就来了。这其实是一场一方为当事的个人而另一方为公从的诉讼，但我既看不出有什么可使用的法律条文，也看不出应作出裁决的法官。这时，如果只任由普遍意志来作出决断显然是荒谬的，因为这样的裁决只是一方的结论，对于另一方来说它只是一种个别的意志，这种决断只能偏于不公且容易犯错。因此，正如个别意志不能代表普遍意志，普遍意志一旦有了个别意志也就改变性质了，它将不再是普遍意志，就不能再以其普遍性来对人和事作出公平的裁决。举个例子，当雅典人民任命或废除他们的领袖，对一些人施加惩罚而对另一些人授予荣耀，通过许多个别的政令行使着政府的职能，这样他们就不再是主权体了，已经与行政官员无异。这好像与通常的观点不太一致，但你们必须要给我点时间来详细阐明我的观点。

从上述可见，普遍意志的存在并不取决于参与投票者的数目，而在于能够联系起这些投票者的共同利益，在这种体制下，每个人必须要服从于他加给其他人的同一个条件，这就是利益与正义的共存共荣，它使得集体的协商具有平等的特点。这时，一旦有个别事件或对象加入了讨论，这种公平性便不复存在，因为此时不再有将法官的裁决和当事方的规则完美结合的共同利益。

无论从哪个角度来探究这个原则，我们都会回归到同一点，即社会契约在公民之间建立了一种平等，公民受同一条件制约，也享有同样的权利。也就是说，根据社会契约的本质，任何主权的约定，即真正属于公意的每个约定，都平等地约束或关怀着每个公民。这样一来，主权体只认得国家这一个实体，而不再区分其作为成员的单独个人。那么，确切地说，什么是主权约定呢？它不是上级和下级之间的协约，而是共同体和它每个成员之间的约定。它是一种合法的约定，因为它所依据的是社会契约；它是一种公平的约定，因为它对所有人一视同仁；它是一种实用的约定，因为它只以为人民谋福利为己任；它是一种持久的约定，因

社会契约论
The Social Contract

为它以公众力量和最高权力为支持。在这样一种约定下，只要公民遵从，那他们其实就是在遵从自己的意志，并不受制于任何人。至于主权体和公民各自的权利可以延伸到什么程度，就要看每个公民对自身的约束可以达到什么程度了，每个人要对全体负责，全体对每个人也要负责。

由此可见，主权权力尽管是绝对的、神圣的、不可侵犯的，它却不能超越、也不会超越普遍约定的范畴，每个人都可以根据自己的意愿来充分支配这些约定所规定给他的财产和自由。结果，主权体永远无权对某个臣民施加比其他臣民多的负担，因为那样一来，就变成个别情况了，就超越了主权体的权限。

如果我们看到了这种区别，那么，那种断言个人由于社会契约而确实失去权利的说法就是错误的了。事实上，当个人进入社会契约中，他会发现自己处于一种比过去更优越的环境中；他们不但没有失去任何东西，反而进行了一次有利的交易，用一种动荡不安的生活非常得利地换取了一种更稳固美好的生活；用对自然的依赖换取了独立自由；不必再对别人进行暴力侵犯就可以保证自己的安全；用他们可能被战胜的力量换取了社会联合体所带来的不可征服性的权利。他们奉献给国家生活，从而获得了国家的保护；当他们冒着生命危险去捍卫国家时，不就是在回报从国家那里得到的保护吗？而且，他们如此冒险所做的，不正是在自然国度里也必须更经常更危险地去做以保障自身的生存吗？确实，当国家需要时，所有的人都需要为国家而战，但同时人们就不必再为自己而战了。联合之前我们需要冒很大的危险去保全自己，联合之后我们只需冒部分危险来保卫国家，两相比较，难道不是有很大的改善吗？

【原注1】各位细心的读者，请不要过早地指责我的前后矛盾，我由于语言能力有限，无法避免用词上的矛盾，但还是请诸位等我把话说完吧。

第五章
论生死权

有人也许会问：既然个人都没有处置自己生命的权利，那他又怎么可能有权把这样的权利转让给主权体呢？这个问题之所以难以回答，是因为它问的方式不对。每个人都有为了保护自己的生命而冒生命危险的权利，一个人为了从火灾中逃生而从窗口中跳出，难道可以说他这是自杀吗？一个人在出海时被暴风雨吞噬，难道能以明知出海有危险却非要这样做为理由从而强加给他自杀的罪名吗？

社会契约的目的就是要保护各个缔约者。一个想要达到某种目的人，必须会有相应的手段以及运用这种手段所必然存在的危险甚至是牺牲生命。任何人如果想通过牺牲别人而保障自己，他也就必须在必要的时候为他人而牺牲自己。作为一个公民，这时他就不再是自己的主宰了，他所承担的危险必须由法律来决定。当执政者对一个人说：为了国家你必须献身。这个人必须义无反顾地去死，因为这是他一直能够享有安全环境的条件，也因为他的生命已不再是大自然的恩赐，而是国家的有条件的许可。

对罪犯施以死刑也是基于同样的理由，为了避免成为某桩杀人案中的被杀者，每个人就必须得同意，一旦自己成了杀人犯就会被处死。这远不是放弃生命的做法，而是人们认为这样可以使生命安全更有保障，这样做的目的是要保证社会契约的效力，当然无法想象有哪个缔约者在缔结条约时只是希望自己被绞死。

另外，每个犯罪者都是在挑战社会权利，他就会因为这种行为成为国家的叛徒或叛乱者。由于他破坏了国家的法律，他也就不再是国家的成员了，这甚至等于在向自己的国家开战。这种情况下，国家的生存和他的生存就是不相容的了，两者必去其一。如果这个罪犯被处以死刑，他不是以公民的身份，而是以公敌的身份。审判与判决就是为了证明并宣告他破坏了社会契约，他不再是国家的一员。既然他曾是这个国家的一员，或者至少是居住于该国国土上，他就必须遭到放逐或者作为国家公敌被处死。这样的敌人不是一个法人，而是一个实实在在的人，根据战争权，他被处死也是理所应当的。

但是，可能有人会说，对犯罪的惩罚是一种个别行为。没错，因此这样一种职责并不属于主权体，主权体可以给罪犯定罪但是自己却不能亲自执行。我所有的观点都是环环相扣的，只是需要慢慢道来。

过于频繁的惩罚是政府无用或懒惰的表现。无论怎样坏的一个人，总可以使他成为某方面有用的人。如果一个人留存于世并不会对社会造成危险，他就不应该被处死，出于杀一儆百的目的也不行。

至于赦免权，就是对那些受到法律惩罚并由法官强制执行的罪犯施以宽恕或赦免的权利，仅仅属于那个超出法律和法官的主权体。对于对这种权利的规定并不十分明确，因此它很少被使用。在一个法理有序的国家之所以不会有太多的刑罚，并不是因为国家常行使赦免权，而是罪犯数量很少。只有在国家趋于衰亡时，才会有罪犯多而惩罚少的情况。在罗马共和国统治时期，元老院和执政官不曾使用过赦免权，古罗马人也没有这样做，虽然人民有时会撤回裁决。频繁的赦免预示着犯罪行为不久以后将不再需要被赦免，每个人都能看出它所产生的后果。此时，我感到我的心已在阻止我的笔落下。让我们把这个问题留给那些公正人士去讨论吧，他们从不犯错，自己永远不需要任何赦免。

第六章
论法律

社会契约给政治体以存在和生命，接下来的问题就是通过立法为政治体带来意志和行为的力量，因为使政治体得以联合和形成的那种原始行为并没有决定政治体该如何保存自己和发展自己。

第二卷
BOOK TWO

　　事物的美好与合乎秩序是事物的性质使然，与人类的契约无关。一切的公义均来自上帝；只有上帝才是公义的本源。可惜的是，我们不知道该如何去掘取这种源泉，否则我们就将不再需要政府或法律了。毫无疑问，从理性本身就可以找到普世的公义，如果要使所有人都承认，它就必须是互惠的。从人类的角度来看，如果没有任何天然的约束，天然的公义法则在人类中就是虚幻无效的；当正义之士遵守正义法则而其余的人却不照此遵守的话，那么这些正义的法就只能令善者痛恶者快。因此，必须要用协议和法律将权利和义务结合起来，使正义有所伸张。在自然社会中，一切东西都是公共的，对于那些我未曾作出承诺的人，我对他们也没有任何义务，我只承认那些对我无用的东西才属于他人。但是，在公民社会中，情况完全变了，因为一切权利都是由法律规定的。

　　那么，法律究竟是什么呢？如果我们仅局限于形而上学的角度对法律下定义，无论怎么讨论，我们都无法真正地认识它。当我们知道了自然法则的定义时，却依然对国家的法则一无所知。

　　我已经说过，在个别对象上是不会产生公意的，因这样的个别对象不是处于国家之外就是处于国家之内。如果在国家外部，它的意志对于国家来说就属于外来的而不是普遍的意志；如果它在国家内部，它就是国家的一部分，那么整体与部分之间便形成了两个单独个体相对的关系，部分是其中一方，排除了这一部分的整体是另一方。但排除了某个部分的整体便不再是整体；而且只要有这种关系存在，就不再有整体，而是两个不对等的部分。由此导致的结果是，其中一个部分的意愿对于另一部分来说都不能算是公意。

　　但是，当作为整体的人民为整体的人民制订条约的时候，它考虑的便只有自己了；这里如果形成了任何一种关系，那也是一个角度下整体的人民同另一个角度下整体的人民之间的关系，对整体并没有什么破坏。这时人们对某个问题作出约定时就具有了普遍性，正如做出这种约定的意志具有普遍性一样。这样的约定我称之为法律。

社会契约论
The Social Contract

当我说到法律的对象总是普遍性时，我的意思是法律从整体的角度考虑臣民，并抽象地考虑他们所有的行为，它不涉及某个具体的人或某件具体的行为。因此法律可以规定特权，但不能指定哪个具体的人才享有此特权；法律可以把臣民划分为几个等级，甚至规定每个等级的划分标准，但它却不能指名道姓地确定哪个人为哪个阶级；法律可以规定君主政府的世袭制度，却不能指定哪个是君王、哪家是王室。简言之，就是立法权力范围中不能包括针对个别对象的职能。

此时，我们才恍然大悟，我们可以不必问立法权力的归属了，因为法律是公意的约定；我们可以不必问君主是不是高于法律，因为君王不过是国家的一员；我们可以不必问法律是否会不公正，因为没有人会对自己不公正；我们更可以不必问人为何自由却又要遵从法律，因为法律正是我们自己意志的表达。

我们还可以明白，既然法律将意志的普遍性和对象的普遍性结合起来，因此，无论是谁，凭个人的意志擅自下的命令都不称其为法律，就算是主权体针对个别的对象发出的命令也不是法律，而只是一道行政命令，这并不是主权行为，只是政府的行政行为。

因此，对于一切依法而治的国家，不论其行政机构的形式如何，我把他们统称为"共和国"。因为在那里，并且只有在那里，公共利益才能成为主导力量，也才能真正符合"共和"一词的原意。每一个合法的政府都是共和体【原注1】的，我在后面篇章中将会解释何为政府。

确切地说，法律是公民社会得以结合的条件，臣服于法律的人民也是法律的制订者。只有那些构成社会的人们才有权描述他们结成社会的条件，但他们如何来描述这些条件呢？是根据自发的协议还是突发的灵感？政治体是否有一个机构来表达自己的意志？谁会具备这种远见，事先就能明确地知道这些法令并将它们公之于众？或者在需要时他如何宣布这些决定呢？盲目的民众通常并不知道自己想要什么，因为他们往往不能正确判定哪些是对他们有益处的，那么他们靠什么来完成制订法律这样一项伟大而艰巨的重任呢？就民众本身而言，他们总是希求得到对他们有益的东西，可是他们靠自己却很难看清这种利益。公意永远是正确的，可指引公意的判断并非总是明智的，所以必须对它示以事实的本来面目，有时甚至是事物的本质；必须为它指明它所前进的正确道路，不能被个别意志领偏了方向；必须给予它时空观念，使它在权衡眼前利益的同时能看到更长远的未来隐患；个人看到好东西却拒绝它，公众期望好东西却不认识它，两者都需要引导。个人应该用理性来指引自己的欲望，公众应该学会如何发现自己期待的东西。这种公众的启发将会使社会共同体得到理性和意志的结合，使共同体的各部分密切协作，最后形成整体的最大力量。这就需要有一个立法者了。

【原注1】我认为，这个词并不是特指贵族制或民主制，而是在普遍意义上的由公意——也就是法律——指导下的任何政府。一个合法的政府必须不得与主权联合在一起，而只能是一个为主权服务的机构。所以，甚至是君主专制也可以成为共和国。这一点将在本书第三卷中详细论述。

第七章
论立法者

要找到一个适合于所有国家的社会法则，的确需要一种超人的智慧。这种智慧需能理解人类的所有情感但又不卷入其中；要与人类的本性没有任何关系却又对其了如指掌；它的幸福与我们的幸福无关却甘愿为我们着想；最后，它会为了一种遥远的荣耀而一直等待，它在这个时代辛苦劳作，却在下一个时代看到收获的果实【原注1】。真要如此，人类只有等神明来为他们立法了。

关于政治家和君主的界定，柏拉图在他的对话体著作——《政治家》（《The statemans》）中从哲学角度进行了推理论述，卡里古拉也从经验角度进行了同样的

社会契约论
The Social Contract

阐述。如果说伟大的国君很少出现是一个事实，那伟大的立法者的出现又该罕见到什么程度呢？因为国君不过是遵照立法者所提供的政治模型而已。如果说立法者是发明机器的工程师，国君只不过是组装机器的技术工人而已。孟德斯鸠说，当一个政治体诞生时，是共和国的领导者创建了制度，然后制度又反过来塑造领导者。

可以这样说，任何一个敢于承担起创建民族制度重任的人，必须要有改造人性的能力，他要把每个完整而独立的个人转变成一个整体的一部分，到那时，从某种意义上说，这些个体从整体中重新获得了他的生命和存在方式；他要能够弱化人类的原来的组织结构以强化新的政治组织，并用道德性的、集体的存在方式取代人们原来那种天赋自然的生理的、独立的存在方式。总而言之，就是先剥夺一个人的自身原有的力量，再赋予他一种外在的力量，而且这种力量必须在别人的帮助下才能运用。这种自然力量剥夺的越是彻底，他所重新获得的力量越是强大和持久，而新的社会制度就越是稳固而完美。公民没有集体的力量便一无所为，如果集体的力量大于或等于所有个人的自然力量的总和，那我们就可以说，立法已经达到了完美的高度。

立法者在所有方面都是国家中非凡的人。他的非凡不仅表现在他的才华上，还因为他的职位。这种职位既不是行政的也不是主权的，它创建了整个国家的制度，却不在该国家机构中居于任何位置。这是一种超脱于人类权力的独立的高级的职能。因为，治人者不能立法，同样，立法者也不能治人。否则，法律就会被立法者的私人感情所左右，会将不公正地固定下来，立法这项神圣的事业就无法避免地被立法者的个人目的所玷污了。

当莱克古斯为他的国家制订法律时，他先放弃了王位。绝大部分的希腊城邦习惯于请外邦人来为他们制立法律。近代的意大利诸共和国经常效仿这种做法；日内瓦共和国也是如此【原注2】，并发现此法相当有效。而在罗马的鼎盛期，就是因为它的立法权力和主权权力集于一身；暴政统治的种种罪恶不断显现，甚至趋于亡国的边缘。

但是，即使是罗马的十人委员会也从来没有宣称自己拥有绝对的立法权威，他们对人民说："如果没有你们的允许，我们的提议就不能被称为法律。罗马人，你们自己就是法律的制定者，并且用这些法律来维护你们的幸福。"

可见，负责起草法律的人并不拥有立法权，而人民自己，就算有这种意愿，也不能放弃自己这种不可转移的权利；因为根据社会契约，只有公意才能约束个人行为，决定个人意志是否是公意，必须要通过全民自由投票表决之后。——这一点我以前说过，再重复一次并非多余。

由此，我们在立法者的工作中发现两种看似不相容的东西：一项超出人能力之外的任务和缺乏付诸执行的权威。

另外，还有一个难题值得关注。智者往往会用自己的语言而不是通俗的语言来对普通百姓说话，这类语言是不容易被理解的。因为许多思想无法用大众语言来进行表达。正如太遥远的目标无法企及一样，太抽象的概念人们也无法理解。作为个人来说，他只是关心自己的个人利益，对于政府的建构他毫不关心，良好的法律在使他放弃某些私利时能够获得更多的好处，这一点他也很难看到。要使一个新生的民族理解健康的政治原则并遵守国家的基本规则，就必须将原来的因果关系倒置：本应是新的社会制度产物的社会精神反过来支配社会制度的创立，而人民不得不在法律诞生之前就成为了法律将他们塑造成的那个样子。同时，由于立法者既无权通过强权，也不能通过辩论的方式达到他的目的，他必须求助于另一种权威，这种权威必须具有不武自威、不说必服的力量。

这就是为什么历代的开国者都不得不求助于上天的介入，把自己的智慧说成是神的意旨，这样人民才会像服从自然法则般遵从国家的法律，并且认识到正是创造了人类的力量创造了国家，从而使人民自由地服从并温顺地承担起为公共事业谋福祉的责任。

立法者们将这种超乎普通人理解力的崇高道理假托神明之口说出来，目的是用神的威严来引领那些由于人类自身的谨慎而不为所动的人民【原注3】。但并不是什

社会契约论
The Social Contract

么人都可以通过神明立言的，也并不是什么人只要假装是神明的代言人就能够得到人们的信任。立法者的伟大灵魂才是使他能够彰显使命的真正奇迹。任何人一个人都可以去刻一个石碑，或收买一个神谕，或冒称可以和某些神灵秘密沟通，或训练一只小鸟假装在耳边密传神言，或用其他卑劣手段欺骗别人，诸如此类的把戏或许真的能纠集一群愚昧的群众，但不能建立起一个帝国，这种可笑的伎俩将会随着发明人的死去而消失。虚假的权威可以产生一种暂时的聚集，但唯有智慧才能使一种结合长久不衰。犹太法律至今仍然存在，而统治半个世界达十个世纪的伊斯梅尔人后嗣的法律至今仍然在显示着其起草者的丰功伟绩；那些自高自大的哲学和盲目的宗派思想可能会把这些伟人看做侥幸取胜的骗子，但真正的政治家将会在这些制度中认识并崇拜这些使国家长治久安的伟大的天才。

即使如此，我们也不能得出跟瓦伯顿（Warburton）一样的结论，认为政治和宗教对于人的作用是相同的，而应该说，只有在一个民族诞生之初，两者才成为彼此利用的工具。

【原注1】一个民族只有在自己的体制开始衰落时，才会有名气。在希腊其他地方开始谈论之前，我们不知道莱克古斯的制度已经为斯巴达人造福好几个世纪了。

【原注2】那些只是把加尔文看做一个神学家的人并没有认识到其天才的高度。他在我们充满智慧的法令编纂工作中起到了很大的作用，这给他带来的荣誉绝不亚于他的《体制》（《论基督教的体制》）一书。不管我们的教会中会发生怎样的革命，只要对于国家和自由的热爱还没在我们心中泯灭，人们就将永远以崇敬的心情缅怀这位伟大的人物。

【原注3】马基亚维利在文中写道："事实的真相是，在任何国家中都不存在一个杰出的不借助于神明的立法者，如果不借助于神明，他的法律将不被接受。一个智者知道很多有用的真理，但却无法通过一种可以说服人的方式表达出来。"（《李维论》，第五卷，第十一章）【原文为意大利文——译注】

第八章
论人民

　　建筑师在建造一座大厦之前要先勘测和检查地基，看它是否能承受大厦的重量。同样的，一个有智慧的立法者也不会一开始就制订一部本身不错的法律，而是要首先弄清楚这部法律的统治对象能不能接受并支持它。正是这个原因使得柏拉图拒绝为阿卡迪亚人（Arcadian）和昔兰尼人（Cyrenian）制订法律，因为他深知这两个民族都同样富有，是不会接受平等的法律的。克莱特（Crete）就是一个拥有着好的法律和坏的人民的民族的例子，米诺王曾经试图训导的是一些被邪恶所支配的臣民。

　　世界上曾经存在过上千个显赫的民族，但他们并不能遵从好的法律，即使是那些能够接受好法律的民族也只是在其历史上某段短暂的时期具有这种接受的能力。这时的民族就如同一个人，在幼年时期是适合教育的，也愿意接受新的事物，但随着年龄的增长，便越来越顽固和僵化了。一旦这个民族形成了某种习俗，或者某种偏见一旦生根，任何改革都成为冒险且徒劳的事情。一个民族是不会容忍别人触碰它的缺点的，哪怕是别人出于好心想消除这个缺点。这就如同那些愚蠢懦弱的病人往往讳疾忌医，见到医生就发抖。

　　就如同某些疾病可以扰乱病人的大脑，从而使他失去对过去的记忆，有时国家的历史中也会出现某些动乱时期对整个民族产生深重的影响，这种影响就如同重病对病人的影响。这时，人们不是对忘记过去感到恐怖，而是恐慌于对过去的回忆。一个国家只有不忘记过去，才能够在饱经战火的洗礼后重新获得新生，也就是说，能够跳出死亡的拥抱而重获青春。莱克古斯时期的斯巴达，塔尔干王朝之后的罗马，就有着类似的经历，现代社会的荷兰和瑞士在驱逐暴君后也同样重获新生。

　　但这种事例并不常见，它们只是些特殊的例子，这需要从相关国家特殊的制度或历史环境来解释。这些事例甚至不可能在同一个民族中重复发生两次。一个民族的人民追求自由，只有在其未开化之时，当社会的元气耗费殆尽，人民只会在动乱中流离失所，革命也无力挽回这种局面。因为人民身上的锁链一旦被打破，他们就被分解成单独的个体，人民也就不复存在了。因此，人民需要的是一个善于统治的主人而不是解放者。自由的人啊，请你们记住这一句格言：自由可以获得，但绝不可失而复得。

和人的成长一样，一个民族也要经历一个成熟期，这时它才有可能接受法律的制约。但这种成熟期并不是一目了然的，要想识别它并非易事，过早地实施法制往往只会导致失败。民族与民族也不相同，有的民族从诞生时就能接受法律，而有的民族就是等上十个世纪也未必可以。俄罗斯人从未实现过有效的治理，因为他们过早地进行了这种尝试。彼得大帝可以被称为一个极具模仿能力的人，却不能被称为天才。真正的天才具有创造性，能凭空创造一些新的事物。他所做的某些改革是合理的，但更多的是举措失当，他仅看到他治下的人民尚未开化，却未看到他们还没准备好接受政府的治理；此时他要做的只是需要训练他的臣民以使他们成熟，他却要试图使他们成为文明人；他试图将他的臣民改造成德国人或英国人而非俄罗斯人；他强迫他的臣民成为他们本不应该是的样子，却无法成为他们本应该是的样子。这就如同有的法国教师所采取的教育方法，把在童年时期的孩童教得很显赫，在孩子长大后却会一事无成。沙皇俄国企图征服欧洲，最终却发现自己被欧洲征服了。鞑靼人作为它的臣民和邻居将成为它的主人，也是我们的主人：这种革命在我看来已无可避免，欧洲所有的君主都在同心协力地加速这种革命的到来。

第九章
论人民（续）

大自然对正常人的身高给出了一定的界限，超过这个范围的就是巨人症或侏儒症。同样，一个好的国家设置要有一定的幅员限度，它的大小也要有所限制，

第二卷
BOOK TWO

过大往往很难实现好的治理，过小会很难保存自己。每个政治体都有一个它不可逾越的最高国力极限，过度的扩张往往使国力达不到这个最大值。社会纽带延伸得越长就会变得越脆弱，一般说来小国往往在这种比例上要优于大国。

有上千个理由来证明上述说法的准确性。首先，距离越远，行政管理就越难推行，这就如同杠杆越长越难举重的道理。随着国家面积的扩展，行政级别增加，政府加在人民头上的负担便会加重。具体来说吧，在镇这一级人民要支付镇级行政费用，再往上是地区一级，再往上是省，这样层层累积直到更高的行政机构，如总督府和王侯府，而且行政级别越高，花费越大，这层层级别的行政费用最后都落在了倒霉的百姓头上，最后是最高级别的中央政府，它足以压垮所有的人。如此巨大的行政费用层层叠加，使臣民们几近被榨干。在这些超负荷中，臣民们远不是被治理得更好了，实际上，如果只有一级行政权力来管理他们的话，人民远比现在生活得更好。事实上，国家将没有任何可以动用的公共财力来应对紧急事件，一旦有不测发生，国家将会在崩溃的边缘摇摇欲坠。

这还不是全部。太过辽阔的地域不仅使政府没有足够的精力和效率来使人遵守法律、制止不满、防止权力滥用和阻止边远地区发生的叛乱，也使臣民们对于他们永远不得谋面的领袖、广阔无边的国家和大多数形同陌路的同胞们缺乏感情。各个省份因为风尚不同、气候迥异，并不能容忍同一种政府形式，同样的法律并不能同时适合所有的省份，而使用不同的法律则会在人民中间产生误解和混乱，因为这些人民处于同一个管理者的管辖中，并且处于不断地交流中，相互杂居、彼此通婚，不同的规则就会大行其道，人们会逐渐失去对自己传统的承继。当这样一大群彼此陌生的人被聚集到同一片领土上，置于同一至高政府的领导下，才能会被湮没，品德会被漠视，恶行得不到应有的惩罚，执政者有太多的事情要做，以至于他无法做到事必躬亲，他的大权被分化到其下级官吏手中。众多边远地区的官吏们时刻想着要逃避或窃取权力控制，执政者不得不忙于维护这种公共权威，这耗去了他所有的政治精力，以至于再也没有精力去关心百姓的福祉，甚至在必要时无力保卫人民。这样，一个相对于其自身过于庞大的体制就会为其自身重量的压迫所坍塌和毁灭了。

另一方面，如果一个国家想拥有坚实的力量，它就必须为自己打下坚固的根基，这样才能够经得住它必须要经历的种种动荡，并能维护为了自保而做的种种努力。因为所有的民族都有一种离心力，这种离心力使他们之间不断地产生摩擦，并试图牺牲别人的利益来满足自己，就如同笛卡尔所说的旋涡。因此，弱者总是处于被吞没的危险中，除非所有民族都能达到一种平衡状态，使任何地方的人们或多或少地一起承受压力，否则任何民族都不能保全自己。

这就向我们表明，国家扩张有道理，收缩同样有道理，事实上，如果能在扩张与收缩之间找到一种最佳的比例使国家最适合生存，是政治才华中非常重要的方面。一般情况下，领土扩张是外在的相对的，而领土收缩则是内在的绝对的，对外扩张比起对内收缩更不应具有强行性。一个强健的组织体制才应是国家施政的第一目标，因为这种仁政所产生的力量，比起大片领土所产生的物产资源更为可靠。

有人可能会补充说，曾经存在这样政治结构的国家，征服的必要性已经成为它们体制的一部分，它们为了维护自身而被迫不停地扩张自己的领土。也许这些国家曾经为自己的这种必要性而沾沾自喜，殊不知这种必要性会在以后的事实中告诉它们，在它们鼎盛之极的时候，已经暗藏着无可避免的陨落时刻。

第十章
论人民（再续）

可用两种方式来衡量一个政治体：疆域面积和人口数目。国家的最佳大小取决于这两个因素的相对关系，只有人口与土地之间的比例达到平衡，人构成了国家，而土地作为物资来源又养活了人，这两个因素之间的合理比例要求有足够多的土地来养活其居民，同时也要求有足够多的人口来容纳这块土地，只有在这种合适的比例上，一定数量的人民才能实现他们的最大力量。如果疆域过大，势必造成土地耕种不充分而且产出过剩，而过多的物产又会被邻国觊觎，从而容易导致防御性战争；如果情况相反，疆域过少，那这个国家就得依赖从邻国进口资源，受邻国牵制，不久就要引发侵略战争。任何民族如果只能在战争与贸易之间抉择，这样的民族本质是脆弱的，因为它要依赖于事态发展，或者依赖于邻国，它的存在必定是不稳固的和短命的；它或者通过征服他国来改自己的困境，或者被他国征服而不再存在。也就是说，它只能在或收缩或扩张的前提下来保护自己的自由。

在一片给定土地面积的土地上究竟安置多少人口合适，并没有数学上的固定比例。这不仅因为不同土地有不同特点，比如土壤的肥沃程度不同、物产的种类不同以及气候条件各有差异，还因为不同国度的居民素质各不相同，比如一些生活在富饶土地上的居民对土地消耗甚少，而生活在贫瘠土地上的居民则消耗甚多。还需要考虑妇女的生育能力的大小、对国家人口增长的各种有利或不利的土地特征，以及立法者在制定制度时所预期的移民的数量。由此我们可以得知，立法者不应该根据现状而应以对未来的预见作出判断，他不应该只考虑当时人口的情况，同时也要看到人口自然成长的数量会是多少。最后，还会有无数种情况，比如在一些条件特殊的情况下需要或允许人们获取的土地大于所需，在多山的国家，那里的耕地类型主要是森林和牧场，有丰富的自然出产，因此不需要太多的劳作；而且经验证明那里的妇女比平原的妇女具有更强的生育能力；这些地区山坡陡峭，只有很小部分的平地可供耕种；所以人们居住得非常分散。而海边的情况正好相反，人们聚集在一片很小的区域内，甚至可以在贫瘠不毛的礁石区或沙滩上生存。这是因为渔猎可以大量弥补农业产出的不足，人们也需要聚居在一起更好地抵御海盗，还因为他们可以通过海外移民的方式来摆脱人口过剩的负担。

除了上述人类制度的诸多条件，还有一个条件最为重要，这个条件是无可取代的，没有它其他任何条件都不再起作用，这个条件就是：人民必须享有充分的和平。因为国家就如同军营，在初创时期是非常脆弱的，没有抵抗力、最易被消灭。一个国家即使在混乱中也比在酝酿时期更有抵抗能力，因为在国家酝酿期，人们都只考虑自己在国家中所处的地位，而无视公共的危险，如果在这种关键时期遇到战争、饥荒或叛乱，那这个国家将不可避免地被颠覆。

当然，也确曾有过很多在这种动乱中建立起来的政府，但真实的情况是正是这些政府毁灭了自己的国家。那些篡权者往往选择动乱时期，利用公众的恐慌来颁布法律，而这些法律在正常情况是不可能被公众接受的。可以说，要分辨立法者的工作和篡权者的工作，看他们所选择的立法时间就是很明确的方法之一。

那么，什么样的民族适合接受法律呢？我的答案是：一个发现自己已经被某种原始的联合、利益或协议捆绑在了一起，但还未曾受法律真正约束的民族；是一个尚未形成根深蒂固习俗和迷信的民族；是一个不畏惧邻国的突然侵袭、并且不参与到邻国的矛盾中的民族，这个民族能抵挡得住任何一个邻国的干预或能够借助一国的帮助来对付另一国；是一个其中每个成员都被其他成员所知、任何人都不需承担他所承担不起的负担的民族；是一个可以不依靠其他民族就可以生存，并且其他民族不依靠它也能生存的民族【原注1】；是一个既不太富也不太穷能自力更生的民族；最后，它还是一个结合了新生民族的可塑性和古老民族稳定性的民族。立法工作之所以艰难，更多地在于不是要建树什么，而在于要破坏什么；而立法成功的例子之所以稀少，则在于很难将自然的朴素性与社会的需要完美地结合在一起。的确，将上述条件整合在一起是相当困难的，因此，世上也就没有几个体制良好的国家存在。

尽管如此，在欧洲还是有一个能够立法的地方的，那就是科西嘉岛。这个勇敢的民族在恢复和维护它的自由时所表现出的坚定和英勇，使它有资格由一位智者来教导如何保障它的自由。我有一种预感，这个小岛终有一天会使整个欧洲为之震惊的。

【原注1】如果两个比邻而居的民族彼此依存，这种情况对一方是不利的，对于另一方则是危险的。在这种情况下，任何明智的民族都会尽快摆脱这种依赖的局面。斯拉斯加拉共和国处于被墨西哥帝国包围中，那里的人民宁可不用盐也不从墨西哥人那里购买，甚至也不接受他们馈赠的食盐。聪明的斯拉斯加拉人看到了墨西哥人慷慨背后隐藏的阴谋。他们维护了自己的自由，这个处于庞大帝国版图之内的一个小国家最终成为导致那个大帝国灭亡的一个重要因素。

第十一章
论种种不同的法律体系

如果要探究全体人员的最大利益之所在——这原本也应是每个法律体系的宗旨，我们会发现它可被归结为两个主要目标：自由和平等。自由，是因为国家的力量是个体依赖的源泉；平等，是因为如果没有平等，自由亦不复存在。

我已经论述过什么是公民的自由。至于平等，这个词绝不能理解为所有人在权力和财产上都绝对平均分配，而是指权力不能发展为暴力，它只能根据威望和法律才能行使。就财产而言，平等就是没有公民可以富足到可以购买另一个公民，也没有一个公民贫穷到出卖自己【原注1】。这便意味着人们需要节制，位高权重的人应该节制自己的财富与势力，地位相对卑下的人要克服困难，克制自己的贪欲和妄羡。

这就有人会说了：这种平等就是不切实际的幻想，根本不可能在现实中存在。但是，如果明知道滥权是不可避免的，难道就不采取措施加以控制了吗？正由于现实环境总在造成不平等的现象，我们所制定的法律才必须要倾向于保障平等。

这些只是一切完美制度的一般目标，在具体到某个国家时必须针对该国家的地区情况和居民特性所产生的关系来加以更改，正是在这些关系的基础上，每个民族都应该有针对自己的最好制度体系。这种制度本身或许不是最好的，但是对于其针对的国家来说却是最适合的。比如说，你们的土地太过贫瘠吗？你们的领土相对居民人口过于狭小吗？那你们就转向工艺和工业吧，这样就可以用工业产品来换取你们所缺乏的自然资源了。或者相反，你们占据了富饶的平原和辽阔的山川，你们拥有沃土无边却人口稀少，那就全心全力发展农业以增殖人口，并放弃导致人口减少的工业吧，因为工业总会使农业人口减少，并把为数不多的人集中于一定的城市中【原注2】。你们占据了绵长且便利的海岸线吗？那就把海面布满船舶，大力发展商贸，你们将会得到一个短暂却辉煌的文明。沿着你们海岸的，只是海水在拍打无法靠近的岩石吗？那就做个吃鱼的野蛮人吧，你将拥有无比安宁或许更快乐的生活，你也一定更加幸福。总之，除了那些对所有民族都通用的原则外，每个民族都有理由按自己特定的方式生活，实行那些只适合自己的法律。因此，古代的希伯来人和近代的阿拉伯人选择了宗教作为他们的目标；雅典人选择了文学；迦太基人（Carthage）和提尔人（Tyre）选择了贸易；罗德岛（Rhodes）选择了航海；斯巴达选择了战争；罗马选择了美德。《论法的精神》一书的作者采用无数事例证明了立法者是如何艺术地将体制引向这些目标的。

要使一个国家的体制真正做到稳固与持久，必须遵循这样的规则：自然规律与法律在每一点上都能协调一致，而法律也正是用来保障这种和谐的。但如果立法者弄错了他的目标，采取了与国情完全不符合的另一套原则，以至于一方倾向于奴役而另一方需要自由，或者一方追求财富而另一方需要人口增长，或者一方需要和平而另一方追求征服，那么法律就会在不知不觉中被削弱，制度将遭到瓦解，国家就会处于动荡不安中，直至毁灭或更迭，而战无不胜的自然将重新掌握自己的统治。

【原注1】你想让国家内部和谐统一吗？那么就要尽可能使两个极端靠拢。既没有十分富裕的人，也不能有乞丐。因为这两个天然不可分离的阶级对于公共幸福是同等致命的。一方面会产生出暴政的支持者，一方面会产生暴君。经常是这两个阶层之间进行着公共自由的交易：一个买进，一个卖出。

【原注2】阿冉松侯爵说："一般说来，任何对外贸易的部门都只能给王国带来虚幻的利益；它可能会使一部分人、甚至是一些大的城市变得富裕，但是国家作为一个整体并不能从中得到什么，而且人民也不会因此而生活得更好。"

第二卷
BOOK TWO

第十二章
法律的分类

为了使所有事务都井然有序，或者说为了赋予公众尽可能好的法律形式，需要考虑到各种关系，首先是整个政治体对于自身的作用力，即全体与全体的关系，或者说是主权体之于国家的关系，以后我们会看到，这种关系由中间媒介之间的联系构成。

规定着这种关系的法律被称为政治法。如果它制定得当的话，也可称之为基本法。如此称呼不无道理，因为既然一个国家中只有一种最好的制度来治理它，那么已经发现这个制度的民族就应该遵循它。但如果已有的制度不好，那么为什么还要把阻碍人民生活秩序的法律当成基本法呢？另外，一个民族不管在任何情况下都可以做主改变自己的法律，哪怕是最好的法律。如果哪个民族的人们乐于损害自己，那谁还有权不让他们这样做吗？

第二种关系是国家成员间的关系，以及成员同整个政治体之间的关系。成员间的关系应尽可能地受制约，成员同政治体间的关系却是越广泛越好，这样能使每个公民在彼此完全独立的同时又极端依赖国家，这种结果总是通过同一手段达到，因为只有国家的力量才能为每个成员带来自由。这第二种关系产生了民法。

我们还可以考虑第三种关系：个体和法律的关系，也就是违法和惩罚的关系。这种关系使刑法得以形成，从根本上说，刑法与其说是一种特定的法律形态，还不如把它看做对其他一切法律的裁定。

在上述三种法律之外，还应加上第四种法律，也是最为重要的一种，它没被刻在石碑上，也没被刻在铜器上，而是刻在了公民心中。是它形成了国家的真

051

正体制，它每天都在积聚力量，当其他法律过时或消亡的时候，它激励或取代它们；它可以使一个民族保持创造精神，使习惯的力量逐渐代替权威的力量。这里，我说的是道德、习俗，尤其是信仰。这一类法律并不为我们的政治理论家所熟知，但其他一切法律的成败与否都取决于它。伟大的立法者们都懂得秘密关注它，尽管他们表面上只是在制定具体的规章条文，但他们明白这些个别的章节只是制度穹顶的拱架，而缓慢发展的道德与风尚才是形成制度的不可动摇的基石。

在这些不同种类的法律形态中，只有决定政府形式的政治法才是我的题旨所在。

第三巻
BOOK THREE

With regard to the right of conquest it has no other foundation than the law of the strongest. If war does not confer on the victor the right of slaying the vanquished, this right which he does not possess, cannot be the foundation of a right to enslave them. If we have a right to slay an enemy only when it is impossible to enslave him, the right to enslave him is not derived from the right to kill him, it is therefore an iniquitous bargain to make him purchase his life over which the victor has no right, at the cost of his liberty. In establishing the right of life and death upon the right of slavery, and the right of slavery upon the right of life and death, is it not manifest that one falls into a vicious circle?

Jean Jacques Rousseau

在讨论不同的政府形式之前，我们先来确定一下"政府"一词的准确含义，因为迄今为止该词还没被很好地解释过。

第三卷
BOOK THREE

第一章
政府总论

我必须提醒我的读者,你们一定要仔细阅读本章,因为对于那些不打算集中精力的人,我是没办法把这个问题给他们讲清楚的。

任何自由行动的发生都由两个因素共同促成:一个是抽象意义上的因素,即决定这一行动的意愿;一个是物理意义上的因素,即执行这种行动的力量。当我想走向一个目标,首先必须有走向这个目标的意愿,其次是要有行走的能力。一个想走的瘫痪病人和一个不想走的健康人,都只能原地不动。政治体的行为也具有同样的两个因素,我们同样也可将它们划分为意愿和力量,前者被称为立法权力,后者被称为行政权力。如果没有这两种力的同时作用,政治体的任何行动都不能进行。

我们已经知道立法权力属于并只能属于人民。而另一方面,从本书前面章节(第二卷,第四、六章)中所确定的原则中可以看出,行政权力只在特定行为中实施,这种个别行为已经超出了法律的范畴,因此也不属于制定法律的主权范畴,行政权力不能像立法权和主权体一样属于全体人民。

因此,公众的力量需要有一个自己的机构将公共的力量凝聚起来,在普遍意志的指导下行动,作为在国家和主权体之间进行沟通的手段,就如同灵魂与肉体结合为一个人那样把国家和主权体结合起来。这就是国家为什么需要有政府的原因,有时政府被错误地认为是主权体,其实它只是主权体的执行者而已。

那么,究竟什么是政府呢?政府就是为了臣民和主权体相互沟通而建立在两者之间的中介体,负责实施法律、维护政治和社会自由。

该中介体的成员称为行政官员(Magistrates)或国王(Kings),即管理者(Governers),他们被统称为统治者(Prince)【原注1】。这样看来,那种认为人民接受统治者领导的行为不是一种契约的看法完全正确,因为这种约定不过是一种任命或委托而已。在这一过程中,统治者不过是主权体的代理人,他们以主权体的名义行使主权体赋予的权力,主权体可以在任何时候限制、更改或收回这种权力;如果放弃这种权力,就会与社会共同体的本质不相容,就是违背了社会契约的目的。

因此,我把行政权力的合法行使者称为政府或最高行政,把执掌这一行政权力的人或机构称为君主或行政官员。

在政府中,我们可以发现这些中介的力量,它们之间的关系构成了全体与全体的关系以及主权体与国家的关系。后一种关系可被看做首尾两项不断变换的比率关系,而政府就是它们的几何平均数。政府从主权体那里接受命令,然后发布

第三卷
BOOK THREE

给人民，如果想使一个国家处于正常的平衡状态，就必须权衡所有因素，使政府自身的乘积或幂，等于作为臣民的公民和作为主权体公民的乘积或幂。

另外，如果上述三方关系中任意一方发生改变，就必然破坏了原来的等比关系。如果主权体要进行直接治理，或者行政官员想制定法律，或者臣民不服从领导，那么秩序将被混乱的局面取代，力量与意志不再协调行动，国家也会解体，将陷入专制政府或者无政府状态中。最后，正如两个数字之间只能有一个等比中项，一个国家也只可能有一个好政府。但是由于国家政事纷纭，不断改变民族的内部关系，使得不同的民族就应该有不同的政府形态，即使同一个民族在不同的时期也应该有不同的政府。

为了更清楚地说明处于比例两端的关系，我举人口数目作为例子，因为这是一种更容易清楚表达的关系。

假设一个国家有一万名公民，主权体只能被看做一个整体，但作为臣民的每个个人，则被考虑为一个个体。因此主权体相对于一个臣民的比例就是一万比一，就是说，国家的每个成员尽管完全从属于主权体，但它只享有一万分之一的主权权力。如果人口数目增加到十万，臣民的地位没有变化，因为每个臣民同其他臣民一样还要完全遵守法律的约定，但作为主权者，他所分享到的只是十万分之一的表决权，比起以前对制定法律的影响力小了十倍。由于臣民总是作为单一的个体，他和主权体的比率根据公民人口数的增加而增加。由此可得出结论：国家越大，自由越少。

当我说到比率增大时，我的意思是它离平等越来越远了。因此，在几何意义上这个比率越大，在普通意义上就越小。前者考虑的是数量关系，是以指数大小来衡量的；后者考虑的是同一性，判定的是相似性的多少。

个别意志与普遍意志之间的比率越小，即个人原则与法律之间的相似性越少，强制力量就必须越大。因此，如果政府要做到有序行动，随着人口数量增加，它必须相应加强其强制力。

另一方面，由于国家的扩大意味着给公权力的掌握者更大的滥权机会和诱惑，随着政府对人民的控制力加强，主权体对政府的控制力也必须要加强。这里我所说的并不是绝对权力，而是国家不同组成部分之间的相对力量。

从以上双重比率中可以看出，主权体、君主与臣民三者之间的比例绝不是臆造出来的，而是政治体性质的必然结论。我们可以进一步推出，既然连续比率的一端是作为臣民的人民，是作为一个固定的整体，总表现为"一"，所以随着双重比率的增大或缩小，单项比率也会同样地增大或缩小，因此比例中间项也会随之发生变化。这表明，不存在绝对且单一的政府形式，有多少大小不等的国家，就会有多少性质不同的政府形式。

或许有人会嘲笑这一公式，声称如果按照我的观点，找到首尾项的几何平均值建立一个政府，只需计算出人口数字的平方根就可以了。那么我的回答是：我仅仅是举人口数量作为一个例子，而且我所说的各比率不仅取自人口数量，而是要更多地根据众多行为数量来衡量，这些行为的发生又有着数不清的原因。何况，我借用几何学术语只是为了让我的表达更简练，我当然深知道德上的衡量并不像几何学那样精确。

政府就是大的政治体的一个小型化，这个政治体中也包含了政府本身。它是一个被赋予了某些能力的虚拟的人，它像主权体一样主动，像国家一样被动；它可被分解为一些类似的比例关系，产生新的比率，在这些新的比率上，我们可以按照行政官员的官阶继续进行分解，直到分解为一个单一的、不可再分的比率中项，即唯一的首领或最高行政官，我们可把他看成这一比例系列的中心，是逐级演进中一系列分数和一系列整数的那个"一"。

为避免继续在这些复杂比例中纠缠不清，我们就简单地把政府看成是国家中的一个新实体，它有别于人民和主权体，是位于二者之间的中介体。

国家与政府这两个实体有着本质的区别：国家可以独立存在，而政府只能通过主权而存在。因此政府的主导意志应该是、而且必须是公共意愿或者法律，

第三卷
BOOK THREE

它不过集合起公众力量。一旦它试图运用权威进行绝对的独立行动，联结共同体的纽带就开始松懈了。如果政府的个别意志比主权体的公共意志还要活跃，并且为了使人民服从他的个别意志而动用了他手中的公共力量，结果就有了两个主权体，一个是法律上的，一个是事实上的，那么社会共同体将顷刻消亡，政治体也就随之解体了。

然而，为了使政府这个实体能成为真正的存在，具有一个区别于国家实体的真正生命，为了使政府所有成员行动一致，符合建立它的目的，就必须使政府成为一个特定的自我，拥有其成员的共同意识，拥有保障自身的意志和能力。这种特定的存在意味着要有议会制、委员会、磋商和决定的权利、各种权利、君主专属的种种特权以及那种使行政官员随着职责越繁重便越能得到相关回报的地位、头衔和权利。政府这种存在的困难在于，如何找到一种方法，在国家这个大的整体中安置政府这一小的整体，以使政府在强化自身体制的同时又不削弱国家的公共体制，使其能够把保存自身生存的自有力量区别于维持国家生存的公共力量。总之一句话，政府总要做好准备为了人民而牺牲自己，而不是为了政府牺牲人民。

此外，尽管政府这一人为的实体是另一人为实体的产物，它只拥有一种外借的、附属的生命，但并不意味着它不能凭借或多或少的力量和敏捷采取行动，也不影响它享有或多或少的健康。最后，它即使不会完全违背人们建立政府时的目标，但它却可能依照自己的结构方式在某种程度上偏离这个目标。

偶然的特殊的关系会使国家发生改变，政府应根据这些关系和国家保持一定的比例关系。所以，政府应随所属政治体的缺陷而加以改变，否则，即使本身是最好的政府也往往会成为最糟的政府。

【原注1】因此，在威尼斯，即使当大总督不出席的时候，大议会仍被人们称为"最尊敬的君主"。

第二章
论不同政府形式的构成原则

在阐述形成这些不同的一般原因之前，我认为有必要先对政府与君主进行区分，就像我曾经对国家与主权体进行区分一样。

执政者团体中成员的数量或多或少，我们已经说过主权与臣民的比率会随着臣民数目的增加而增长，同理可推之，政府与执政者之间的关系也存在同样的比率。

政府的全部权力在任何时候都等同于国家的权力，这点永远不会改变。因此，政府耗费在自己成员身上的力量越多，余下来用在人民身上的力量就越少。

因此，行政官员数量越多，政府就越弱。这是一个基本的原则，因此我们不妨将它解释得更清楚些。

我们可以在每个行政官员身上区分出三种本质不同的意志。第一种是他的个人意志，它只追求个人私利。第二种是行政官员们的共同意志，它只关心君主的利益，可称之为团体意志。对政府来说它是一种普遍意志，但对于政府从属的国家来说它是个别意志。第三种是人民的意志或主权体的意志，它不论是对于整体的国家，还是对于整体一部分的政府，都是一种普遍意志。

在完善的法律体系中，个别或特殊的意志应该是不起作用的，政府的团体意志也是极其次要的，只有普遍的或主权体的意志才永远居于首位，是所有其他意志的唯一规范者。

然而，在自然规律中，这些不同的意志处于更集中的条件下会变得更加活跃，因此，普遍意志永远最弱，团体意志略强些，而个别意志总是居于首位。结果在政府中，每个成员首先是其自身，然后是行政官，最后才是公民。这一排列

第三卷
BOOK THREE

与社会秩序所要求的次序完全相反。

弄清这一点后，我们再来假定政府是掌握在唯一一个人手里的，此时个人意志和团体意志完全统一在一起，因此团体意志就达到了前所未有的强度。现在，由于权力的实施强度取决于意志的力度，而政府的绝对权力是一个恒量，得出的结论是：最强有力的政府是一个人的政府。

我们再来考虑另一种情况，如果把政府和立法权合并在一起，使主权体就是统治者，每个公民都是行政官员，那么团体意志就会和普遍意志统一起来，团体意志就不会比公意更主动，而个人意志依然保持原来的力度，此时的政府虽然依然拥有着绝对权力，但在相对力量或能动性上却处于最低点。

这些关联是无可辩驳的，对其他方面的考察会对它们进一步证实。例如，处于政府中的行政官员比处于国家中的公民的行动更有能动性，因为政府中的个别意志比主权体约定中的个别意志的影响要大得多，因为每个政府官员总有一些政府职能，而单个的公民却不具有任何主权职能。而且，国家越是扩展，它的力量就会越大，尽管实际力量的增长与地域的扩张并不成正比。但是，如果国家规模一定，行政官员数量增加再多，政府的力量也不会有丝毫增加，因为政府的力量就是国家的力量，而国家的力量并没有变化。在这种情况下，政府的绝对力或实际力量没有增加，它的相对力量或能动性就会降低。

还可以肯定的一点是：参与管事的人越多，公共事务的处理便会越慢；大机构过于强调谨慎，从而坐失良机；遇事往往耽于无休止的讨论，很难作出有效的决定。

我刚才说明的是政府随成员的增加会变得效率降低，前面我还证明过人民数量越多强制力量就应越大。由此可以得出结论，行政官员与政府之间的比率同臣民与主权体之间的比率恰好是相反的。也就是说，国家越扩大，政府就越应精简，所以，行政官员的数量要随着臣民人口的增加而减少。

需要补充的一点是，这里我所论述的是政府的相对权力而不是它应有的本性。因为，行政官员越多，团体意志越接近普遍意志，相反，在只有一个统治者的情况下，如我前面所述，团体意志就只是一种个别意志。在一方面有所失，必定在另一方面有所得，立法者的艺术就在于寻求一个合适的度，将永远成反比的政府的力量和意志得到最恰到好处的结合，使其最有利于国家。

第三章
论政府的分类

在前面一章中，我们已经清楚了为什么要按组成政府的成员人数来划分各种政府形式，本章我们将要探讨的是这种分类是如何进行的。

首先，主权体可将政府置于全体人民或绝大多数人民的手中，这样，作为政府官员的公民数量就会比作为普通个人的公民要多。我们把这种政府形式称为民主制。

或者，主权体将政府交付到少数人手中，使普通公民的数量多于行政官员，这种政府形式称为贵族制。

最后，主权体可以把整个政府都集中于一个人手里，其他官员都从这个当权者手里获得权力。这种形式是最为常见的，称为君主制或皇室政府制。

应该注意的是，所有这些形式，至少是前两种，行政官员的数量可以有或多或少的浮动，甚至可以有相当显著程度的变动。民主制形式可以从全体人民到半数人民；贵族制可以从半数人民到极少数人；即使是君主制政府也存在分权的可能。根据斯巴达的宪法，国家可以并存两个国王。罗马帝国甚至曾经同时拥有八个皇帝却没有破坏它的统一。因此每种政府形式都可能在某一点上与另一种形式重合。尽管只有三种名称，但实际上一个国家拥有多少公民数目，就有可能存在多少种政府形式。

再者，同一政府可能在某些方面再分为各种不同的机构，每个机构都可以采取不同的行政方式，三种政府形式便可结合起来产生很多种混合形式，每种混合

第三卷
BOOK THREE

形式都可从这三种单一的形式中演变出来。

历朝历代人们都在争论这个问题：什么是最好的政府形式？殊不知，任何一种形式都可能在某种情况下是最好的，而在另一种情况下却可能最坏。

如果说，在一个国家中最高行政官员的数量应与公民人数成反比，那么一般说来，民主政府适合小国，贵族制政府适合中等国家，而君主制则适合大的国家。这一法则直接从我们已建立的原则中得出，但是我们该如何考量那些大量的例外情况呢？

第四章
论民主制度

立法者比任何人都更清楚该如何解释法律和执行法律，于是看上去似乎最好的国家组织形式应该是执法权力与立法权力的结合。但是事实上，正是这种结合使这种政府在某些方面存在缺陷，因为它将本该分离的权力结合了起来，如果君主与主权体成为了同一个人，那么可以说，建构起来的是一个没有政府的政府。

由制定法律的人来执行法律，或者作为结合体的人民将注意力从全面的角度转向个别的对象，这都并非好事。公众事务中最危险的莫过于私人利益的影响了，政府对法律权力的滥用也比不上立法者追求个人利益的危害更为严重。一旦这种腐败行为发生了，国家肌体将遭到破坏，那么任何改革都无法挽回了。一个从不滥用政府权力的民族也不会滥用独立，一个始终自我治理良好的民族也不需要由别人管理。

从严格意义上说，真正的民主制从未存在过，也永远不会存在。由多数人统治少数人是违反自然原则的。我们无法想象，人民需要不断地集合起来处理公共事务，而一旦人民为此设立一些专门机构，很容易看出的是，行政形式便随之改变了。

社会契约论
The Social Contract

我确信这样一个公理：如果政府的职能被许多机构分别掌握了，那么，那些人数少的机构会慢慢获得最大的权威，仅仅因为他们处理事务的便捷也会迟早将他们引向这一步。

何况，要建立一个民主制政府需要多少难以凑齐的先决条件啊，首先，国家要十分小，以便使人民易于集合而彼此认识。其次，习俗和道德要极其简洁，以避免繁多的事务和棘手的讨论。第三，社会等级和财富要实现高度平等，否则权利和权威上的平等难以持久。最后，杜绝奢侈现象。因为奢侈是财富过多造成的，或者使得财富成为一种必需，它既腐蚀富人，也腐蚀穷人，使国家陷入了萎靡和虚荣之中，它使一些人沦为其他一些人的奴隶，或者让所有人都成为公共舆论的奴隶时，国家便失去了所有的公民。

这就是为什么一个著名作家【译注1】把美德作为共和国的基本原则，因为没有美德，其他所有条件都无法维持。但是这位伟大的天才却没有对事务进行必要的区分，所以他的论述常常不够精确，有时甚至不清晰，他没有看到既然主权在哪里都是一样的，同样的原则应在所有体制良好的国家内都适用。当然由于政府形式不同，它们的影响力也会有或大或小的差异。

还要补充的是，民主制政府或人民制政府比其他任何形式的政府都更可能出现内战或动乱，因为没有任何政府如此经常地、如此强烈地倾向于改变自己的形式，或者需要如此的警觉与勇气来维持现有的形式。总之，在民主制度下，公民必须要时刻充满力量与坚定，他要终其一生地、每天都从心底重复着德高望重的侯爵【原注1】在波兰议会上所说的话："我宁要动荡中的自由，也不要平静中的奴役。"

如果有一个神的国度，他们可能会采用民主制来治理，但这种政府并不适合人类。

【原注1】波兹南侯爵，1704~1735年曾为波兰国王。
【译注1】孟德斯鸠的《论法的精神》。

第三卷
BOOK THREE

第五章
论贵族制

这里我们有两个完全不同的法人，即政府和主权体，因此就有了两个普遍意志，一个是相对于全体公民而言的，另一个是相对于行政当局的成员而言的。因此，尽管政府可以任意对自己的内部事务作出规定，但它只能以主权体的名义，也就是人民自身的名义，否则它无权对人民发号施令，这一点我们必须牢记。

最初的社会形态都是按照贵族制来进行治理的，家族的家长们聚在一起商讨公共事务，年轻人心甘情愿地服从于经验的权威，于是有了长老、元老、尊长、长官这些称呼。北美的土著人直到今天仍然采用这种治理方式，而且治理得相当不错。

但是当社会发展到一定程度，人为的不平等逐渐战胜自然的平等，财富和权力[原注1]取代了年龄开始为人看重，贵族制就变为选举了。最后，权力与财产的父子相传造就了贵族世家，这使政府也变成世袭制，有时甚至会出现二十岁的元老。

所以有三种贵族制，即自然的、选举的和世袭的。第一种只适用于原始部族，第三种是所有政府形式中最糟糕的。第二种是最好的，它体现了真正意义上的贵族制。

实行选举的贵族制除了有将主权体与政府两权分离的好处，还有着可以选择政府官员的好处。在民主制中，所有公民生而为行政官员，但贵族制把官员局限为少数人，他们只能由选举产生[原注2]，这种方式使得诚实、贤明、经验以及其他受公民看重和尊重的品质成为一个明智政府的保障。

社会契约论
The Social Contract

再一点就是集会更易举行，事务也能得到更好的讨论，进而可以有序地将这些事务处理得井井有条。在外国人眼中，德高望重的元老们比那些不知名的或被人鄙视的群众更能很好地维护国家的名望。

总而言之，如果能够确定他们是为了民众的利益而不是自己的利益而去治理民众的话，那么让贤明之士来治理民众这种方式是最好最符合自然法则的安排了。这样就无需增加管辖范围，选举出一百个人就能干好的事，就无需使用两万个人了。但必须要注意团体意志就此产生，它并不会严格地按照普遍意志来指导国家力量，而且一部分行政权力将不可避免地逃避法律的约束。

至于建构这种政府形式的特殊要求，它并不要求国家足够小，或者人民必须十分淳朴正直，以便像好的民主制那样使法律的执行能直接来自公众意志。但它要求国家也不能太大，因为国家很大会导致四散分开的官员们可能在自己的辖地内取得主权者的权利，继而谋求自身独立，直至最终成为那块土地的主人。

尽管贵族制并不像民主制那样要求人民具有一定水准的美德，但它有着其他方面的德行要求，比如富人的节制和穷人的满足，因为严格意义上的平等是不会存在的，即使在斯巴达也不例外。

然而，虽说这种政府形式允许一定的财富不公存在，那也只是为了在一般情况下使公共事务的管理被托付给那些能够付出他所有时间的人，而不是如亚里士多德所认为的富人理应受到重视。相反，有时相反的选择是非常有必要的，它可以教育人民，优秀的品质比富有更为重要。

【原注1】很明显，古代人使用"贵族"一词并不是表示最好，而是最强有力的意思。

【原注2】把执政者的选举用法律规定下来是极为重要的，因为如果把这项权力留给统治者的意志来决定，难免会落入世袭的贵族制，就如威尼斯共和国和波尼尔共和国所发生的那样。前一个国家早已分裂，后个国家是靠元老院的超人智慧才得以维持，这是一个值得尊敬但对于国家治理来说非常危险的例外。

第三卷
BOOK THREE

第六章
论君主制

之前，我们一直把统治者视作一个由法律力量结合起来的法人，被赋予了国家和集体的行政权力。现在，我们所要考虑的是，当这些权力集中于一个真正的自然人、一个实实在在的人的手里，并且只有他才能行使由法律授权的权力时，这个人就是我们所说的君主，或国王。

在其他政府形式中，是由一个集体的法人代表来代表一个人执政，而在君主制中，一个个人代表了一个集体的存在，构成统治者的统一体是抽象的，但同时也是一个具体的人；在其他政府形式中，法律要花费很大精力将这些权力结合在一起，而在君主制中，这些很自然地就实现了。

这样，人民的意志、统治者的意志、国家的公共力量、政府的个别力量，统统服务于一个驱动者；机器的所有机关都控制在一个人手里，一切都朝着同一目标迈进，而并无相互的矛盾来破坏这种前进。我们很难想象还有其他政府形式能用更小的力量产生比这更大的能量。在我看来，静静坐在河边，却能毫不费力地拖动一艘大船的阿基米德就如同一位精明的国君。这样的国君貌似不动声色，却能运筹于千里之外，坐在暖阁中就将自己的辽阔王国治理得井然有序。

然而，如果说没有任何政府形式比君主制更有活力，但是，也没有任何政府形式中的个人意志像君主制这样更具支配力。尽管在君主制下，一切都朝着同一目标迈进，但这个目标并非为了人民福祉，也正是这种行政力量在不断削弱国家的力量。

国王们总想拥有绝对的权威，但是来自遥远地区的百姓的呼声却告诉他们：

社会契约论
The Social Contract

要想拥有至高无上的权威，最好的方法就是受到人民的爱戴。这是一条很好的法则，并且在某些方面非常正确。不幸的是，这条法则只是朝堂上的一个笑柄。这种建立在人民爱戴基础上的权力当然是最强大的，但这种力量却也是不确定和短暂的，国王们当然不会满足于此。就是最好的国王也想在自己乐意的时候做点坏事并且不妨碍他继续做主子。政治布道家可能会游说国王，说既然人民的力量就是国王的力量，那国王的最大利益莫过于使百姓繁荣富强、人丁兴旺、英勇坚强。但国王们深知事实并非如此，他们的个人利益首先在于，要使人民虚弱贫困，从而永远无法反抗他们。我承认，如果国王的臣民们总是完全服从的话，那么人民的强大就是国王的力量，并且能使邻国都畏惧他的力量。但这只是第二位的从属的利益，并且力量与彻底的服从总是不兼容的，所以国王们总是自然地偏好那些对他们来说更直接有用的原则。这是撒姆尔对希伯来人所强调过的，也是马基亚维利【译注1】所清楚证明的——他借口指导国王，实际上是在向人民宣讲，他的《君主论》可以成为共和主义者的手册【原注1】。

在由前面的一般性比率进行讨论时我们发现，君主制只适用于大的国家，而通过对君主制本身的研究，也会得到同一结果。公共行政人员越多，统治者与臣民间的比例就越少而使两者趋于相等，成为一比一或实现民主制中的平等。这个比率又会随着政府人员的收缩而变大，并在政府集权于一个人时达到最大。但是这样，统治者与人民间的距离会过大，国家缺乏凝聚力，必须有中间阶层的出现来弥补这种缺陷，这些中间阶层包括亲王、总督、大臣等。但所有这些并不适用于小国，小的国家会为这层层的社会规则所毁灭。

但是，如果说治理好一个大国很困难，由一个人来治理就更困难了。每个人都明白当国王一旦通过代理人来进行统治会发生什么事情。

君主制政府有一个本质的不可避免的缺陷，这使它劣于共和制政府：在共和制中，人民总是把有才能的人推到高位，这些人也总能以此为荣而很好地履行他们的职责；而在君主制下，得势的却往往是无赖、骗子和阴谋家，这些人凭着小

第三卷
BOOK THREE

聪明爬到高位，而一旦置于高位就会向公众暴露出自己的无能和不称职。显然，人民在择人方面比君主犯的错误要少。君主制内阁中真正优秀的人和共和制政府首脑中愚蠢的笨蛋同样少见。因此，如果有这样一种幸运的机会，一个天生有统治才能的君主开始执掌一个被投机钻营者们败坏了的国家，每个人将会震惊于他所发掘出的能量，而这位君主的出现便成为这个国家历史上划时代的大事。

君主制国家若想治理得好，它的人口和幅员大小就必须依治理者的才能而定。显然，夺天下易，治天下难。如果有足够长的杠杆，一根指头就可以反转世界，但要想支撑这个世界，非要有大力士赫尔格利斯的肩膀【译注2】了。国家稍微大一点，君主治理起来就会力不从心了。如果情况相反，国家的疆域相对于君主的能力太小时——当然这种情况比较少——国家依然治理不好，因为君主为了自己的宏伟理想，往往会忘记人民的利益，结果他会滥用自己超凡的才能扩张，如此，带给人民的苦难并不亚于一个能力不足的庸主。可以说，一个国家的扩张或收缩都是依照君主的能力而定，相反，民主制国家中，元老院的治理能力更容易保持在一个固定的水平，国家会拥有固定不变的疆域，治理也不会更坏。

一人执掌的政府有一个可怕的缺陷，就是缺乏继承的连续性，在其他两种政府体系中，这种连续性为统一提供了永不间断的纽带。当一位君王去世后，便需要选出另一位新主，选举期便成为一个暴风骤雨般的动荡期。这时，除非这种政府中的公民比一般情况下更无私与忠诚——而这根本不可能——否则贿赂与阴谋就会乘虚而入，靠收买而执掌了国政的人上台后，很难保证他不再次把国家出卖，以从弱者身上捞回以前被强者搜刮走的钱财。在这样的政府中，卖官鬻爵盛行，一切都成为金钱交易，人们在有国王统治时享受到的这种和平比王位空缺时的混乱更糟糕啊。

人们为了防止这样的邪恶曾做了些什么呢？曾使王位在某些家族中代代相传，并确定了继承的秩序以防止在国王驾崩时发生争端。也就是说，用摄政的缺陷取代了选举的缺陷，这表明人们偏爱表面的安定胜过贤明的行政，人们宁愿让未成年的孩子、怪物、智障来当政，也不愿冒着发生冲突的危险去选择贤主。人们没有意识到，当他们冒着危险做出这种两难的选择时，他们已使一切机会都对他们不利了。小狄俄尼索斯曾为了一桩不光彩的事遭到父亲的指责："我为你做出过这种榜样吗？"小狄俄尼索斯狡猾地回答："您的父亲不是国王啊！"

当一个人从小就被培养如何去命令别人，那所有一切会使他最容易丧失公正和理性。据说，人们常会煞费苦心教会一个年轻的王子以统治艺术，但结果显示，这种教育对他来说没有任何益处，反而教给他如何服从会更有效些。历史上那些名垂千古的君主并不是从小接受统治教育的人，因为统治是这样一种学问，学得越多，掌握得越少，服从要比命令更能使人掌握它。"辨别好与坏的最有效和最迅捷的方法是把自己放在别人而不是国王的角度上来思考自己想要什么或不想要什么。"【原注2】

政府缺乏连续性的一个后果就是王室政权的不稳定性。政府有时执行这个计划，有时又有了另一种计划，这完全取决于当时进行统治的国王或者代他统治的人的秉性，因此，无法在较长时间内形成一个固定目标或连贯的政策，这种不确定性让国家朝令夕改，摇移不定，而这种情况在其他政府形式下是不会发生的，因为那些政府的统治者是同一的。由此可见，一般情况下，皇室宫廷多阴谋，共和体的元老院多智慧；共和制国家沿着稳定而有效的指导方向向着固定的目标前进，而君主制政府每一次变更都带来国家的巨大变化，因为所有的大臣和大部分的国王都会翻转他们前任所制定的政策，这几乎成为一条普遍的准则。

这种不连贯性同时可以驳斥保皇派政治家们常用的诡辩，这种诡辩不仅包括了前面我已经反驳过的谬论，即把公民政府喻为家庭管理，把国王比作一家之主，它还包括了把所有君主都想象成拥有一个君主所应具备的德行，并把君主设想成他们所应有的样子。在这种假定下，君主政府显然明显优于其他政府形式，因为它毫无疑问是最强的政府，如果它的团体意志更符合普遍意志的话，那它也是最好的政府了。

第三卷
BOOK THREE

但是，正如柏拉图所言，一个有天赋的国王是十分罕见的。那自然和命运要多久才能交汇在一起造就出如此的明君呢？如果皇室的教育只会腐蚀接受这种教育的人，那么对于那些世袭的君主我们还能期待什么呢？因此，把君主政府等同于明君政府简直就是自欺欺人。要看清君主政府的本质，就必须观察它在最无能最邪恶的君主治下的状况，因为如果君王不是在登基之前就无能与邪恶，那就一定是在登上王位之后才变得无能与邪恶的。

我们的理论家们不是没看到这些困难，但他们并不为此感到为难，他们告诉我们，解决的办法就是要默默地服从。上帝在盛怒之中降下了昏君，人民应该把那当做神的惩罚而忍受。的确，这种观点相当有启发性，但我认为，把它放在教堂里进行布道应该比放在一本政治理论书里更合适。如果一个医生承诺会创造奇迹，而他的全部医术只是鼓励病人一味地忍受病痛，对这样的医生我们还能说什么呢？

每个人都知道，当我们已经有一个坏政府时我们只能去忍受它，但我认为更好的解决办法是如何去寻找一个好的政府。

【原注1】马基亚维利是一位绅士和好公民；但因其从属于美第奇（Medici）家族，他被迫在祖国深受压迫时掩饰他对自由的热爱。他在书中选择了一个令人憎恨的主人公便清楚地显示了他秘密的意图，他在《君主论》中的原则和《李维论》、《佛罗伦萨史》中的原则相互矛盾，显示这个深刻的政治思想家至今都只拥有一些肤浅堕落的读者。罗马宫廷严禁了他的作品，我对此非常理解，因为在他的作品中清晰地描绘了这个宫廷。

【原注2】此文原文为拉丁语，为罗马皇帝戈尔巴的演说词，见塔西图，《历史》第一卷。

【译注1】马基亚维利（Niccolo Machiavelli）（1469–1527），意大利政治理论家。1513年创作《君主论》，书中的原则后来为很多人治国所借鉴，拿破仑、希特勒、墨索里尼都曾把它作为案头书。

【译注2】希腊神话中的大力神，曾用一臂替人扛天。

第七章
论混合形式的政府

严格来说，单一形式的政府是不存在的。一个唯一的统治者手下必须有一群从属的官员；一个民主政府也要有一个首领。因此，在行政权力的分配中，必定有一个从大到小的级别，区别是有时少数依赖多数，有时多数依赖少数。

有时也有权力均等的情况，这种情况的发生或者是因为政府各组成部分相互依赖，如英国政府；或者是各部门虽拥有独立的权威但并不完善，如波兰政府。后一种形式不足取，因为政府并非统一的整体，国家也缺乏联系的纽带。

那么哪种政府形式更好呢？混合还是单一？政治理论家们对这个问题争论不休，至于我的回答，与早些时候关于政府形式的回答是一样的。

就本身而言，单一形式的政府最好，正是因为它简单。但是当行政权不完全依附于立法权时，也就是说，当统治者与主权体的比例大于人民——君主的比例时，就应当重新分割政府予以弥补。这样一来，政府各部门就对臣民的权威并没有减少，但对他们的分割使他们总体上不如主权体力量强大。

这种失衡还可以通过设置中间官员来弥补。这种官员可以平衡并维持两边各自的权力，从而使政府不必被分割。这时，政府并没有变成混合型的，而是采用了协同的形式。

相反的缺陷也可用同样的方法来修正：当政府结构松散时，可以建立一些机构来使它变得集中。在前一种情况下，政府被分割以削弱它的力量；在第二种情况下，则是为了加强它的力量。这是所有民主制国家都在实践的。在单一的政府形式中同时存在着最强的力量和最弱的力量。而混合形式的政府却具有适中的力量。

第三卷
BOOK THREE

第八章
论任何一种政府形式都不能适用于所有国家

自由不是任何气候都能长出的果实,因此它并非任何民族都能获得。孟德斯鸠提出了这一学说,人们对它越是深究,就越能体味它的真理性;对它越是反驳,就越能有机会得到新的证据来证明它的正确性。

世界上任何政府中,公务人员都是只消耗而不能生产。那些他们所消费的东西来源于何方呢?都是各国成员的劳动所得,正是个人产品的过剩来支持了这一公共需求。从这一点看,只有当人们的劳动生产出比自己的所需更多的产品时,才会存在政府机构。

但这种过剩在不同的国家是不相同的。有些国家剩余多些,有些国家剩余少些,而另外一些国家剩余为零,还有一些国家甚至产出不敷消耗。这种情况取决于各国气候的好坏、土壤所需要的劳动种类、出产的种类、当地居民的体力、居民需要的消费品的数量,以及促成这种关系得以形成的其他一些因素。

另一方面,不同的政府特性不同。有些政府消耗多些,有些消耗少些。这种不同是基于另一种原则:税收离其源头愈远,它的负担就越大。在这里,衡量税收负担的依据不应是捐税的数量,而是税收从来源再回到纳税人手里所经过的距离。当这一循环迅速而顺畅时,赋税多少是无关紧要的,人民总是富足而国家财政总是良好。相反,如果人民的持续纳税得不到回馈,那无论税赋有多轻,其源泉终归会在不断的榨取中变得干涸,这样,国家永远不会富裕,人民永远贫困。

由此可见,人民与政府的距离越远,他们的赋税就越沉重。所以,在民主制国家中,人民的税收负担最轻;贵族制国家中,负担要重一些;在君主制国家中,负担最重。因此君主制只适用富裕的国家,贵族制适合财富和疆域都中等的国家,而民主制则适合小而穷的国家。

社会契约论
The Social Contract

的确，我们越是多加思索，就越能在自由国家和君主国家之间发现诸多不同：前者，一切都为了公众利益；后者的公众力量和私人力量成反比，一个增长会导致另一个减少。最终，君主专制政府不仅不会为了臣民的幸福而进行统治，反而要把人民拖入悲惨的境地以便治理。

以下要讲的是每种气候条件下都有一些自然因素，根据这些自然因素来决定最适合该气候的政府形式，甚至可以说出这种气候下的居民类型。

那些贫瘠的不毛之地根本不值得开垦，那就任由它们荒芜、闲置，或者由原始人去住；那些劳动仅够民生所用的地区应由野蛮人居住，这些地方都不可能有政治社会；那些劳动产出比生活所需略有超出但超出不多的地区，适合自由的民族居住；那些拥有富饶肥沃的土地、劳动不多而所得丰盛的地区，适宜建立君主制，以使君主的奢侈生活能够消耗掉臣民的大量劳动剩余，因为这种剩余由政府来吸收要比个人浪费掉要好得多。我知道会有例外的情况存在，但这些例外也会证实以上的规律，因为这些例外的国家迟早都将引发革命，从而又恢复到自然的安排。

我们必须要永远将一般规律同影响一般规律的特殊规律区别开来。即便所有的南方地区都是共和制国家，而所有的北部地区都是君主专制国家，上述规律依然正确，即在只考虑气候的因素下，专制制度适合气候炎热的国家，野蛮的制度适合气候寒冷的国家，而优秀的政治体制只适合在气候温和的地区存在。我知道这一观点虽得到人们的认可，但在具体应用上仍会为人诟病。有人可能会说：寒冷地带也有肥沃的土地，而热带国家也可以十分贫瘠。这一问题对于那些从不全面考虑问题的人才称其为难题，我们必须，正如我所提到的那样，要考虑到劳动、力量、消费等各种因素。

假定有两块同等大小的土地，一块的产量为五，另一块的产量为十。如果第一块土地上居民的消耗为四，第二块土地上居民的消耗为九，那前者的剩余为五分之一，而后者的剩余为十分之一。这两者剩余的比率和它们产出的比率成反比，产量为五的土地所剩余的是产量为十的土地剩余的两倍。

第三卷
BOOK THREE

但这里并不存在双倍产量的问题。我认为,一般不会有人将寒冷国度的肥沃程度等同于热带国家的肥沃程度。不过,我们姑且假定这种相等吧,比方说,英国等于西西里,波兰等于埃及,再往南一点就是非洲与印度,再往北一点就什么都没有了。那么怎样的农业技术会使它们的物产量相等呢?在西西里,只需刮刮地皮就能大量收获,而在英国就得花大力气耕作。如果在某国需要增加大量的人力来生产与其他国家同样的物产,那这个国家的劳动剩余量必定少于他国。此外,我们还要考虑同样多的人在热带国家消耗量相对少得多的事实。在这样的气候中,人必须节制食欲才能保证健康。欧洲人到了热带国家,如果还像以前一样饮食,就会死于消化不良和痢疾。沙尔丹说:"与亚洲人相比,我们就是如狼似虎的食肉动物。有人将波斯人的节俭归因于他们国家的不宜耕作。但我认为,他们之所以土地出产不丰是因为其居民所需不多。"他接着写道:"如果他们的节约是由于土地贫瘠的结果,那就应该只有穷人才吃得少,但事实是每个人都是如此。而且人们发现,这里的人并没有根据省份的不同,或根据土地的肥沃程度吃得有多有少,这个国家任何一个地方都同样的节俭。他们满足于自己的生活方式,称只要看一看他们的肤色就可以知道他们的生活方式比其他国家要好得多。确实如此,波斯人面色干净,他们的皮肤美丽、细腻又光滑,而附属于他们的亚美尼亚人,由于按照欧洲人的方式生活,皮肤粗糙而暗沉,身躯肥胖又笨重。"

越是靠近赤道,人们吃得越少,他们几乎不食用任何肉类,大米、玉米、粗麦粉、小米、木薯是他们的日常食物。在印度,数以百万的人每天消耗的食物价值不到一便士。即使同在欧洲,北部人同南部人的胃口也迥然不同,一个德国人的一顿晚餐足够一个西班牙人吃上一礼拜。在那些胃口较大的国家,人们的奢侈也充分体现在吃的方面,如在英国,奢侈就是满桌的大鱼大肉;而到了意大利,则会受到糖与鲜花的款待。

服饰上的奢侈也体现出了类似的差异。在那些季节变化急遽且迅猛的地区,人们的衣着质地优良且简单;在那些衣服仅是一种装饰的地区,人们追求的是一

社会契约论
The Social Contract

种炫耀而不是实用，衣着本身就成为奢侈。在那不勒斯，你每天都可以看到有人沿着博西利普山上散步，他们穿着镶了金边的上衣，却赤着足。建筑方面也是如此，当完全不必担心风吹日晒时，人们便开始追求建筑物的富丽堂皇了。在巴黎和伦敦，人们想的是如何能住得温暖而舒适。在马德里，人们虽拥有极为讲究的客厅，但是窗户大开，而他们所睡的卧室却像老鼠洞。

热带国家的食物更有营养而美味，这是第三种因素，它必然影响上述的第二种因素。意大利人为什么吃那么多的蔬菜？因为那里的蔬菜质量好，营养高且味道佳。法国的蔬菜只是靠浇水长成的，并无多少营养，在餐桌上也没什么价值。但即使这样，它们也没少占用土地，栽种时花费的力气也和意大利的蔬菜同样多。实验证明，西西里的小麦虽然质量不如法国小麦，但磨出来的面粉要多得多，而法国小麦磨出的面粉比北方小麦又多得多。由此我们可以推出，一般而言，从赤道到北极存在着一个类似的渐变过程。这样，从同样数量的产品中却获得了较少的出产，这难道不是一个很明显的不利条件吗？

除了上述各种各样的差别，我还要补充一点，它从前面各因素中推出，又可以对它们进行强化。这个因素是：热带国家比寒冷国家所需的居民要少，能供养的人口却多，这便为专制政府提供了一个双倍的剩余。相同数量的人民占据的地方越大，反抗就越发困难，因为他们不能迅速且秘密地聚集在一起进行筹划，政府就总可以轻易发现他们的密谋并及时切断通信。相反，人口越是集中，政府就越不容易侵犯主权者；首领们可以如君主身处内阁中议事一样安全地在家中策划；民众也可以如士兵在军营中集合一样，迅速地在广场集合。因此，距离越远，对于暴君的统治越有好处，只要政府能为自己提供一个强有力的支点，根据杠杆原理【原注1】，政府的统治力量会随着距离的增长而增强。相反，人民的力量却是越集中才越有效。一旦这种力量分散开来，便会烟消云散，就如同火药散在地上后只能星星点点地燃烧。人口最稀少的国家最适合暴君的专制，凶猛的野兽只有在荒野里才能称王称霸。

第三卷
BOOK THREE

【原注1】这与我在前面所说的（第二卷第九章）大国的不利条件并不矛盾。因为我在那里论述的是政府对其成员的权威，而在此我考察的是政府对臣民的权威。政府分散的成员就像许多杠杆的支点，通过它们作用于边远的百姓，但政府并没有一个对其成员自身的杠杆支点。因此，杠杆的长度在一种情况下是弱点，而在另一种情况下则是优点。

第九章
论一个好政府的标志

如果人们一定要问什么是绝对意义上的最好政府，那么这个问题是无法回答的，因为它无法确定，或者可以说，各民族的绝对处境和相对处境有多少种可能的组合，就有多少种正确答案。

但是如果有人问：判断某个特定民族是否得到了良好的治理或不好的治理的标志是什么？这就是另一个问题了，对于这个实际问题则是可以给出回答的。

然而，这个问题也不能得到切实的回答，因为每个人都会以自己的方式来回答这个问题。臣民们要求的是公共安全，公民们颂扬的是个人自由；前者希望财产有保障，后者希望人身有保障；臣民们认为政府要尽量严厉，公民们认为政府要尽量宽容；前者提倡惩治犯罪，后者提倡预防犯罪；前者觉得自己的国家被邻国惧怕是好事，后者觉得自己的国家被邻国遗忘是好事；前者乐于金钱流通，后者则要求人民丰衣足食。但是，即使我们能在上述问题和类似问题上达成共识，我们的认识就真的深入了吗？道德是没有精确衡量标准的，即使我们能对一些衡量标志达成一致，我们又如何能在评估方式上达成一致呢？

对我而言，我总是诧异于人们不能够认识到如此简单的一个标志，或者别有用心地拒绝承认。政治结合的目的是什么？就是对其成员的保护和使之繁荣兴旺。它的成员得到保护和走向兴旺的最确定的标志是什么？就是它们的人口数

社会契约论
The Social Contract

量。我们不必再去寻找这个标志之外的那些颇有争议的尺度了。假定其他所有条件都是相等的，在某个政府的治理下，不借助归化、移民和殖民等外来手段，其公民数量增长最快最多的政府便是最好的政府。在其治理下人民数量减少、逐渐衰弱的政府无疑是最坏的政府。统计学家们，接下来就是你们的任务了：就请点数、计算、比较吧。【原注1】

【原注1】人们应该根据同一个原则来判断哪个世纪更有利于人类的繁荣。人们曾经过分地尊崇艺术和文学繁荣的世纪，却不能洞察到这些文化背后的秘密企图。"无知者称之为'人道'的，其实那是奴役的开始。"（引自塔西图的《阿格瑞科拉传》，塔西图：罗马历史学家）难道我们在读到这些箴言时，不能看出其背后所包括的促使作者如此写作的那些个人利益吗？不，不管他们说了些什么，也不管文化有多么灿烂，如果国家的人口减少了，就不能说这个国家治理良好。一个诗人在他的时代即使能收入十万里弗，也不足以说明他所处的时代就是所有时代中最好的。一场冰雹可能会使几个地区受灾，但它很少会造成饥荒。叛乱和内战可能会使统治者极其惊慌，但对人民来说并不是真正的灾难，因为当统治阶层都忙于争权夺利时，人民甚至可以得到几个月的喘息机会，他们的灾难和兴旺都来自于那种永久不变的生存状态。当所有人都在枷锁下变得懒怠时，一切都开始毁灭了，这时，统治者就可以肆意地摧残他们，"当他们的国土沦为废墟的时候，他们便说和平来临了。"（选自塔西图《阿格瑞科拉传》）当高官们的纠葛搅扰得法兰西王国不得安宁，当巴黎的副主教怀揣一把匕首参加议会时，法国人民依然生活幸福、人口繁盛、自由而富庶。以前，古希腊在最残酷的战争中繁荣起来，即使在暴乱中血流成河，但整个国家反而人丁兴旺。马基亚维利说："看上去，在暗杀、流放和内战中，我们的共和国似乎变得更为强大。公民的品德、精神和独立性对共和国的巩固作用比所有的纷争对共和国的消弱作用更为有效。"些许的动荡可以赋予灵魂以活力，真正使人类繁茂的更多的不是和平，而是自由。

第十章
论政府的滥用权力和它衰退的倾向

正如特殊意志总是不断反抗普遍意志，政府也总是不断与主权体作对。这种对抗的力量越大，政府机构就越腐败，而且因为这里没有一个独立的团体意志来制衡它，因此君主意志迟早要不可避免地压制主权体，从而破坏社会契约。从政治体诞生之日起，这一内在的必然缺陷就不断地使它走向衰落，就如衰老和死亡不断在破坏人的机体一样。

政府的退化有两种方式：一种是政府自身的收缩，另一种是国家的解体。

当政府的成员数目由多变少时，也就是从民主制走向贵族制，从贵族制走向君主制时，政府就发生了收缩。这是它的自然趋势[原注1]。如果政府的成员人数朝另一个方面发展，即由少到多时，政府结构便松弛了，但这种逆向的发展是不可能发生的。

事实上，除非一个政府的能量被耗尽、衰弱到不能维持现状时，否则它是永远也不可能改变它的形式的。一个政府如果随着扩张而扩展自身，那么它的力量会减少为零，从而使自身难以继续维持。所以，当一个政府开始变得松弛时，它必须上紧发条使自身机构紧凑起来，否则它支撑的国家就会走向消亡。

国家的解体可以通过两种方式发生。

第一种，它发生在统治者不再依法治国，而是篡夺了主权体的权力时。这时发生了一个明显的变化，即不是政府在收缩，而是国家在收缩。我的意思是，国家作为一个整体解体了，而另一个国家又在它的体内形成，新的国家成员只包括原来政府的成员，对于其余的人民来说，这个新的国家只是一个彻底的暴君和主人。因此，一旦政府颠覆了主权体，社会契约立刻破灭，所有的公民理所当然又重新收回了他们天然的权利，但他们的服从仅仅是强力的胁迫，并非出于道德的义务。

社会契约论
The Social Contract

相同的情况还发生在当政府成员分别篡夺了他们本应作为一个整体来行使的权力的时候。这并不仅是一种违法行为，它会引发更大的动乱，可以这样说，有多少个行政官员就可能有多少个君主，而国家也像政府一样四分五裂，然后不是走向消亡，就是改变形式。

当国家解体时，不论政府的滥权为何种形式，都可被统称为无政府状态。更精确地说，就是民主制退化成暴民统治，贵族制成为了寡头政治。再补充一点，君主制变成暴君制，因为最后这个词含义不清，需要另行解释清楚。

人们通常理解的暴君是指统治残暴、无视正义与法律的国王。而在确切意义上，暴君是指那些本无任何皇家权利但窃取了这一权力的人。希腊人就是这样来理解"暴君"一词的含义的。他们不加区别地把这个称谓用于非法登基的国王，而不论其是好君主还是坏君主[原注2]。因此，暴君和篡权者是同义词。为了使不同的事物具有不同的名称，我把王权权威的篡夺者称为"暴君"，把主权权力的篡夺者称为"专制君主"。暴君虽然违背法律掌握政权，但却依照法律进行统治；专制君主却是将自己的权力置于法律之上。因此，暴君不一定是专制君主，专制君主却一定是暴君。

【原注1】威尼斯共和国在一片礁湖中缓慢形成和发展，为这一过程提供了显著的例证；令人惊讶的是，经过一千二百年之后，威尼斯人似乎依然处在1198年由西拉尔·康塞里奥开始的第二阶段。至于人们所谴责的那些古代的大公们，不论《威尼斯自由论》这本书怎么说，都可以证明大公们原来不是他们的主权者。

肯定有人会提出罗马共和国的例子来反驳我，说他们遵循了一个完全相反的过程，从君主制过渡到贵族制，又从贵族制过渡到民主制。但我绝不同意这种看法。

罗穆鲁斯建立的第一个政府是混合政府，它随即堕落成为专制政府。由于一些特殊原因，国家过早灭亡了，就像人们所看到的一个婴儿在未成年前就夭折一样。塔尔干王朝的被驱逐才标志着罗马共和国的真正诞生。但一开始它没有采用一种固定的形式，因为罗马人没能够废除贵族等级使得这一事业半途而废了。世袭贵族制作为合法行政机构中最糟糕的那一种，不断地与民主制发生冲突，正如马基亚维利所证明的，政府形式一直处于变化与不确定中直到有了保民官后才确定下来，从这时起才有了真正的政府和真正的民主制。这时，人民不仅是主权者，还是行政官和法官。元老院只是一个附属机构，来制约和集中政府的力量。执政官本人尽管是贵族、首席执政官、战争中的绝对统帅，但在罗马，他只是人民的管家而已。

正是从这时起，罗马政府开始依照它的自然走向，强烈地趋向了贵族制。当贵族们好像是废除了自己的等级，贵族制不再像日内瓦和威尼斯那样存在于贵族等级的实体中，而是存在于贵族和平民们共同构成的元老院实体中，甚至是存在于篡夺了实际权力时的保民官实体里；因为名称并不能改变事物性质，当人民有了代表自己进行治理的首领时，不论这些首领有着怎样的名称，他们实际上就是贵族制。

贵族制权力的滥用导致了内战和三方执政。苏拉、尤利西斯·恺撒和奥古斯都都成为了事实上的君主，最后，国家在提贝留乌斯的专制下终于解体。如此看来，罗马历史并没有否定我的原则，而是恰恰证明了它。

【原注2】"在一个习惯了自由的城邦中，那些保有永久权力的人都会被认为和称为暴君。"（见科尔纳留斯·尼波斯的《米提阿底斯传》。的确，亚里士多德在他的《尼各马可伦理学》第八卷第十章中曾区分过暴君和国王，把两者差别的关键定为前者统治是为了自己的利益，而后者是为了其臣民的利益；然而，所有的希腊作家通常都使用另一层意思来使用暴君这个词，就如色诺芬的《希罗》所清楚显示的那样。当然，根据亚里士多德的那一区分准则进行推论，从世界产生以来还从未出现过一个真正的国王。

第十一章
论政治体的灭亡

这就是政府形式自然的、无法挽回的趋势，哪怕它是最好的政府。如果斯巴达和罗马都灭亡了，那我们还能期待什么样的国家能够永世长存呢？如果我们希望建立一种持久的制度，就不要梦想什么永恒了吧。如果想要成功，就不要去尝试那些不可能的事，也不要愚昧地自夸人类所创造的哪样东西是牢不可破的，因为人世间是不存在永恒的。

政治体如同人的身体，从出生那刻起就注定要死亡，而且它自身就存在着使自己死亡的原因。但这两者身上都有着或强或弱的机制，使它们能在或长或短的时期内维持着自己的生存。人体的结构是大自然的产物,而国家结构是人为的作品。人类无法延长自己的寿命,但他们可以赋予国家一个好的体制,从而使国家尽可能久地存在下去。尽管结构最佳的国家最后也要消亡,但如果没有意外事件使它早亡的话,它的存在必然要长于其他国家。

政治生命的关键在于主权权威,立法权力是国家的心脏,行政权力是指挥各部门运行的大脑。如果大脑瘫痪了,人还可以继续存活,尽管成了痴呆,却依然活着。然而,一旦心脏停止了跳动,它所属的身体就死去了。

国家的生存靠的不是法律,而是立法权力。昨天的法律不能约束今天,但基于沉默在某种程度上就是默许,如果主权体在它能废除法律时却没有采取行动,那么它就不断地被认为它认可了那些法律。那么,主权体过去所声明的意愿就依然是它现在的意愿,除非它否决了过去的声明。

那么为什么古老的法律能获得人们的尊重呢?正是因为它们的古老。人们或许认为是古代法律的完美卓越使它们长久地保存下来;但事实上,如果不是主权体不断承认它们有益,它们可能已经被废除过一千遍了。所以,在一个体制良好的国家里,法律不但不会变弱,反而会不断增加新的力量。对古老东西的偏爱使这些法律日益受到人们的尊重。当法律随着年代的久远而不断削弱,就表明立法权力已经不存在了,国家离死亡不远了。

第十二章
论如何维持主权权威

除了立法权力之外,主权体再无其他任何力量,它只能通过法律来发挥作用。既然法律只是普遍意志的真实表达,所以只有当人们聚在一起时,主权体才能有所体现。"将人民聚集在一起?"人们会说:"那不是天方夜谭嘛!"这在今天看来是一种天方夜谭,但在两千年前却是现实。难道人类的本性改变了吗?

道德范畴所能达到的可能极限并不像我们所想象的那般狭窄,正是我们的软弱、邪恶和偏见使这些界限变窄了。正如卑劣的灵魂不相信存在伟大的人,低贱的奴隶会嘲笑"自由"这个字眼。

让我们借已经发生的事情来考察一下人类能够做到的事情。我就不说古希腊共和国了,在我看来,罗马共和国就是一个庞大的国家。罗马城是个很大的城市,该城的最后一次人口普查显示,这里有四十万武装公民,而整个罗马帝国最后一次人口普查的结果是四百多万公民,这还不算那些臣民、异邦人、妇女、儿童和奴隶。

真是很难想象,如何将首都及其周围市郊如此众多的人民聚集在一起开会。而事实上,罗马市民很少有哪几周不集会的,有时甚至一周集会数次。人民不仅行使主权权力,还执行一部分政府功能。他们处理某些事物,审判某些案件,在这种公众集会中,罗马人民不仅是公民,还是执政官员。

上溯至各国的发轫时期,我们会发现在大多数古代政府中,甚至像马其顿人和法兰克人那样的君主制政府,都有着类似的集会。无论如何,我所引的这个无可辩驳的事实就回答了我的问题,在我看来,从事实中导出的可能发生的事情是符合逻辑的。

第十三章
论如何维持主权权威(续)

仅仅在人民的某次集会上批准了一套法律体系并决定了国家的体制,这是不够的;人民建立了一个永久的政府或一劳永逸地提出了行政官员的选举办法,这也是不够的。除了那些因意外事件的发生所必须举行的特殊集会外,还要有固定的、定期的集会，而且不能任意取消或推迟。这样，到了规定集会的日子，人民便会依据法律规定而合法地集合起来，而不需要其他正式通知。

但是，除了这些依法定日期举行的合法会议，人民的其他任何集会，如果没有经过专门负责此事的官员通过预定的形式召集，都应该被视为非法，会上所有的决议也将视为无效，因为集会本身的命令就应该由法律发出。

至于合法集会的频率，因受太多因素的制约，不能给出明确的规定。我们只能说，一般而言，政府力量越大，主权体就越应频繁地出面表达自己。

或许有人会说，这对于单一的城镇来说或许可行，但如果一个国家包括若干个城市，又当如何处理？是把主权权威进行平分呢？还是把主权集中于某个特定的城镇而使其他的城镇从属于它？

我的回答是两者都不可行，首先，主权权威作为一个单一的整体，一旦把它分割开就等于毁灭它。第二，正如一个国家不能合法地从属于另一个国家，一个城镇也不能合法地从属于另一个城镇，因为政治体的本质就是服从和自由的统一，"臣民"和"主权者"两个词的含义完全对等，两者的意义结合为"公民"一词。

我还要进一步回答说，把若干城邦联合成为一个国家总是一个错误，任何一个希望如此做的人就不要再埋怨无法避免自然的种种不便。不能因大国的泛滥就去反对那些只喜欢小国的人们。但是，怎样才能使小国拥有足够的力量去抗拒大国呢？就如古代的希腊城邦反抗强国国王，或者更近些时候的荷兰和瑞士抵御奥地利王室那样。

当然，如果无法把国家的领土限定在适当的范围内，还有一个办法，就是不设立固定的首都，将政府的驻地轮流设置在各个城市，并且使国家财产在各地轮流循环。

让人口均衡地分布于国土之上，使相同的权利扩展到国家的每个角落，让财富和生机充盈整个国家，只有这样，国家才能最大限度地发挥自身的力量，才能得到最好的治理。请记住，城市的高墙都是以乡间的房屋化为瓦砾为代表建造起来的，每当我在首都看到又一座辉煌的宫殿拔地而起时，我就好像看到整个乡间遍布了茅屋。

第十四章
论如何维持主权权威（再续）

一旦人民作为主体者合法地进行集会，政府的一切权限就要停止，行政权力也暂停行使，即便是最卑贱的公民也和最高等的行政官员一样神圣不可侵犯，因为既然被代表者已经亲自前来，也就不需要什么代表了。发生在罗马公民集会上的大部分骚乱都是由于对这一准则的忽视或无知所致。这时的执政官仅仅是人民的主持者，保民官只是发言人【原注1】，而元老院则什么都不是。

对于政府的成员们来说，这种权力暂时停顿的间隙期是很可怕的，因为此时他们只得承认或被迫承认自己存在一个上级；这种人民集会作为政治体的保护者和政府权力的约束者，总是时时成为官员们的噩梦；于是，这些人总是不遗余力地设置障碍、制造麻烦以及滥许诺言，以使公民与集会作对。如果公民贪婪、胆怯、倦怠，或者热爱安逸胜过自由时，他们就不能长久地抵制政府的一再攻势了。于是，随着政府的对抗力量不断增加，主权权威将最终消失。大多数的共和政体都过早地衰弱、灭亡了。

但是，在主权权威与独裁的政府之间，有时会出现一种中间力量，接下来我们就来说一说这种力量。

【原注1】这个词语在这里的意思有点类似于它在英国议会中的含义。即使所有的权力都被暂时中止，这些职能上的相似也会使执政官和保民官发生对立。

第十五章
论议员或代表

　　一旦公众服务不再是公民关心的重点、公民开始使用他们的钱包而不是自身来为国家提供服务时，国家也就离毁灭不远了。国家需要出兵作战吗？公民会出钱雇佣军队而自己待在家里；到了日期需要参加集会吗？公民会指派代表而非自己亲自出席。花钱和懒惰的结果是，他们最后将祖国交由军队来奴役、交由代表来出卖。

　　正是由于人们忙于商业和手工业，忙于对利润的追逐，也由于人们的软弱和贪图安逸，使得个人服务用金钱代替。公民放弃了他们的一部分利益以便随心所欲地追逐其他利益。赶快利用金钱吧！你们很快就被金钱所奴役。"代役费"一词就是奴隶的词语，在共和国中，人们是不知这个词为何物的。在一个真正自由的国度，公民是用自己的双手而非金钱来完成任何事情的。他们绝不会为了逃避责任而花费金钱，反而会花钱使自己履行义务。在这里，我的想法和世俗的观点截然不同：我认为税收比义务性服务更不利于人们的自由。

　　国家的结构越是良好，公共事务在公民头脑中就越是优先于私人事务。事实上，并不存在那么多的私人利益，因为公共福利就是为每个人的绝大部分幸福所在，所以个人也就不必使用个人手段来谋此福利了。在治理良好的国家里，一有公共集会，人们都会飞奔而去；而在坏政府的治下，谁都懒得挪动一步，因为没人对集会上讨论的事情感兴趣，人们都料到了主导集会的不是公共意志，最后，公民把精力完全投入在自家的私事上。好的法律能使人们制定出更好的法律，而坏的法律将会带来更坏的法律。一旦有人在谈论国事时说"这与我何干？"时，我们就可以预料：这个国家快完了。

　　爱国热情的冷却、私人活动的勃兴、国土的辽阔、四处征讨和政府的滥权——所有这一切都暗示着在国家集会中需要有议员或人民代表的出现。有些国

第三卷
BOOK THREE

家甚至公然把这些代表称为第三等级,这就意味着第一等级和第二等级代表私人利益,而公众利益已经退居第三等级了。

正如主权是不能被转让的,它也不能被人代表,主权的本质是公共意志,而公共意志是不能被代表的:它要么是公共意志,要么是别的意志,不存在任何中间的可能。所以,人民代表不是也不能是人民的代表,他们只是人民的代理人,他们不能最后决定任何事情,任何法律不经人民的亲自认可都是无效的,根本不成为法律。英国人认为自己是自由的,但他们犯了一个严重的错误,他们只有在推选议会成员时才是自由的,一旦议会成员被选举出来,他们就开始遭受奴役,什么也不是了。在获得自由的短暂时间里,英国人利用自由的这种方式使他们注定失去自由。

代表的概念是近代才有的,它来自于那个使人类蒙羞,并且使这个称号名不符实的不公正且荒唐的封建政府。在共和制度下,甚至在古代的君主制国家中,人民从来就没有代表,这个词根本不存在。罗马便是一个很好的例子,保民官是如此神圣,以至于没有人能想象到他们可能会篡夺人民的权力,而在盛大的群众集会中,也没有人试图将自己的权威转让。这一点可参照在格拉古斯发生过的由于集会人数太多而造成的麻烦事,许多群众不得已,只能从屋顶上扔下他们的投票。

在权利和自由得到充分体现的地方,那些不方便也就算不得什么了。这些聪明的古罗马人民把所有的事情安排得恰到好处,他们让扈从们[译注1]去做他们的保民官不敢做的事,而人民并不担心这些扈从有代表人民的企图。

要了解保民官是如何代表人民的,只要理解政府是如何代表主权体的就可以了。既然法律只是公共意志的表达,显然人民在行使立法权力时是不能被代表的,但是当行使行政权力时,人民可以也应该有代表,因为行政权力不过是履行法律的手段。这样说来,如果仔细考察,世界上只有少数几个国家拥有法律。不管如何,可以肯定的是,不具有任何行政权力的保民官是不能通过自己职务权力来代表罗马人民的,他们只能在僭越了元老院的权力之后才能代表人民。

在希腊,人民必须做的所有事人民都会自己来完成。他们不断地在户外集

社会契约论
The Social Contract

会。希腊人生活在温和的气候中，他们不贪婪，奴隶们把工作都做完了，他们主要关心的就是他们的自由。如果没有了这些有利条件，又怎能保持同等的权利呢？你们的恶劣气候增加了你们的需求[原注1]，一年之中有六个月公共场地是不能使用的，在开阔的空气中你们微弱的声音根本无法让别人听到。这时，你们关心利益超过了关心自由，而且你们害怕贫困已经超过了害怕受奴役。

什么？难道自由只能借助于奴隶制的支持才能存在吗？也许是吧。这是两个极端的融合。一切不符合自然的事物都是有缺陷的，而政治社会比其他一切缺陷更多。有这样一些很不幸的情况：一个人要想保持住自己的自由必须以牺牲另一个人的自由为代价；只有在奴隶是绝对的奴隶时，公民才是完全自由的公民。斯巴达的情况就是如此。至于你们这些现代人，你们没有奴隶，但你们自己就是奴隶，你们用自身偿付了你们自己自由的代价。不管你们怎么为你们的取舍而得意，我从中看到的更多是懦弱，而不是人道。

我并不是想通过这些论述来说明奴隶制是必须的，或者蓄奴制是合法的，因为我已经证明这是不正确的了。我只是想说明为何自以为自由的现代人需要代表，而古代人民却没有代表的原因。无论如何，一旦一个民族的人民为自己选出了代表，那他们就不再自由，也就不再称其为人民了。

通过仔细地通盘考虑，我在像我们一样的人民中，看不出任何主权者可以行使其权力的可能性，除非是一个很小的共和国。但如果一个共和国很小，它会不会被其他国家颠覆呢？不会的。我会在以后[原注2]讲述如何把小国的易于管理和秩序良好与强大民族的对外力量结合起来。

【原注1】如果寒冷国家的人也像东方人一样过着奢侈和怠惰的生活，那么就等于给自己戴上了枷锁，并且比东方人更不可避免地顺从于这种枷锁。

【原注2】这是我在本书的后续著作中想要讨论的，在探讨对外关系的处理时我想到了联邦制。这是一个相当新的课题，其中的原则还有待确立。

【译注1】古罗马公共场合下在官员前负责开道的随从人员。

第三卷
BOOK THREE

第十六章
论政府的建立不是一项契约

立法权力一经确立，接下来就是确立行政权力，因为后者是通过一些个别行为来运作，所以与立法权有着本质的不同，所以两者自然是分开的。如果主权体按照主权的本意而言，也能够拥有行政权力的话，法律和实际就会相互混淆，人们就无法区别什么是法律和什么不是法律了。陷入歧途的政治体不久将成为暴力的牺牲品，而政治体的建立本来是为了防止这种暴力的。

按照社会契约，所有的公民都是平等的，任何人都可以提出所有人应该做什么，但任何人都没有权力要求别人去做他自己都不去做的事。但这项权力对于维系政治体的生存和运转是必不可少的，主权体在创立政府时授予统治者的正是这项权力。

有些政治理论家曾经声称，建立政府的行为是人民和他们所选择的统治者之间形成的契约，这个契约规定了双方的责任，即一方负责发布命令而另一方负责服从。我确信这是一个非常莫名其妙的契约，就让我们来看看这种理论是否站得住脚。

首先，最高权威是不能改变的，正如它不能转让；对它的限制也就是对它的毁灭。主权者把一个更高的权威放在自己之上是荒谬的、自相矛盾的；如果让主权服从一个主人，人民又将恢复到原有的自然状态中去。

其次，很显然，人民和某些人之间的这种契约是一种特殊的行为。由此可知，这种契约不可能是法律的或主权的行为，因此，它只可能是非法的。

还可以进一步看到，订立契约的双方只是处于自然法则下，他们之间的相互约定得不到任何保证，这种情况是与社会状态相违背的。如果拥有权力的人做什么事都可以随心所欲，那么假如一个人对另一个人说："我把自己的一切都给你，条件是你想还我多少就还多少。"这种行为也可以被冠以"契约"的名称了。

国家中只有一个契约，即结成共同体的契约，它排斥了所有其他的契约。我们难以想象有其他公共契约的存在而不会破坏这份原始的约定。

第十七章
论政府的建立

我们该如何来考虑政府建制这一行为呢？我首先得指出这一行为是复杂的，或者说它由其他两种行为构成，即法律的制定和法律的执行。

在第一种行为中，主权者决议应该按一定的规则或形式来建立政府；很显然，这种行为就是法律。

在第二种行为中，人民任命官员在建立起来的政府中任职。这种任命是特殊行为，所以它不是第二种法律，只是第一种行为的结果和政府的行为。

困难在于政府产生以前，如何理解政府行为的产生，以及作为主权者和臣民的人民如何在某种情况下成为统治者和行政官员。

在这里，政治体显示出了它一个令人吃惊的特性，这一特性把政治体两个相互矛盾的行为协调运作起来了。因为这一特性是由于主权突然转变成民主制而形成的，这种转变使变化几乎看不见，仅仅由一种新的全体对全体的关系，公民就变成了行政官员，普遍行为变成了特殊行为，法律转变成法律的执行了。

这种关系的转变并不是没有现实例子的玄虚理论，它在英国议院中每天都要上演。在那里，为了更好地磋商国事，下议院会在某些特定情况下把自己转变成一个议会委员会，因此，刚才它还是一个主权者的会场，现在变成了主权者的一个简单的委员会；之后，它要以议会委员会的身份就刚才已经做出的决定向作为下议院的它本身作出汇报，并且又要以一方的名义对以另一方的名义针对作出决议的问题再次进行讨论。

民主制政府的特有好处就在于它只要通过公共意志的一次简单行为就可以确立起来。随后，如果这种形式被采纳后，那么这一临时政府仍旧可以继续存在下去，或者会以主权者的名义按法律规定建立任何政府。到那时，一切就走上了正轨。除此之外，除非抛弃我前面章节中的原则，否则在建立政府制度方面不存在任何其他的合法方式。

第十八章
论防止政府篡权的方法

从第十六章确立的观点来看，组成政府制度的不是一种契约行为，而是法律行为；行政权力的掌握者不是人民的主人，而是人民的雇员，人民可以在适当的时候随意任命或罢免他们，而这里并不存在一个与他们缔约的问题。在完成国家交给他们的职责时，他们只是在以公民的身份履行责任，并没有任何权利对条件进行讨价还价。

因此，当人民建立起一个世袭政府时，不管它是一个在家族内部继承的君主制，还是一个在一定阶层的公民中世袭的贵族制，人民在此并不需要做出任何承诺；世袭政府只是人民所组织的行政机构的临时形式，人民可以随时决定采用其他行政方式。

社会契约论
The Social Contract

　　当然，这种变化总是相当危险的，除非现有政府与公众利益的矛盾到了不可调和的地步，否则就不要改变已经建立起来的政府；但这种慎重只是政治策略而非法律规定，国家不一定要把公共权威交到行政官手中，就如不一定要把军事权威交到将军手里。

　　当然，在一些情况下，尽管人们已经很循规蹈矩了，但仍然不能使用合理的程序来将一场正当合法的行为与煽动性的鼓吹、整个人民的意志与部分人的喧嚷区分开来。但是，非常重要的是，人们对于那些对社会有害而被要求的屈服，一定不能超出法律许可的范围。正是由于这种一定程度的屈服，使统治者获得了一个很好的机会可以不顾人民意愿地维护自己的权力，而又不被说成是篡权。因为从表面上看，统治者只是在行使自己的权力，但是他又很容易扩展这种权力，在维护公共安全的借口下，阻止为修正政府滥权而举行的公众集会。他阻止人们打破现状，这样，人们的沉默便被统治者利用为默许自己统治的证明，而由此引起的骚乱成为压制那些敢于抗议者的原因。罗马十人委员会就是这样做的，他们在某一年被选举出来之后，便不断地连任，试图用阻止罗马公民集会的方式来保持永远的权威；正是通过这种简单的方式，世界上所有的政府在获得公权力之后，迟早都会篡夺主权权威。

　　我前面所说的召开周期性的集会的方式是阻止或推迟这种不法行为最好的方式，特别是那类不需要正式召集的集会，这样，政府也就无法加以阻挡，否则它就等于公开申明自己是违法者和国家公敌。

　　在这些以维护社会契约为唯一目的集会上，都应该由两个议题的表决开始，这两个议题永远不能被废除，而且每个议题都要独立地表决。

　　第一个是："主权者是否希望保留现有的政府形式？"

　　第二个是："人民是否愿意仍然让现任的行政官员管理国家行政事务？"

　　至此，我认为我已经清楚地证明了我的观点，那就是，国家中的任何法律都是可以被撤销的，甚至包括社会契约在内。因为如果全体公民举行集会一致同意

第三卷
BOOK THREE

结束社会契约,毫无疑问,这个契约就被合法地取消了。格劳秀斯就认为任何人都可以放弃自己是某国成员的身份,离开这个国家后[原注1]恢复其天然的自由和财产。独自一个人都可以这样做,如果说全体公民联合起来却不能这样做,那当然是荒谬的。

[原注1] 当然,任何人都不能为了逃避义务而离开自己的国家,也不能在国家需要他的时候拒绝挽救他的国家。在这种情况下,逃避就是有罪的,应该受到惩罚。因为这种情况下的离开不是撤销身份,而是背叛。

第四巻
BOOK FOUR

With regard to the right of conquest, it has no other foundation than the law of the strongest. If war does not confer on the victor the right of slaying the vanquished, this right, which he does not possess, cannot be the foundation of a right to enslave them. If we have a right to slay an enemy only when it is impossible to enslave him, the right to enslave him is not derived from the right to kill him, it is therefore an iniquitous bargain to make him purchase his life, over which the victor has no right, at the cost of his liberty. In establishing the right of life and death upon the right of slavery, and the right of slavery upon the right of life and death, is it not manifest that one falls into a vicious circle?

Jean-Jacques Rousseau

第四卷
BOOK FOUR

第一章
论公意是不可摧毁的

只要有一些人联合在一起，并认为他们是一个整体，那么他们就有了唯一的意志，这个意志指向他们的共同生存和公共福利。这时，使国家运转的力量就会简单而富有生机，它的原则也一目了然，没有任何错综而矛盾的利益冲突，共同的利益会明明白白地显露出来，使任何人只需要常识就能发现它。和平、团结、平等与政治阴谋是天敌。正直和纯朴的人难以被欺骗，正因为他们是单纯的。诱惑和花言巧语是骗不了他们的，因为他们不够工于心计，所以不会因诱惑而上当。在世界上那些最幸福的民族中，成群的农民在橡树下处理国家事务，并且总是处理得极为明智。看到此情此景，我们如何不蔑视其他那些在政治上玩弄术权的民族呢？他们巧施各种技巧和玄虚，却使得自己的国家因陷入绝境而为世人所不齿。

用如此方法治理的国家只需要很少的法律，而且一旦要颁布某个新法律时，人们都能看到这个法律的必要性。所以这项法律的第一个提议者不过是表达出了所有人的感觉而已，一旦确定其他人都有同样的想法，那么就是把所有人都同意去做的事情制定为法律。这无需阴谋，也无需雄辩。

理论家们往往被误导，因为他们只看到了那些从一开始构建就很差的国家，所以他们就想当然地认为在那些国家维持上述那种治理方式是不可能的事。一想到一个聪明的骗子或一个善辩的演说家能使巴黎或伦敦人民受到愚弄摆布，他们就发笑。他们不知道克伦威尔【译注1】曾经被伯尔尼人民判处过强制劳动，波伏公爵【译注2】也曾被日内瓦人民囚禁起来。

可是，当社会纽带开始松弛，国家开始衰弱，当私利能够为人民感知，小集体开始影响大社会时，共同利益便开始发生变化并遇到反对者，投票时再也没有一致通过的情况了，普遍意志从此不再是所有公民的总体意志，冲突和争论随即出现，即使是最明智的观点也要经过一番争论方能通过。

最后，当国家濒于灭亡，其存在只是流于空洞和虚幻的形式时，当连接社会的所有纽带都在人民心中断裂时，当最卑鄙的私利也厚颜无耻地打着公益的幌子招摇过市时，普遍意志已经变成了哑巴，每个人都在打自己的小算盘，不再作为公民发表意见了，仿佛国家从未存在过一样；人民开始弄虚作假，借法律之名去制定一些纯粹为追逐个人利益的不公正法令。

从上面所述的一切是否就能说公共意志消亡或堕落了？不能，公意永远是不变的，纯净而不会被腐蚀。但它被其他流行的意志压倒而处于了屈从的地位。

每个人在将自己的个人利益从公共利益中分离出来时，就清楚地知道他无法完全脱离公共利益，但是与他所捞取的想要据为已有的好处相比，他那一份公共的坏处就好像微不足道了。除了这些私人利益，为了自己的利益，他也会像其他人一样强烈地为公共利益着想。哪怕是他为了金钱而出卖了自己的选票时，他也没有泯灭他内心的公意，只是躲避了而已。他所犯的错误是改变了问题的性质，而且对问题答非所问，也就是说，通过他的选票，他没有回答"这一方案对国家有利"，而是说"这一方案对某个人或某个团体是有利的"。由于这个原因，调整公民集会的法律目的不仅是要维护公民内心的公意，还要确保公意总会被询问到，而且问题也总能得到答复。

关于在所有主权行为中简单的投票权，我打算做进一步的详谈，因为这是每个公民都不可剥夺的权利。我还想再深入探讨一下政府总是极力局限在政府内部的发言权、建议权、分析权和讨论权。但这个重要课题需要再单独写一文章了，我在本章中无法尽述。

【译注1】克伦威尔（1588-1658），英国17世纪资产阶级的领导者，推翻并处死了国王查理一世，建立了共和国，但也成为事实上的独裁者。
【译注2】波伏公爵（1616-1669），法国贵族，投石党运动领袖之一，被称为"菜市场之王"。

第二章
论投票权

从前面章节的论述我们可以清楚地看到，公共事务的处理方式是观照公众道德和政治体健康与否的一个相当准确的标志。集会中达成协议的步调越是一致，就意味着人们的观点越是统一，公共意志也就越占主导地位；而长久的争论、分

社会契约论
The Social Contract

歧和吵嚷则意味着个人私利的盛行和国家的衰落。

当国家结构中包括两个或几个等级时，上述规则就不甚明显了。以罗马为例，就是在共和国的鼎盛时期，罗马的贵族和平民间的争吵也常常扰乱公民集会。但这种例外更多是表面现象而非真实情况。因为这种情况下，由于政治体的内在缺陷，可以说罗马这个国家存在着两个国家，上述规则对于这两部分合起来虽说是不正确的，但对于每个单独的部分来说却是正确的。而且事实上，即使在最动荡的年代，只要元老院不干涉，罗马公民的投票会和平地进行，并且政令的颁布多是根据多数选票来进行的。由于公民只有一种利益，所以人民也就只有一个意志。

全民一致的情况也会发生在另一极端，那就是当公民完全陷入奴役状态，不再具有自由和意志的时候。这时，恐惧和谄媚把投票行为变成了附和，人们不再有什么讨论，有的只是崇拜或者咒骂。这便是在罗马皇帝的统治下元老院卑鄙的表达方式。有时，元老们做这些事情时小心得可笑，据塔西陀的记载，在奥托的治下，那些元老们在争相批判维提留斯的同时又制造一场喧闹，这样做的原因是，即使维提留斯将来有机会控制政权，他也无法分辨出元老们分别说过什么。

这各种考虑都提示了一些基本原则的必要性，人们应该根据这些原则，根据普遍意志被认知的难易程度和国家衰落的程度，对计算选票和比较民意的方式作出规定。

本质上只有一种法律是需要全体人民一致同意的，这就是社会契约。既然公民联合在一起是世界上最自愿的行为，每个人都是天生自由的，都天生是自己的主人，任何人不能以任何借口不经某人的同意强制他做任何事情。称一个女奴的儿子天生是奴隶，就相当于断言他生来就不是人类。

因此，如果在缔结社会契约时有反对的声音，那么这种反对并不能使社会契约无效；只不过是反对的人将自己排除在了社会契约之外而已。这些反对者就是公民中的异族人。国家一旦形成，居住就意味着认可：居住在一块领土之内就等于是承认了它的主权权威【原注1】。

除了这个原始契约之外,多数人的决定总能制约其他少数人的决定,这也是契约本身的一种结果。可能有人要问:一个人怎么能做到既是自由的,同时又不得不遵从那些并非他自己的意志呢?那些反对的少数人怎么可能既是自由的,又要服从于那些他们不曾同意的法律呢?

我的回答是,这一问题本身就问错了。公民是同意所有法律的,即使是那些违背他意志而通过的法律,甚至是那些如果公民胆敢违反就要对他施加惩罚的法律。国家中所有成员的固定意志就是公共意志,通过这个公共意志,他们成为公民,获得了自由【原注2】。当人民在集会上提议一个法律时,人们被问的问题并不是他们是赞成还是反对这个提议,而是这个提议是否与属于他们的公共意志相符合。每个人通过投票表达自己对这一问题的看法,而从对票数进行计算,公共意志就得到宣告了。当与我相反的观点胜出时,只能表明我犯错误了,我所认为的公共意志并不是真的公共意志。如果我的个别意见竟胜过公意成为主导,这时我所做的就非我所愿了,我也就不再自由了。

这表明公共意志的全部特性仍然体现在多数人中,如果它不在多数人中,不论人们作出何种选择,都不再有自由可言了。

之前我在阐述个别意志是如何在公众的讨论中取代普遍意志时,我曾详细地论述了防止这种滥权的具体方法,以后我还会对此进一步讨论。至于普遍意志的宣告所应达到的投票比例,我也曾给出了一些原则,根据这些原则,人们就可确定这一比例。一票之差就可以打破双方对等的局面,一票反对就可以破坏全体通过。在全体一致通过和双方均等之间,还存在着多种不均等的分配情况,根据政治实体的状况和需要来进行分配,其中任何一种都可以成为合适的投票比例。

有两个普遍性的准则可以用来规定这些比例,第一个是:要决定的事情越是严肃和重要,占上风的观点就越应接近全体一致;第二个是:要决定的事情越是需要快速解决,绝大多数的数量就越要降低;而对于当时就要做决定的问题,一票的优势就足够了。第一个准则似乎更适合制定法律,后一个准则则适合行政事务的迅速处理。无论如何,决定性多数的宣布所需要的最佳比例是以二者的结合来确定的。

【原注1】这一点当然总应该理解为一个自由国家的情况;因为在其他地方,家庭、财产、无容身之所、贫穷或暴力都可能违背人的意愿使其滞留在一个国家,如此一来,他这种单纯的居住就不再说明他对社会契约是认可还是违反了。

【原注2】在热那亚,人们可以在监狱门前和犯人的脚镣上看到"自由"一词。此处题铭的用法是极正确且公正的。因为在所有的国家,正是犯罪者妨碍公民获得自由。如果在一个国家里,所有这样的人都被关进监狱,人们将会享受到最完美的自由。

第三章
论选举

我曾经说过,统治者和行政官员的选举是一种相当复杂的行为,可以通过两种方式进行,即投票推选或抽签。这两种方式在不同的共和国中都被使用过。在威尼斯的总督选举中,我们甚至可以看到这两种方式的复杂结合。

孟德斯鸠说:"通过抽签进行的选举,是民主制的特征。"我同意这一点,但为什么是这样呢?他继续说:"抽签是一种使任何人都不感到苦恼的选举方式,并且它给予每个公民为他的国家服务的合理希望。"但这并不是一个好的理由。

如果我们还记得首领的选举是一项政府职能而非主权职能的话,那么我们就会明白为什么抽签的方式更符合民主制的本质,因为民主制中没有那么多的行政行为,所以行政效果才更好。

在真正的民主制度中,行政官的职位并不是一种特权,而是一种沉重的责

第四卷
BOOK FOUR

任,这样,人们如果把它加于一个人身上,而不加于另一个人身上,就有失公正。唯有法律才能把这份负担加之于某个抽到签的人,因为抽签时,条件对每个人都是相等的,而且选举的结果并不取决于任何人的意志,法律的普遍性也没有因为任何特殊的应用而遭到破坏。

在贵族制中,是君主选择君主,政府自己维护自己,这种情况下,投票选举才是最合适的方式。

威尼斯总督选举的例子非但没有否定这两种方式的区别,恰恰证实了这种区别。这种混合的形式正适合混合政府,因为将威尼斯政府视作真正的贵族制是错误的,虽然人民无权分享政府的行政权力,威尼斯贵族本身便是另外一种人民。一群贫困的"马拿波特"【译注1】与任何行政官员的职位都是无缘的,他们的贵族身份只体现在空洞的"阁下"这个虚名和旁听大议会的权利上。既然这种大议会就像我们日内瓦全民会议一样人数众多,他们显赫的贵族成员也不会比我们普通的公民拥有更多的特权。毫无疑问,除了两个共和国的极端差别,日内瓦的市民完全对应于威尼斯的贵族,我们的土著和居民对应于威尼斯的市民和人民,我们的农民对应于威尼斯大陆上的臣民。总而言之,不管以什么样的观点考察威尼斯共和国,不考虑面积大小,它的政府并不比我们的政府更贵族化。所有的区别就在于:因为没有一个终身执掌政权的国家首领,我们不需采用抽签的选举法方式。

在真正的民主制中,抽签选举并没什么不好。因为在那里,所有人不论在品质和能力上,还是在准则与财产上,都是平等的,因此无论谁当选,都没什么不同。但正如我曾经说过的,世上并没有真正的民主制。

当投票和抽签两种选举方式同时进行时,投票选举应该被用于填充那些需要特殊才能的官职,如军事指挥;而抽签则应该用来产生那些只需理性、公正和诚实就能担任的官职,比如行政职位,因为在一个建制良好的国家,这些优点是所有公民都具有的。

在君主制政府中,抽签与投票都不存在。因为君主是法定的、唯一的统治者和行政官员，所以对附属于君主的官员的选举权利仅仅属于君主自己。当圣彼埃尔神甫提议增加法兰西国王议会的数量，并且通过不记名投票的方式选举议会成员时，他并没有意识到他是在提议改变政府的结构。

我还应该再谈一下人民集会中投票和计票的方式，但是罗马体制的发展史可以更生动、也更强有力地论证我所要确立的所有原则。如果花上一些时间来详细考察一下一个由二十万人组成的集会是如何处理公共事务和私人事务的，这对于善于思考的读者来说是绝对值得的。

【译注1】威尼斯的贵族分为贵爵和巴拿波特，巴拿波特是贫穷的贵族。

第四章
论罗马的人民大会

有关罗马的早期历史，我们并没有非常确切的文献资料，而且我们听到的大部分关于罗马的说法极有可能只是神话[原注1]。按照一般准则，一个民族的编年史中最有指导意义的部分，就是他们的政治制度史，而这部分也正是我们最缺乏的。经验虽然每天都在告诉我们各帝国兴衰的原因，但由于各个民族的形成期已经过去，我们只能靠推测来解释他们曾经是怎样形成的。

从那些人们已经发现的各种确立的习俗中，至少可以得出结论：这些习俗必定有其形成的根源。传统就是由这些根源发展而来，那些能得到最大的权威支持和最好的理性确证的传统应被看成是最可靠的。这便是我在考察世界上最自由最强大的民族如何行使他们的最高权力时所力图遵循的原则。

罗马建国之后，新生的共和国，也就是由阿尔巴人、萨比人和外邦人组成的

第四卷
BOOK FOUR

建国者的军队，被分为三个种类，正由于这种划分，有了部族的名称。这些部族中的每一个又被分为十个库里亚，每个库里亚又被分成十个德库里亚，其首领被称为库里昂或德库里昂。

除此之外，又从每个部族中抽出一个由一百名骑兵或骑士组成的一个团队，称为百人团。因为在城市中没有这种划分的必要，因此我们可以推定这种划分的最初目的是纯军事性的。但是，罗马这个小城看上去似乎有一种追求伟大的天分，这种天分引导它在一开始就为自己提供了一套适用于世界首都的组织系统。

然而，这种最初的划分很快便显出了一种缺陷，即阿尔巴人的部族和萨比人的部族总是维持不变，而外邦人的部族随着外族人的不断迁入而人数不断增多，因此其力量很快就超过了另外两族。塞尔维乌斯对这一危险弊端的解决办法是改革划分的方式，他废除了原来按种族划分的制度，代之以基于部族在城中所占地区的划分制度。他划分出了四个部族，取消了原来的三个。每个部族占有罗马的一座小山，并以山的名字命名。这样，塞尔维乌斯不仅修正了现有的不平等，还防止了未来的不平等。为了保证这种划分是针对种族，而不是地区，他禁止一个区域中的居民迁移到另一个区域，从而防止了种族间的混杂。

他还把原先的三个百人团增加一倍，另外又新设了十二个百人团，但他保留了原有的名称。这是一个简单又慎重的方法，他用这种方法把武士群体和人民群体区分开来，而没有引起后者的抱怨。

在这四个城镇部族的基础上，塞尔维乌斯另增加了十五个部族，称为乡村部族，因为它们由分布在十五个州府的乡村居民组成。之后，又不断设立其他的新部族，直到最后，罗马人民被分为三十五个部族，这个数字在共和国结束之前一直是固定的。

城市部族和乡村部族的区分产生的结果是十分值得人们关注的，因为在此之前从未有过这种先例，还因为罗马人道德的维持和罗马帝国的成长都要归因于此。人们可能会认为这种划分之后，城市部族很快就会独揽大权和所有的荣耀，从而极大地降低乡村部族的声望。但事实恰恰相反，古代罗马人对乡村生活的品味是众所周知的，这种品味来自他们明智的创建者，这些创建者把自由与乡村劳动、军事服役结合起来，而把艺术、工艺、阴谋、财富和奴役留给了城市。

于是，既然杰出的罗马公民都居住在乡下勤于垦种，去乡间寻找共和国的中流砥柱就成为一种惯例。由于这是最高贵的贵族生活方式，因而得到了所有人的尊崇。人们喜爱乡村居民的简单而勤劳的生活胜过罗马市民的闲散而懒惰的生活。而且，一个人在城市如果只是个穷困的无产者，但只要他去乡间耕地，就会成为受人尊敬的公民。瓦罗说："我们高贵的祖先选择了在乡村建立培养那些健壮勇敢男儿的基地，让他们在战争时保卫自己，在平时供养自己，这些不是没有道理的。"普林尼也肯定地说，乡村部族受人尊敬是因为他们部族的人，如果要贬低一个懦夫，就把这个人转移到城市部族去羞辱他。当萨宾人阿皮乌斯·克劳狄乌斯载誉而归，来到罗马住的时候，就被编入了一个乡村部族，这个部族随后就以他的名字命名。最后，那些被解放的奴隶全部被编入了城市部族，没有一个加入乡村部族。整个罗马共和国也没有任何一个被释放的奴隶担任执政官的例子，即使他们已经成为合法的公民。

尽管这是一个极好的原则，但它被过分地实行，最后发生了变化，也就导致了政治权力的滥用。

首先，督察官长期把持着任意把公民从一个部族转移到另一个部族的权力，后来甚至允许大多数人根据自己的选择编入某个部族，这种让步是没有任何益处的，它使督察行为失去了一个主要的职能。此外，所有那些高贵的和有权势的人都跑去了乡下，而获得自由的奴隶和普通人则留在了城里，这样一来，部族不再具有任何地区或者领土的基础，所有部族如此混合在一起，人们只能通过户口簿才能识别出某个部族的成员身份了。这就是"部族"一词逐渐具有了人格上的意义，而不再具有领地的意义，或者说已经没有任何意义。

第四卷
BOOK FOUR

还有一个结果,就是由于集会的地点往往靠近乌合之众居多的城市部族,由于近水楼台之便,城市部族常常是人民集会中最强大的群体,他们会把国家出卖给那些胆敢从构成集会的无耻之徒手中购买选票的人。

至于库里亚,既然建国者在每一部族中立有十个库里亚,那么那时被围入罗马城墙之内的罗马人民就有三十个库里亚,每一个都有自己的庙宇、神明、官员、祭司,还有自己的节日,被称为"大路节",有点类似于后来乡村部族举办的乡村节。

当塞尔维乌斯做出这样的划分时,三十个区并不能被平均分配到四个部族里,而他又不想改变这一数字,于是就有了独立于部族的库里亚,这成为划分罗马居民的另一种方法。但在乡村部族或是组成乡村部族的人民中间都没有库里亚,因为部族成为纯粹的民间机构之后,罗马便设置了另一种制度征募军队,罗穆鲁斯时代的军事划分方法已经成为多余了。这样,尽管每个公民都是某部族的成员,很多人却不属于任何库里亚。

塞尔维乌斯还实行了第三种划分,这种划分与前两种没有任何关系,但由它实施的效果来看,它却成为所有划分法中最重要的一种。他把整个罗马人民分成六个等级,这种分法既不根据人的身份,也不按居住区域,而是按财产来划分,所以第一等级中全是富人,而最后一个等级中全是穷人,中间等级则由中等富裕的人构成。这六个等级又被细分为一百九十三个团体,命名为百人团。这些群体的分配非常不均,第一等级占据了其中半数的百人团,而最后一个等级单独构成了一个团,这样就导致了人数最少的等级却拥有数量最多的百人团,而最末的等级却只当做一个团来计算,尽管这一个等级包括了罗马半数以上的居民。

为了使这种划分形式的含义不那么露骨,塞尔维乌斯把它伪装成一种军事形式:他在第二个等级中安插了两个军械士百人团,在第四个等级安插了两个兵器制造的百人团。除了最末一个等级,他还在每个等级中做了老幼的划分,就是说,把那些有义务服兵役的人和那些因年龄大而依法免兵役的人区别开来;这种区分方法

社会契约论
The Social Contract

与按财产进行划分的方法相比，需要更经常性的人口普查。最后，他又规定集会在玛尔提乌斯运动场举行，所有达到服兵役年龄的人都必须携带武器参加。

塞尔维乌斯没有在最后一个等级中也对年轻人和老年人做出区分，原因在于这些最普通的国民没有拿起武器为他的国家服务的荣誉；一个人必须先有一个家，然后才有权利保卫这个家园。今天的国王军队里充斥着数不清的乞丐，若是在那个士兵作为自由捍卫者的时代，这些人恐怕没有一个不被轻蔑地从罗马步兵队伍里排斥出去。

然而，就是在最低等级中，也对其中的无产者和所谓按人头计数的人做出了区分。前者还不是完全的一无所有，至少他们还能为国家提供公民，在紧急的时候甚至能提供兵源。但是后者，那些一无所有而且只能通过数人头来计数的人，则完全被视为一无所用了，马瑞乌斯是第一个肯屈尊招募他们的人。

我在这里姑且不谈这三种划分方式本身是好是坏，我可以肯定地说，只有在早期，罗马人的简单淳朴、他们对农业的热爱以及他们对商业和牟取暴利行为的轻蔑，才使这种划分行得通。而现代人无厌的贪欲、浮躁的内心、无休止的奔波以及反复无常的祸福变换，哪个现代民族能使这样的制度维持二十年而不颠覆呢？我们也应该注意到罗马人民的道德和监察制度比这个制度更强大并且足以纠正这个制度的弊病。如果一个富人过分地炫耀他的财富，那么他将被贬斥到穷人的队伍中去。

从上述的一切便很容易理解，为什么罗马尽管有六个等级，但人们常常提起的只有五个。因为第六等级既不能加入军队，也不能去玛尔提乌斯运动场参加公民投票【原注2】，他们在共和国几乎一无用处，所以也就很少得到人们的关注。

以上就是罗马人民的各种分类方式，接下来让我们考察一下这些划分对公民集会的效果。合法召集的公民集会被称为人民大会，通常在罗马广场或玛尔提乌斯运动场上举行。根据集会的召开所依据的三种形式分为库里亚大会、百人团大会和部族大会。库里亚大会是由罗穆鲁斯创立的，百人团大会则由塞尔维乌斯

第四卷
BOOK FOUR

首创，而部族公民会议则起源于保民官。只有在这些人民大会上，才可以通过法律，才可以选举行政官员，而且由于每个公民都是被编入库里亚、百人团或部族的，所以每个公民都没有被排除在投票权之外，罗马人民是法律和事实上的真正主权者。

要使人民大会的召开具有合法性，会议上通过的决议具有法律的力量，必须具备下列三个条件：第一，召集会议的团体或官员必须具有相应的权威；第二，大会必须在法定的日子举行；第三，天象占卜必须为吉兆。

第一条规则的原因不需要解释了，第二条是一项管理方面的规定，集会不应当在节假日或有集市的日子举行，因为进城办事的乡民们没有时间在广场待上一天。第三条规则可以使元老院能够制约那些骄傲而且不安宁的人，并且可以消减保民官们煽动性的热情，尽管保民官会找出种种办法来摆脱这种约束。

法律和官员选举并非是提交集会决定的唯一内容，既然罗马人民已经篡取了政府最重要的职能，可以说整个欧洲的命运就是在那些集会上决定的。要处理的公共事务各种各样，这些决定了集会所要采取的不同形式。

要想评判这些不同的大会形式，只需对它们进行一下比较就可以了。罗穆鲁斯建立库里亚的目的是要让元老院制衡人民的力量，人民又反过来制约元老院，而他自己则可以驾驭这两方了。他的这种安排给予了人民人数上的权威，以平衡他留给贵族的权力和财富上的权威。然而，按照君主制的精神，他还是留给贵族们更多有利条件，贵族可以通过贿买他们的被保护者在投票上保持优势。这种令人赞叹的保护者和被保护者的制度实在是一项政治和人道的杰作，没有它，和共和制精神相背离的贵族统治就不可能维系下去。只有罗马才会有此殊荣为世界做出良好榜样，尽管这一制度从未产生过任何弊病，但它在其他地方从未被效仿过。

库里亚这种形式在所有王权时期直到塞尔维乌斯时代都一直存在着，由于塔尔干王朝末期的统治被认为是不合法的，因此王权时期的法律整体上被称作库里亚法。

社会契约论
The Social Contract

在共和制时期,由于库里亚一直局限于四个城市部族,并且仅仅包括罗马城的居民,所以这种形式既不能适用于领导贵族阶层的元老院,也不能适用于虽然自己身为平民但却领导着一群有钱公民的保民官。这样,库里亚就失去了威信,每况愈下,以至于只要他们的三十个扈从集合起来,就可以处理那些本应在库里亚大会上处理的事情了。

百人团的划分对元老院如此有利,以至于我们一开始很难看明白,为什么元老院在那个被称为百人团集会的大会中不能占主导地位,去选举执政官、监察官和其他高级行政官员呢?因为事实上,在那个由全体罗马人民六个等级所形成的一百九十三个百人团中,第一等级就占了九十八个,而选票是以百人团的数目来计算的,那么第一等级就拥有了超出其他所有等级数的多数。如果第一等级所有百人团意见达成一致的话,其他等级的投票数就不用再统计了,这样,由少数人作出的决定就被看做是大多数人的决定;因此可以这么说,在百人团集会中的事务是以财富的多数而不是以投票的多数来决定。

但是,这种极端的权威在两方面遭到制约。首先,保民官往往是富人等级,而许多平民也属于富人等级,他们的存在制约了第一等贵族的影响力。

其次,按规定,百人团并不按等级次序进行投票,因为这样的话,第一个等级的百人团总是首先投票。相反,人们先通过抽签的办法选出一个百人团【原注3】,由该团单独进行选举,之后在另一天,所有其他百人团被召集起来再重复这一选举,其结果通常接近前一结果。于是,对应民主制的原则,示范的权威便由地位转移到了抽签上。

这一做法还会有另一个好处,就是乡下的公民可以利用两次选举的间隔来了解临时被任命的候选人的品行,因而就不会再盲目投票了。但这个办法最终在加快选举进程的借口下被废除了,两个选举被放在同一天举行。

严格来说,部族集会才是罗马人民真正的议会,它只能由保民官来召集,而正是这种集会上选出了保民官,并通过了全民制定的法律。元老院不仅在此毫无

第四卷
BOOK FOUR

地位，甚至无权参加部族集会，不得不服从他们未能参加表决的法律。从这方面来说，元老们的自由还比不上那些最末等的公民。但这一不公正的规定完全是一种拙劣的做法，这个未曾得到全体成员认可的体系足以使它产生的政令无效。如果所有的贵族都凭着自己作为公民的权利参加了这些集会，他们按照人头计算的投票就会跟普通人一样，做出的决定也不会产生多大的影响力，因为在这里，最卑微的无产者也同最高贵的元老是同等重要的。

可以看到，由如此庞大的人群举行集会进行投票，除了收集选票的种种不同制度产生不同次序外，这些投票产生的形式本身也并非无关紧要的，而是每种形式都有与其意图相联系的效果，而这种意图恰是导致这一办法被选中的原因。

不必再进一步阐述更多细节，我们可以从前面的解释中得出结论，部族大会是对民主政治更有利的一种集会，百人团集会则对贵族制更为有利。至于罗马市民占大多数的库里亚大会，由于它们只适宜于推行暴政和设计阴谋，因而名誉扫地，就是那些叛乱分子也避免利用这种集会，以防止把自己的计划暴露出去。毫无疑问，罗马人民的尊严只有在百人团集会中才能找到。这种大会是唯一完整的公民集会，因为乡村部族不参加库里亚大会，而部族集会又把元老院和贵族排斥在外。

至于计票方式，尽管还比不上斯巴达的方式那样简单，但早期罗马人所实行的计票方式也很简单，就如同他们淳朴的道德和习俗。每个人大声报出自己的选票，由职员负责记录。每个部族内部的大多数选票决定了该部族的决定，大多数部族的投票结果便代表了所有人民的决定，库里亚和百人团的表决方式与此相同。如果公民们都是诚实的，每个人都耻于在公开场合下投票支持那些提出不公措施或不合格的候选人，那么这种投票方法是可行的。但是，当民风败坏，选票开始可以买卖时，就应该使用秘密投票的方式，以使收买选票的人因不信任出卖选票的人而受到限制，而且也使恶棍们不至于成为叛国者。

我知道西塞罗谴责这种投票方式的改变，他将共和国灭亡的原因部分地归结于此。但是，尽管我知道西塞罗可能具有的权威力量，但我对他的这个观点不敢苟同。相反，我认为正是由于类似的改革太少了，才加速了罗马共和国的灭亡。正如健康人的食谱不适宜于病人，适宜于正直民族的法律也不能用于治理一个开始堕落了的民族。对这一原则最好的例证莫过于威尼斯共和国那长久的历史了，迄今为至，它余波仍在，唯一的原因就是它的法律是专为不道德的人制定的。

现在，每个罗马公民在投票时都会分得一块方板，这样他们在写下自己选择时别人就无从知道了。人们也制定出了收集方板、统计选票、比较票数等事务的新程序。尽管如此，也没能使那些负责这些职能[原注4]的官员免除作弊的嫌疑。最后，人们还制定了一些用来防止投票舞弊和收买选票的法令，但这些法令的名目繁多显示了它们的无效。

到了罗马共和国的后期，人们经常不得不诉诸非常性的权宜之计来弥补法律的不足。有时他们会假托神迹，但这种办法骗得了人民，却骗不了统治人民的人；有时他们会在候选人还来不及收买选票时就突然召集会议；有时当人民已经被说服并且即将做出错误决定时就将整个会议耗费在聊天中。但是最后，野心还是战胜了试图制约它的一切；所有这些中最令人不可思议的是，尽管有如此种种弊端，这个庞大的民族还是借助了古老的规则，继续选举他们的官员、制定法律、审理案件、处理公私事务，其表现出来的智慧同元老院无异。

【原注1】"罗马"一词据说源自罗穆鲁斯，其实它是希腊文，意思为"力量"。"弩玛"一词也为希腊文，意思是"法律"。难道说这个城市最初的两个国王在他们统治之前就提前使用了与他们后来的所为相关的名字？

【原注2】我说去"玛尔提乌斯教场"是因为这是百人团集会的地点；在其他两种集会时，人民在市场或其他地方召开会议，这时，按人头计算者和最显贵的公民平起平坐，有着一样的影响力和权威。

【原注3】如此通过抽签选出的百人团被称为特权团（proerogativa），因为它是第一个被要求表决的，特权（prerogative）一词由此而来。

【原注4】这里指的是选票的保管、分发和回收。

第五章
论保民官制

当人们不能在国家各组成部门之间确立一个精确的比例时,或者当一些无法控制的原因不断改变它们之间的关系时,就需要建立一个独立于其他部门的特殊机构,它能使国家的各组成部分处于一种良好的平衡中,在统治者和人民之间,或者在君主和主权体之间,成为一种中介或纽带,如果需要,它甚至可以同时调节以上两种关系。

我将这种制度称之为保民官制度,它是法律和立法权的维护者。它有时为了保护主权体而与政府作斗争,就像以前罗马的保民官一样;有时,它也为了支持政府而反对人民,就如同现在的威尼斯十人委员会;有时它又用以维持双方的平衡,就像从前斯巴达的监察官所起的作用。

保民官制度不属于共和制的组成部分,它不应享有任何立法权和行政权,但也正是因为这一点,它的权力才最大,它虽然自身什么也不能做,但它可以阻止其他机构所做的任何事情。作为法律的护卫者,它比执行法律的统治者和制定法律的主权者都要更为神圣和受人尊崇。这一点,在罗马显而易见,那些总是鄙视全体人民的自命不凡的贵族,却不得不屈从于一个既不神圣、又无审判权的普通保民官。

一个调节得当的保民官制度是国家良好体制的最强有力的支持者;但是,一旦它的权力多于它所必需的范围,哪怕是多出一丁点,它就会扰乱整个国家。保民官制在本质上并不是一种易于屈服的力量,一旦它掌握了一定的权力,它所发挥的力量永远不会劣于它所应有的状况。

当保民官篡夺了那些他们本来是只作为调节者的行政权力,或是他们试图去制定那些本应只是他们保护的法律，保民官制就堕落成暴政了。尽管斯巴达的监察院拥有巨大的权力，这在斯巴达还保持着一定道德水准时并没有更多的危险，但一旦其道德开始堕落，这个危险便愈演愈烈了。这些篡位暴君谋杀阿基斯的血债，由他的继承者讨了回来。但这些监察官们所犯的罪行和所受的惩罚加速了共和国的灭亡；到了克里奥门尼斯之后，斯巴达就不值一提了。罗马也是以同样的方式走向灭亡，保民官们逐步篡夺了过度的权力，借助于为自由而制定的法律，他们甚至成为破坏自由的皇帝的保护者。至于威尼斯的十人委员会，根本就是一个血腥的审判所，对于贵族和平民同样的可怕，它远不是崇高地保护法律，而是把法律贬得很低。在蜕变之后，它只是在暗中施放一些见不得人的冷枪暗箭。

就如政府一样，保民官制度的力量也随着人数的增加而削弱。罗马人民的保民官最初是两人，后来成了五个。当他们试图把这个数目增加一倍时，得到了元老院的支持，元老院自信可以利用其中一些人去控制另外一些，而最后这些都如其所愿地发生了。

要防止这样一个拥有强大力量的机构篡权——尽管还没有任何政府试图这样做——最佳方法就是不要让保民官成为常设机构，可以让它周期性存在，限定一些间歇，但这些间隔时间不能太长，以免权力滥用有足够的时间生根发芽。具体的间隔期可以通过法律作出一些规定，以便于在需要的时候可以根据规定来缩短间隔期。

在我看来，这样的安排没什么不好，因为我已经说过，保民官制度不是国家体制的一部分，将它暂停也不至于产生什么损害。而且我还认为这是一种很有效的安排，因为机构重新运作后的新任官员不是以他的前任所拥有的权力为起点，而只是拥有法律赋予他的权力。

第六章
论独裁制

法律的缺乏弹性使它不能根据具体事件而有所变通，这在特定情况下是有害的，在危机出现的时候甚至能导致国家灭亡。法定程式的种种规定以及拖沓的程序往往会耗费一定的时间，而现实环境往往等不了这么长时间。可能出现的无数种情况都是立法者始料不及的，当然，如果懂得他们不可能预见所有的事情，这就是一种了不起的预见了。

正是由于这个原因，所以人们不应该试图把政治机构建立得如此僵硬，以至于剥夺了人们中止法律执行的权力。即使是斯巴达有时也会停止法律的运行。

但是，冒着很大的危险去改变公共秩序只有在面临更大更紧急事件的危险时，只有在国家面临生死存亡时，才可以暂停法律的神圣权力。在这些罕见而又显见的情况下，人们可以通过一种特殊的约定来维护国家的公共安全，把这一责任放在一个最值得信赖的人手中。根据危险的性质，这种责任可以使用两种方式授权。

如果只需调动政府的能动性就足以应付危险，那么就可以把它的权力集中在政府的一两个成员手中。在此，并不是法律的权威发生了改变，只是执行法律的形式变了。如果危险太大，法律规定的本身已经成为有效行动的障碍，那就必须任命一个至高无上的首领，使他有权力让法律沉默，并且暂时搁置立法者的权威。在此情形下，普遍意志应是无可置疑的，因为很显然，此时人民最关心的就是不使国家灭亡。因而立法权威暂时搁置并不是要废除它，使法律暂时沉默的官员并不能使它开口；他可以主导立法权威，但没有权力代表它；他什么都可以做，就是不能制定法律。

罗马的元老院曾依据一种神圣的仪式把维护国家安全的责任赋予它的执政官，他们采用的便是这两种方法中的第一种；而当罗马两个执政官中的一个被指定为独裁官时【原注1】，便是采用了第二种方法。这种最初方法始自阿尔巴·隆伽。

社会契约论
The Social Contract

在共和国建立初期，罗马人经常诉诸独裁官制，因为国家的根基尚不稳定，还不具备维护自身的力量。而且在这一时期，人民的道德特征使在其他情况下的预防措施都成为不必要，人们不必担心独裁者会滥权或试图延长他的任期。相反，这一巨大的权力对于执掌它的人来说似乎是一种负担，因为他们总是试图尽快摆脱它，就好像取代了法律的职位对于自己有太多的困难和危险一样。

在罗马早期就实行这种独裁制度的不明智做法颇受人诟病，并不是因为它存在滥权的危险，而正是因为这种职位的权力会有贬值的危险。因为当这种独裁官被随意地滥用于选举、祝圣和纯粹的礼仪事务时，人们就有必要担心，这种制度在真正需要时就不会那么令人生畏了，因为人们已经习惯于认为它只是一个用于空洞仪式的空洞头衔。

接近共和国的末期，罗马人变得小心起来，此时他们在运用这种独裁制上的保守程度，同他们曾经在运用这种制度的滥权一样毫无道理。我们很容易就能看出他们的担心是毫无根据的，当时罗马的虚弱反倒成了一种自我保护，可以对抗夹在中间的行政官，而一个独裁者在特定情况下是要在保卫公共自由的同时又不侵犯到这一自由。罗马的束缚不是来自它本身，而是在罗马军队里形成的，马留乌斯对苏拉、庞贝对恺撒几乎都没有什么抵抗，这清楚地显示了在面对外部压力时，内部权威的可能作为。

这一过失使罗马人犯了很大的错误，比如，他们在卡提里那【译注1】事件中没有任命一个独裁官；因为这一事件只是涉及罗马城内部，至多是关联到意大利的几个省份，那么凭借法律所赋予独裁官的无限权威本可以使这次阴谋很容易就被挫败，但事实上，只是在种种偶然幸运事件凑在一起才使这次阴谋没有得逞，可人类是不应指望幸运的偶然的。

元老院没有任命一个独裁官，只是把自己的所有权力交给了执政官们。正因为这样，西塞罗为了更有效地行动，不得不在关键时刻逾越了这一权力，尽管一开始，罗马人在喜悦的激动情绪中支持了他的行动，但是后来人们便要求他为民众在这一破坏法律的行为中所流的血负责了，而这件事如果发生在一个独裁官身上，人们就无法指责他。不过这位执政官的能言善辩压过了一切。尽管他是罗马人，但他爱自己的荣誉胜过爱自己的祖国，他不是去积极寻找拯救自己国家的最确定最合适的方法，而是想办法从这件事上获得荣耀【原注2】。因此他作为罗马的解放者受到人们的尊敬是很公正的，但作为罗马法律的破坏者，他也同样公正地受到了惩罚。不管后来对他流放的撤销是多么的精彩，但毫无疑问这只是一种赦免。

此外，不论以何种方式授权这样一种重要的任命，重要的一点是，要把其任期规定到一段非常短的时期，并且这一任期不能延长。在需要独裁者出现的紧急关头，国家要么很快灭亡要么得到拯救。一旦这种危机过去，独裁要么变成暴政，要么有名无实。罗马的独裁官任期为六个月，大部分人在自己任期结束前就辞职告退了。如果这一期限更长的话，他们可能还想延长，就像十人委员会一样，任期为一年。发生危机需要推举独裁官，那么独裁官的任期只要足够应付这个危机就够了，这样他才没有时间作任何其他的打算。

【原注1】这种任命是在夜间秘密进行的，好像把一个人置于法律之上是非常可耻的一件事似的。
【原注2】如果他提议任命一个独裁官的话，他就不能确定能否得到这种荣耀了，因为他不敢毛遂自荐做独裁官，也不确定他的同僚是否会提名他。
【译注1】卡提里那（公元前108-62年），罗马政治阴谋家。曾试图武装夺取执政官一职，演说家西塞罗得知这一阴谋后，不顾恺撒的请求，逮捕并处死了卡提里那在罗马的阴谋同伙，一个月后，卡提里那在战争中败亡。

第七章
论监察官制

正像公共意志是由法律来申明一样，公众判断是由监察机构来阐明的；公共的意见即舆论是另一种法律形式，监察官就是这种法律的执行者。而且依照君主的形式，他只是把这一法律应用于个别事件。

监察官只是人民舆论的发言人，而绝不是人民舆论的权威，一旦它偏离了这一点，它的决定就失去了效用。

将一个民族的道德和尊崇对象区分开来是没有意义的，因为两者基于相同的原则，而且必然会融合到一起。在世界上所有的民族中，决定他们喜好选择的并不是天性，而是舆论。端正了人们的舆论，人类的道德自然就会纯正起来。人们总是热爱美好的东西，或者说热爱他们认为美好的东西，但正是在这个判断中会发生错误，那就必须对这种判断作出规范。对道德的评判就是对他们所尊崇的东西作出评判，而要对他们所尊崇的东西做出评判，则要看人们观念的尺度。

一个民族的观念源自它的政体，尽管法律并不对道德作出规定，但道德却从立法中得来；当立法薄弱的时候，道德就开始退化，但是此时，法律做不到的事情，监察官也不能做到了。

从这一点可以知道，监察官制对维持道德是有作用的，但却不能重建道德。所以要在法律还有活力的时候设置监察官制，因为一旦这种活力消失了，任何事情都失去了希望；当法律失去了自身的力量，一切合法的权力也都不再有力量了。

监察官制度通过以下几种方式来维持道德：阻止人们观念的腐蚀；通过以贤明的裁决保持舆论的正确性；有时甚至在舆论还不确定的时候把它确定下来。比如，在决斗中使用助手曾在法兰西王国盛行一时，但这一习惯由于国王的诏书里的几个字"至于那些使用助手的懦夫们……"就被废止了。由于这一判断预见了公共的判断，因此一下就把公共的判断确定下来了。但是如果试图以同样的诏书宣布决斗也是一种懦弱的行为，尽管决斗确实也是懦弱的表现，但这与舆论的观点不符，公众就会嘲笑这个决定，因为公众对决斗的评判早已形成了。

我在别的地方已经说过[原注1]，公共舆论是不能受到限制的，在代表舆论的法庭上是不应该存在任何舆论受限制的痕迹的。因此，对于这种罗马人用高超的技巧所使用、拉西第蒙人使用得更加巧妙、而现代人完全丢失了的方法，我们怎么推崇都不过分。

第四卷
BOOK FOUR

以前一个品行不端的人在斯巴达的议会上提出了一个很好的建议,监察院未予理睬,却让另一个德高望重的公民重新提出了同一建议。尽管没有对哪一方做出赞美或指责,但这种做法对一方是多大的荣誉,而对另一方是多大的羞辱啊!有些来自萨莫斯【原注2】的醉汉们曾弄脏了监察院的法庭,第二天就有公共的法令允许萨莫斯人可以做下流的事情。而这种惩罚比任何实际的惩罚来得更严重。当斯巴达宣布哪些是正当的,哪些是不正当的,希腊人对这种判断未加任何争辩。

【原注1】我在本章中只是提出了我的观点,而在我的《至达朗贝先生书》中对此有详细阐述。
【原注2】他们其实是来自另外一个岛的,但我们语言的微妙不允许我在这里写出它的名字。

第八章
论公民宗教

人类最初并没有国王,有的只是神祇,没有政府,而只有神权政治。他们像卡里古拉那样进行思考,而在当时的环境中,那种方式也是对的。在经历了感情上和观念上的漫长改造过程,人类才最终决定接受他们同类中的某一个作为自己的主人,并幻想从这一切中获得好处。

由这一个事实来看,每个政治社会膜拜一个神,由此可以得出结论,有多少个民族就有多少个神。两个相异的、甚至是敌对的民族是不可能长期事奉同一个主人的,正如两支敌对的军队不可能受同一个指挥官统领。因此,民族的区分形成了多神制,而多神制进而产生了宗教和政治上的不相容,而这两种不相容在本质上是相同的,这一点我在后面还要阐述。

社会契约论
The Social Contract

希腊人曾经有一种幻想，他们在野蛮民族所崇拜的神中发现自己的神，这种想法源自他们荒唐地把自己视为了那些民族的天然主权者。但在我们的时代，研究不同民族的神的同一性是一种荒唐且拙劣的学问，就好像莫洛克、萨士林、克罗诺斯可能是同一个神，腓尼基人的巴尔、希腊人的宙斯和罗马人的朱庇特可能是同一个神，这就仿佛在这些名字不同的虚构者之间存在着某些共同点似的。

但是，如果有人问为什么在异教信仰的时代，每个国家都有自己的宗教仪式和不同的神明，却没有发生过宗教战争呢？我的回答是：正是由于这样一个事实，即每个国家都有自己的信仰和政府，所以国家对神灵和法律并不加以区分。政治的战争也就是宗教上的战争，可以这样说，神的疆域是由国家的疆域所决定的。一个民族的神没有任何控制另一个民族的神的权力。异教徒的神灵绝不是嫉妒的神灵；这些神把整个世界的统治范围进行了划分；甚至连摩西和希伯来人也默认这一主张，并在谈话时会提到以色列的神。当然，他们并不承认迦南人的神，认为迦南是个被流放的、命中注定要毁灭的民族，国土应该被其他民族所占领。但是，考虑一下他们是如何评说相邻民族是如何神圣而不可侵犯的吧，耶弗塔对亚扪人说："你们的神基抹所拥有的难道不是你们的合法所有物吗？""因此我们同样有资格拥有由我们的神占领的土地。"【原注1】在我看来，这就相当于承认基抹和以色列的神权力是相当的。

犹太人曾先后臣服于巴比伦王国和叙利亚王国的统治，但是他们坚决拒绝承认除了自己上帝之外的任何其他神灵，这种拒绝便被认为是对征服者的一种反抗，因此为他们招致了种种迫害，这一点我们可从他们的历史中频频读到，在基督教之前这是史无前例的【原注2】。

既然每种宗教都唯一地附属于相关国家的法律并受其规范，除了征服之外，没有别的办法使一个民族改变自己的信仰，那么唯一的传教士就是征服者；既然改信宗教的义务是由征服强加的，那么在任何宗教进行传播之前就必须先完成征服。正如《荷马史诗》中所描写的，远不是人类为神而战，而是神为人而战。每

第四卷
BOOK FOUR

个民族都在向自己的神祈求胜利，并且开设新的圣坛来感谢神的庇护。罗马人每在攻取一个新的城镇之前，都要先诏令该处的神放弃这个地方。他们之所以允许塔伦坦人保留其愤怒的神灵，是因为他们认为塔伦坦人的神已经服从了罗马人的神，并且要向罗马的神效忠。他们把自己的神留给被征服者就相当于把自己的法律留给了被征服者。向罗马的加比多尔神殿中的朱庇特进献一顶皇冠经常是罗马人索要的唯一供品。

最终，当罗马人在随着帝国的扩张不断把他们的宗教和神到处传播的时候，当他们通过被征服民族接受他们的公民身份而吸收了这些民族的信仰和神灵的时候，这个巨大帝国的人民逐渐发现他们拥有众多的神灵和宗教，并且几乎在其他地方也是完全一样的，就这样，异教信仰最终成为整个已知世界的统一信仰。

正是在这种形势下，耶稣来到世上建立了一个精神的王国。这个王国将神学体系和政治体系分离开来，这就意味着国家不再是一个统一体，它造成的内部分裂使基督教世界的人民动荡不安。这个另一世界中王国的新思想始终不能被异教徒所理解，基督徒于是成了异教徒眼中一伙表面逆来顺受的虚伪的臣服者，会伺机阴谋独立并夺取权力，在自己虚弱时会狡猾地篡夺他们假装尊重过的权威。这便是基督徒遭到迫害的原因。

异教徒所担心的事情终于发生了：一切事情都换了面貌，曾经谦卑的基督徒也一改往日谦卑的腔调，这个所谓在另一个世界有着看不见的统治的精神王国，很快在一个看得见的首领[译注1]领导下成为这个世界上最暴烈的现实统治。

但是，由于统治者和公民法律是一直存在的，这两种权力就会不断地在基督教国家发生权限冲突，这种冲突使得一切基督教国家都不可能得到良好的治理，因为人们不知道到底应该服从统治者还是服从教士。

有很多民族，甚至包括欧洲和附近地区的民族，都曾试图保留或重建原有的体制，但都没能成功，基督教精神获得了完全的胜利。对神的崇拜总是会保持或重新得到其对主权的独立，并且不必同国家有任何关联了。穆罕默德对此很有见地，他将政教很好地实现了统一，只要他的继承人哈里发继续将这种政府形式保存下去，这个政府就会得以保存完整，这种政府形式就不会分裂。但是，后来阿拉伯人变得繁荣了、开化了、优雅了、娇气了、柔弱了，最后被野蛮人征服了，结果两种权力又重新开始分裂。尽管这种分裂在穆斯林中不如基督教中那么明显，但它确实存在，特别是在阿里教派下，在某些国家如波斯，我们能一直感受到这种分裂的存在。

在我们当中，英格兰国王已经把自己变为教会的首领，沙皇也如法炮制；但他们的这一头衔与其说是使他们成为教会的主人，不如说是变成了大臣。因为他们除了取得维持教会的权力外，并没有取得改变教会的权力。因此他们不是立法者，只是管理者。在任何神职人员构成一个集团【原注3】的地方，都会产生自己的主人和立法者。所以英国、俄国其实和其他地方一样，都存在着两种权力，两个主权体。

在所有的基督教作家中，哲学家霍布斯是唯一一个清楚地看到其中弊病并能开出药方的人，他大胆地提出将鹰的两个头重新合在一起，把一切彻底归于政治统一中，如果失去了这种政治统一，政府和国家都永远不会有良好的结构。但他大概也看到了基督教的专制与他的学说体系并不相容，教士的利益总是强于国家的利益。霍布斯的政治体系之所以被人憎恶，并不是因为其中虚假和可怕的部分，而正是因为其中正确和真实的部分【原注4】。

我相信，如果从这一点上来阐述历史，我们就可以轻易地驳斥贝尔和瓦伯顿的两种相互对立的观点，他们一个声称任何宗教对政治实体都一无用处，另一个则说，不对，基督教是政治实体的最坚实的支持。我们可以向第一个证明：任何一个国家的建立都是以宗教为基础的。对于第二个人，我们则可以告诉他：事实上，基督教的法律对于一个国家的建构害处远大于利处。为了使我的观点更加清晰，只需稍微明确几个与我主题相关的宗教概念。

就宗教与社会的关系来说，即根据这一关系是普遍的还是个别的，可以把宗

第四卷
BOOK FOUR

教分成两类，即人的宗教和公民的宗教。第一种宗教，没有庙宇、祭坛和祭祀，纯粹是出于一种发自内心地对至高无上的神灵的虔诚，以及对于道德的永恒责任感，这种宗教是简朴和纯粹的福音的宗教，是真正的有神论，可以称之为神圣的自然法律。第二种公民的宗教是建立于特定的国家，为该国提供了自己的神灵，规定了这个国家的保护神；它有它的教条、祭祀仪式，和由法律规定的外在崇拜形式；对于执行这种宗教的国家来说，一旦出了这个国家的疆域便是不忠、异端和野蛮的行为；它将人的权利和责任都局限于它的祭坛所在的地方。所有原始民族的宗教都属于这种情况，我们可以把这种宗教称为公民的或正式的神圣宗教。

还有第三种更加奇特的宗教形式，它在给人提供两套法律、两个统治者和两个祖国的同时，让人们服从两种相互矛盾的义务，使人们无法同时既是信徒又是公民。喇嘛教是这样的，日本人的宗教是这样的，罗马的天主教也是这样。我们可以把这种宗教称为牧师的宗教，它产生了一种无可名状的混合的、非社会的法律体系。

如果从政治角度来考察这三种宗教，它们每一种都有其弊病。第三种宗教的坏处是如此的明显，以至于再去证明其缺陷根本就是浪费时间。任何破坏社会统一的东西都是没有价值的，任何体制如果使人民处于自我矛盾之中也毫无价值。

第二种宗教的好处在于它把对于神的崇拜和对法律的热爱结合到了一起，在于它通过把祖国变成公民崇拜的对象，教导公民为国家服务就是为保护他们的神灵服务。这是一种神权政治，除了统治者之外没有其他教主，除了行政官员之外没有其他牧师。所以为国捐躯就是殉教，违犯法律就是亵渎神灵，让一个犯罪的人接受公众的憎恨就是把他交给了神威的惩罚：让他受到谴责吧。

但是，由于这种宗教是建立在错误和谎言的基础上的，它欺骗人民，使人民轻信和迷信，它把对神灵的神圣崇拜埋没在无聊空洞的仪式中，这些都是它的缺点。它的坏处还在于，当它变得唯我独尊并且专横暴虐时，它会使整个民族都变得嗜杀且不宽容。这样，人们沉浸于虐杀和屠戮之中，他们会相信杀死那些不接

社会契约论
The Social Contract

受他们神的人是一种神圣的行为。这便会把这个民族和其他民族置于一种天然的战争状态中，这对于其他民族和这个民族都是极具破坏力的。

剩下要说的便是人的宗教或基督教了。这里所说的并不是今天的基督教，而是福音书的基督教，这两者是完全不同的。通过这一神圣的、崇高的、真正的宗教，人类作为同属于上帝的子民，彼此之间成为兄弟，人们所由此而聚合成的社会即使灭亡也不会解体。

然而，这种宗教不和政治体发生特别的联系，所以法律只能从自身寻求力量，而这种宗教不会为法律提供新的力量，于是，维持社会的一个重要纽带就很难起到什么作用了。更糟的是，它使公民淡然出世，因此远不是使公民心系国家，而是使公民远离国家，就像远离了俗世上的一切东西一样。由我看来，恐怕没有什么比这更背离社会精神了。

有人说由真正的基督徒所构成的社会能成为可以想象出来的最完美的社会。我在这种假说中看到的只是一个巨大的困难，那就是一个由真正基督徒构成的社会将不再是人的社会。

我甚至还要说，正因为它的完美，所以这一假想中的社会既不是最强大的，也不会长久。正因为它的完美，所以它缺乏凝聚力，正是它的完美产生了导致它毁灭的缺陷。

在这种社会里，每个人都会履行自己的义务，人民遵纪守法，统治者公正而节制，官员们诚实而廉洁，士兵们会英勇地蔑视死亡，在这里不会存在虚荣和奢侈。所有这一切都令人崇敬，但让我们接着往下看。

基督教是一种精神至上的宗教，关心的只是天国的事情，基督徒在这个世界上是不存在祖国的。他们的确在履行自己的义务，但他们在尽义务时对自己所作努力的成败漠不关心。如果他们对于自身没有什么可指责的，那么世界变得是好是坏都与他们无关。如果国家兴旺，他们几乎不敢享受公共的喜悦，害怕自己因国家的光荣而变得过分骄傲；如果国家没落了，他们还会祈祷上帝之手惩罚了他的子民。

第四卷
BOOK FOUR

这个假想社会要想获得和平，保持永久的和谐，所有公民都必须无一例外地成为同等好的基督徒。但如果公民中不幸出现了一个野心家，一个伪善的人，例如，一个卡提里那或克伦威尔，那么这个人就可以很容易利用他虔诚的同胞们，因为基督徒的仁爱思想不允许把别人想得太坏。当一个狡猾的人发现了某种欺骗同胞的办法，并且因此而取得了一部分公权力，他就会成为权力的化身，上帝的意愿是让他必须受到尊敬；当他大权独揽后，上帝又会让人们服从他；如果他滥用了这一权力呢？那他就会成为上帝借以惩罚自己子民的鞭子。基督徒在要不要驱逐这个篡权者的问题上也会犹豫不决，因为那需要扰乱公共的和平，使用暴力、流血，所有这些都是与基督温和的教义相违背的。毕竟，既然人世间是充满苦难的，一个人是自由人或者是奴隶又有什么区别呢？最重要的是升入天堂，而逆来顺受是升入天堂的一条重要途径。

如果一场与他国的战争爆发，公民们会心甘情愿地奔向战场，谁也不会想到逃跑。每个人都将履行自己的义务，但他们在履行这一义务时是没有任何夺取胜利的热情的；他们对死亡的认识要远远多于对战胜敌人的认识。对他们来说，是战胜者还是被征服者与他们没有任何关系，上帝不是比他们更知道他们需要什么吗？可以想象一下，一个骄横、充满激情且士气高昂的敌人会从这种斯多葛学派中获得怎样的好处。如果他们置于一场与心中充满了荣誉以及对祖国充满了热情的勇敢民族作战的战争中，想象基督徒共和国面对的敌人是斯巴达人或罗马人，虔诚的基督徒们在还没反应过来时就已经被击溃、被粉碎、被毁灭了，当然，他们或许也会由于敌人对他们的蔑视而得以保全性命。

我认为法比乌斯的士兵所发下的誓言是极好的，他们并不发誓是要战胜或战死，而是发誓要以征服者的身份凯旋，而他们也的确遵守了自己的诺言。基督徒们从来就不敢这样做，他们会感觉这是在试探上帝。

但是当我说到"基督徒共和国"时犯了一个错误：这两个词是互不相容的。基督教宣扬的是服从或奴役，其精神对暴政来说太有利了，这让暴政无法不对其加以利用。真正的基督徒就是用来做奴隶的，他们知道这一点，对此也毫不在乎，因为对他们来说，人短暂的生命几乎没有任何价值。

有人说，基督徒的军队是极好的军队。我否认这一点。请说这话的人举出一个这样的基督徒军队给我看看。就我个人而言，我不知道有这样的军队。有人可能会以十字军为例来反驳我，但这里我不为十字军的战斗力争辩，我只想指出他们远不是基督徒，而只是牧师的士兵和教会的公民；他们是为了精神上的家园而战，但这一家园却不知被教会采用什么方式变成了现世的家园了。严格地讲，十字军之战可被归入异教的主题之下，既然福音书并不是哪一国宗教，因此基督徒中任何圣战都是不可能的。

在异教徒的国王的统治下，基督徒士兵是英勇的。所有的基督徒作家都告诉我们这一点，我也相信他们。但是这些士兵只是为了与异教徒军队争夺荣誉，一旦国王也变成了基督徒，这种争夺就停止了。当十字架驱走了鹰饰，罗马人的所有活力都消失了。

但是，让我们先将政治的考虑放到一边，回到权力的问题上来，在这个重要问题上确立起我们的原则。如我已经说过的那样，社会契约赋予主权置于臣民之上的权力，但绝不能超出公共利益的范围【原注5】。臣民不应在信仰等观念上对主权者负责，除非这一观念对社会极其重要。对国家来说，当每个公民所信奉的宗教能使自己更热爱自己的责任时，这个宗教才是十分重要的。但是，除非是这种宗教的教义涉及道德风尚及自己对于他人的责任时，否则它与国家及成员都不相关。此外，每个人都可以拥有他选择的任何观点，这并不在主权者的管理范围之内，因为主权者是管不着另外一个世界的。只要臣民在今生是个好公民，他在来世的命运如何就与主权者没有任何关系了。

因此，可以有一个纯粹的对于社会信仰的公民宣言，宣言的条文可由主权者拟定。这不是严格的宗教教义，而是一种社会性的情感，如果没有这些，一个人就不能成为一个好公民，也无法做一个忠实的臣民【原注6】。尽管主权者不会强制任

第四卷
BOOK FOUR

何人去信仰这些条款，但可以驱逐任何不相信此信仰的人，驱逐他的理由并不是因为他的不虔诚，而是因为他反社会，因为他不能真诚地热爱法律和正义，不能在需要的时候为了责任而奉献生命。如果有人在公开场合承认那些条款，但在行动上却好像并不相信它们，那就应该将他处死，因为他犯了所有罪行的首恶：他在法律面前撒了谎。

公民宗教的教义应该简单、条款少，表达准确而不必解释或说明。一个强大的、睿智的、仁慈的和具有远见的万能上帝的存在；来世的生命；正直者的幸福；对邪恶之人的惩罚；社会契约和法律的神圣性——这些都是正面的教义。至于负面的教义，我把它归结为一点：不宽容。我们应该把不宽容从所有宗教教义中排除出去。

在我看来，那些把公民的不宽容和宗教的不宽容区别开来的看法是相当错误的。这两种不宽容是不可分割的。人们不可能与一个他们认为应该受到诅咒的人和平相处；爱这些人就是憎恨惩罚他们的上帝；一定要让他们迷途知返或是让他们深受折磨。不论在哪里，当宗教的不宽容为人接受，它就不能不产生某种社会上的结果[原注7]，而这种结果一旦产生，主权体就不再是主权体了，即使在世俗领域内也不是了。从那时起，教士就成为真正的主人，而国王只是他们的官员而已。

既然现在不存在，也不能再存在一个唯一的民族宗教，所以教义中不包括任何违背公民责任的内容，所有容忍了其他宗教存在的宗教也应该被其他宗教所容忍。但是如果任何人敢说"在教会之外不存在救赎"，他就应该被从国家中驱逐出去，除非国家是教会而国王是主教。这种教条只有在神权政府下才是好的，在任何其他政府中都是致命的。传说的亨利四世接受罗马宗教所依据的理由，本应使所有诚实的人都背离罗马宗教，更何况一个善于思考的君主呢。

【原注1】"Nonne ea quae possidet Chamos deus tuus, tibi jure debentur?"这是拉丁文圣经的原文。贾立埃神父将他译为："难道你们不相信你们有权拥有你们的神基抹所拥有的土地吗？"我不知道希伯来文原文的

社会契约论
The Social Contract

含义，但我在拉丁文圣经里发现耶弗塔正面承认了神基抹的权利，而法文圣文加上了原拉丁文中没有的"据你的说法"，这就弱化了原文的含义。

【原注2】非常明显，被称为"圣战"的弗凯亚人的战争并不是宗教战争，其目的是为了惩罚渎圣者，而不是征服非基督徒。

【原注3】应该注意到，把教士联合为一个群体，并不是像法国的集会那样形式很正式的集会，而只是通过教会的圣餐仪式。圣餐仪式和开除教籍仪式是教士们的社会契约，凭借这一契约，他们就总是人民和国王的主人。所有一起交流的教士都是同胞公民，哪怕他们来自地球的两极。这种发明是一大政治杰作。在异教的教士中不曾有过这样的事，因此也就从未组织过教士的群体。

【原注4】此外，请参看格劳秀斯于1643年4月11日写给他兄弟的信，从中我们可以看到这个博学之士对霍布斯的《公民论》赞成什么和谴责什么。事实上，他因为偏爱作者的优点而轻易原谅了书中坏的一部分，但并不是每一个人都如此宽容。

【原注5】阿冉松侯爵说："在共和国里，每个人在不伤害他人的情况下是可以拥有做任何事情的自由的。"这是永恒不变的做人底限，无法更确切地表达这句话了。尽管他的这部手稿不为人所尽知，但我不能否认我在援引手稿中内容时的愉快心情，以向这位杰出而又伟大的人表达我的敬意。他直至入阁后也一直保持着一颗真正公民的心灵，并且对于他国家的政府持有一种公正且有益的观点。

【原注6】恺撒在为卡提里那辩护时，曾试图确定灵魂不能长存的教条。卡图和西塞罗在反驳恺撒的时候没有将时间浪费在纠缠哲学问题上；他们只是指出恺撒在辩护时像是一个不良公民，正试图推行一个对国家有害的教义。事实上，元老院应该对此作出裁判，而不是一个神学问题。

【原注7】举例来说，婚姻就是一种公民的契约，会产生社会影响，没有这项契约，社会根本无以为继。让我们设想一下，某教士把订立婚姻的约定权力掌握在自己手中，在一切不宽容的宗教中，神职人员必定会争取这一权力。他就此在提高教会权威中也使君主的权威有名无实，一旦这一切成真，那么君主除了教士愿意留给他的臣民，便不再拥有其他臣民了。如果教士可以根据人们是否接受这样那样的教义、是否接受这样那样的规矩、对他是否虔诚来主宰着是否允许别人婚礼的进行，接下来的事就很明显了，因为如果教士谨慎行事并坚持到底，他最后会获得对以下事情的完全控制：继承、公职、公民等事务，甚至包括治理国家。因为这时国家只是由私生子组成了，再也无法维持下去，一切难道不是很清楚了吗？有人会说，对这种滥权可以申诉，可以对教士进行传唤、命令，甚至占领教会的财产。多么可怜的见解！教士只要稍有一点点常识——我就不说有一点点勇气了，他会任凭一切自然发展。他会平静地接受人民的控告，由他们去传唤、去命令和接管财产，他最终仍然会恢复他所有的一切的。在我看来，当一个人有把握获得一切时，放弃一部分并不是什么巨大的牺牲。

【译注1】指作为天主教首领的教皇。

第四卷
BOOK FOUR

【译注2】斯多葛学派是塞浦路斯岛人芝诺于公元前300年左右在雅典创立的学派。斯多葛派认为神性是世界的主宰,个人不过是神的整体中的一分子,强调顺从天命,安于自己在社会中所处的地位。这一派认为,国家不是人们的意志达成协议的结果,而是自然的创造物。

第九章
结语

一旦确定了政治权力的真正原则,并在这些原则的基础上建立了国家,剩下要做的就是考虑对外关系,包括国际公法、商业、战争法和征服权、公共法律、联盟、谈判、条约,等等。但是这一切对于我狭窄的视野来说确实是一个过于庞大的课题,我还是把视线放在我力所能及的范围之内吧。

第一巻
BOOK ONE

PREFATORY NOTE

This little treatise is extracted from a larger work undertaken at an earlier time without consideration of my capacity, and long since abandoned. Of the various fragments that might be selected from what was accomplished, the following is the most considerable, and appears to me the least unworthy of being offered to the public. The rest of the work is no longer in existence.

社会契约论
The Social Contract

I wish to enquire whether, taking men as they are and laws as they can be made, it is possible to establish some just and certain rule of administration in civil affairs. In this investigation I shall always strive to reconcile what right permits with what interest prescribes, so that justice and utility may not be severed.

I enter upon this enquiry without demonstrating the importance of my subject. I shall be asked whether I am a prince or a legislator that I write on politics. I reply that I am not; and that it is for this very reason that I write on politics. If I were a prince or a legislator, I should not waste my time in saying what ought to be done; I should do it or remain silent.

Having been born a citizen of a free state, and a member of the sovereign body, however feeble an influence my voice may have in public affairs, the right to vote upon them is sufficient to impose on me the duty of informing myself about them; and I feel happy, whenever I meditate on governments, always to discover in my researches new reasons for loving that of my own country.

BOOK ONE

With regard to the right of conquest it has no other foundation than the law of the stronger. If war does not confer on the victor the right of slaying the vanquished, this right, which he does not possess, cannot be the foundation of a right to enslave them. If we have a right to slay an enemy only when it is impossible to enslave him, the right to enslave him is not derived from the right to kill him, it is, therefore, an iniquitous bargain to make him purchase his life, over which the victor has no right, at the cost of his liberty. In establishing the right of life and death upon the right of slavery, and the right of slavery upon the right of life and death, is it not manifest that one falls into a vicious circle?

Jean-Jacques Rousseau

BOOK ONE
第一卷

CHAPTER 1
Subject of the First Book

Man is born free, and everywhere he is in chains. Many a one believes himself the master of others, and yet he is a greater slave than they. How has this change come about? I do not know. What can render it legitimate? I believe that I can settle this question.

If I considered only force and the results that proceed from it, I should say that so long as a people is compelled to obey and does obey, it does well; but that, so soon as it can shake off the yoke and does shake it off, it does better; for, if men recover their freedom by virtue of the same right by which it was taken away, either they are justified in resuming it, or there was no justification for depriving them of it. But the social order is a sacred right which serves as a foundation for all others. This right, however, does not come from nature. It is therefore based on conventions. The question is to know what these conventions are. Before coming to that, I must establish what I have just laid down.

CHAPTER 2
Primitive Societies

The earliest of all societies, and the only natural one, is the family;yet children remain attached to their father only so long as they have need of him for their own preservation. As soon as this need ceases, the natural bond is dissolved. The children being freed from the obedience which they owed to their father, and the father from the cares which he owed to his children, become equally independent. If they remain united, it is no longer naturally but voluntarily; and the family itself is kept together only by convention.

This common liberty is a consequence of man's nature. His first law is to attend to his own preservation, his first cares are those which he owes to himself; and as soon as he comes to years of discretion, being sole judge of the means adapted for his own preservation, he becomes his own master.

The family is, then, if you will, the primitive model of political societies; the chief is the analogue of the father, while the people represent the children; and all, being born free and equal, alienate their liberty only for their own advantage. The whole difference is that, in the family, the father's love for his children repays him for the care that he bestow upon them; while, in the state, the pleasure of ruling makes up for the chief's lack of love for his people.

Grotius denies that all human authority is established for the benefit of the governed, and he cites slavery as an instance. His invariable mode of reasoning is to establish right by fact. ①A juster method might be employed, but none more favourable to tyrants.

It is doubtful, then, according to Grotius, whether the human race belongs to a hundred men, or whether these hundred men belong to the human race; and he appears throughout his book to incline to the former opinion, which is also that of Hobbes. In this way we have mankind divided like herds of cattle, each of which has a master, who looks after it in order to devour it.

Just as a herdsman is superior in nature to his herd, so chiefs, who are the herdsmen of men, are superior in nature to their people. Thus, according to Philo's account, the Emperor Caligula reasoned, inferring truly enough from this analogy that kings are gods, or that men are brutes.

The reasoning of Caligula is tantamount to that of Hobbes and Grotius. Aristotle, before them all, had likewise said that men are not naturally equal, but that some are born for slavery and others for dominion.

Aristotle was right but he mistook the effect for the cause. Every man born in slavery is born for slavery; nothing is more certain. Slaves lose everything in their bonds, even the desire to escape from them; they love their servitude as the companions of Ulysses loved their brutishness. ②If, then, there are slaves by nature, it is because there have been slaves contrary to nature. The first slaves were made such by force; their cowardice kept them in bondage.

I have said nothing about King Adam nor about Emperor Noah, the father of three great monarchs who shared the universe, like the children of Saturn with whom they are supposed to be identical. I hope that my moderation will give satisfaction; for, as I am a direct descendant of one of these princes, and perhaps of the eldest branch, how do I know whether, by examination of titles, I might not find myself the lawful king of the human race? Be that as it may, it cannot be denied that Adam was sovereign of the world, as Robinson was of his island, so long as he was its sole inhabitant; and it was an agreeable feature of that empire that the monarch, secure on his throne, had nothing to fear from rebellions, or wars, or conspirators.

> ①Learned researches in public law are often nothing but the history of ancient abuses; and to devote much labour to studying them is misplaced pertinacity'(Treatise on the Interests of France in Relation to her Neighbours, by the Marquis d'Argenson). That is exactly what Grotius did.
> ②See a small treatise by Plutarch, entitled That Brutes Employ Reason.

CHAPTER 3
The Right of the Strongest

The strongest man is never strong enough to be always master, unless he transforms his power into right, and obedience into duty. Hence the right of the strongest —a right apparently assumed in irony, and really established in principle. But will this phrase never be explained to us? Force is a physical power; I do not see what morality can result from its effects. To yield to force is an act of necessity, not of will; it is at most an act of prudence. In what sense can it be a duty?

Let us assume for a moment this pretended right. I say that nothing results from it but inexplicable nonsense; for if force constitutes right, the effect changes with the cause, and any force which overcomes the first succeeds to its rights. As soon as men can disobey with impunity, they may do so legitimately; and since the strongest is always in the right, the only thing is to act in such a way that one may be the strongest. But what sort of a right is it that perishes when force ceases? If it is necessary to obey by compulsion, there is no need to obey from duty; and if men are no longer forced to obey, obligation is at an end. We see, then, that this word right adds nothing to force; it here means nothing at all.

Obey the powers that be. If that means, yield to force, the precept is good but superfluous; I reply that it will never be violated. All power comes from God, I admit; but every disease comes from him too; does it follow that we are prohibited from calling in a physician? If a brigand should surprise me in the recesses of a wood, am I bound not only to give up my purse when forced, but am I also morally bound to do so when I might conceal it? For, in effect, the pistol which he holds is a superior force.

Let us agree, then, that might does not make right, and that we are bound to obey none but lawful authorities. Thus my original question ever recurs.

CHAPTER 4
Slavery

Since no man has any natural authority over his fellow men, and since force is not the source of right, conventions remain as the basis of all lawful authority among men.

If an individual, says Grotius, can alienate his liberty and become the slave of a master, why should not a whole people be able to alienate theirs, and become subject to a king? In this there are many equivocal terms requiring explanation; but let us confine ourselves to the word alienate. To alienate is to give or sell. Now, a man who becomes another's slave does not give himself; he sells himself at the very least for his subsistence. But why does a nation sell itself? So far from a king supplying his subjects with their subsistence, he draws his from them; and, according to Rabelais, a king does not live on a little. Do subjects, then, give up their persons on condition that their property also shall be taken? I do not see what is left for them to keep.

It will be said that the despot secures to his subjects civil peace. Be it so; but what do they gain by that, if the wars which his ambition brings upon them, together with his insatiable greed and the vexations of his administration, harass them more than their own dissensions would? What do they gain by it if this tranquillity is itself one of their miseries? Men live tranquilly also in dungeons; is that enough to make them contented there? The Greeks confined in the cave of the Cyclops lived 'peacefully until their turn came to be devoured.

To say that a man gives himself for nothing is to say what is absurd and inconceivable; such an act is illegitimate and invalid, for the simple reason that he who performs it is not in his right mind. To say the same thing of a whole nation is to suppose a nation of fools; and madness does not confer rights.

Even if each person could alienate himself, he could not alienate his children; they are born free men; their liberty belongs to them, and no one has a right to dispose of it except themselves. Before they have come to years of discretion, the father can, in their name, stipulate conditions for their preservation and welfare, but not surrender them irrevocably and unconditionally; for such a gift is contrary to the ends of nature, and exceeds the rights of paternity. In order, then, that an arbitrary government might be legitimate, it would be necessary that the people in each generation should have the option of accepting or rejecting it; but in that case such a government would no longer be arbitrary.

To renounce one's liberty is to renounce one's quality as a man, the rights and also the duties of humanity. For him who renounces everything there is no possible compensation. Such a renunciation is incompatible with man's nature, for to take away all freedom from his will is to take away all morality from his actions. In short, a convention which stipulates absolute authority on the one side and unlimited obedience on the other is vain and contradictory. Is it not clear that we are under no obligations whatsoever towards a man from whom we have a right to demand everything? And does not this single condition, without equivalent, without exchange, involve the nullity of the act? For what right would my slave have against me since all that he has belongs to me? His rights being mine, this right of me against myself is a meaningless phrase.

第一卷
BOOK ONE

Grotius and others derive from war another origin for the pretended right of slavery. The victor having, according to them, the right of slaying the vanquished, the latter may purchase his life at the cost of his freedom; an agreement so much the more legitimate that it turns to the advantage of both.

But it is manifest that this pretended right of slaying the vanquished in no way results from the state of war. Men are not naturally enemies, if only for the reason that, living in their primitive independence, they have no mutual relations sufficiently durable to constitute a state of peace or a state of war. It is the relation of things and not of men which constitutes war; and since the state of war cannot arise from simple personal relations, but only from real relations, private war, or war between man and man cannot exist either in the state of nature, where there is no settled ownership, or in the social state, where everything is under the authority of the laws.

Private combats, duels, and encounters are acts which do not constitute a state of war; and with regard to the private wars authorised by the Establishments of Louis IX, king of France, and suspended by the Peace of God, they were abuses of the feudal government, an absurd system if ever there was one, contrary both to the principles of natural right and to all sound government.

War, then, is not a relation between man and man, but a relation between state and state, in which individuals are enemies only by accident, not as men, nor even as citizens,[①] but as soldiers; not as members of the fatherland, but as its defenders. In short, each state can have as enemies only other states and not individual men, inasmuch as it is impossible to fix any true relation between things of different kinds.

This principle is also conformable to the established maxims of all ages and to the invariable practice of all civilised nations. Declarations of war are not so much warnings to the powers as to their subjects. The foreigner, whether king, or nation, or private person, that robs, slays, or detains subjects without declaring war against the government, is not an enemy, but a brigand. Even in open war, a just prince, while he rightly takes possession of all that belongs to the state in an enemy's country, respects the person and

143

property of individuals; he respects the rights on which his own are based. The aim of war being the destruction of the hostile state, we have a right to slay its defenders so long as they have arms in their hands; but as soon as they lay them down and surrender, ceasing to be enemies or instruments of the enemy, they become again simply men, and no one has any further right over their lives. Sometimes it is possible to destroy the state without killing a single one of its members; but war confers no right except what is necessary to its end. These are not the principles of Grotius; they are not based on the authority of poets, but are derived from the nature of things, and are founded on reason.

With regard to the right of conquest, it has no other foundation than the law of the strongest. If war does not confer on the victor the right of slaying the vanquished, this right, which he does not possess, cannot be the foundation of a right to enslave them. If we have a right to slay an enemy only when it is impossible to enslave him, the right to enslave him is not derived from the right to kill him; it is, therefore, an iniquitous bargain to make him purchase his life, over which the victor has no right, at the cost of his liberty. In establishing the right of life and death upon the right of slavery, and the right of slavery upon the right of life and death, is it not manifest that one falls into a vicious circle?

Even if we grant this terrible right of killing everybody, I say that a slave made in war, or a conquered nation, is under no obligation at all to a master, except to obey him so far as compelled. In taking an equivalent for his life the victor has conferred no favour on the slave; instead of killing him unprofitably, he has destroyed him for his own advantage. Far, then, from having acquired over him any authority in addition to that of force, the state of war subsists between them as before, their relation even is the effect of it; and the exercise of the rights of war supposes that there is no treaty of peace. They have made a convention. Be it so; but this convention, far from terminating the state of war, supposes its continuance.

Thus, in whatever way we regard things, the right of slavery is invalid, not only because it is illegitimate, but because it is absurd and meaningless. These terms, slavery and right, are contradictory and mutually exclusive. Whether addressed by a man to a

BOOK ONE

man, or by a man to a nation, such a speech as this will always be equally foolish: 'I make an agreement with you wholly at your expense and wholly for my benefit, and I shall observe it as long as I please, while you also shall observe it as long as I please.'

> [1] The Romans, who understood and respected the rights of war better than any nation in the world, carried their scruples so far in this respect that no citizen was allowed to serve as a volunteer without enlisting expressly against the enemy, and by name against a certain enemy. A legion in which Cato the younger made his first campaign under Popilius having been re-formed, Cato the elder wrote to Popilius that, if he consented to his son's continuing to serve under him, it was necessary that he should take a new military oath, because, the first being annulled, he could no longer bear arms against the enemy (Cicero, De Officiis i, 11). And Cato also wrote to his son to abstain from appearing in battle until he had taken this new oath. I know that it will be possible to urge against me the siege of Clusium and other particular cases; but I cite laws and customs (Livy, v, 35-37). No nation has transgressed its laws less frequently than the Romans and no nation has had laws so admirable.

CHAPTER 5
That It Is Always Necessary to Go Back to a First Convention

If I should concede all that I have so far refuted, those who favour despotism would be no farther advanced. There will always be a great difference between subduing a multitude and ruling a society. When isolated men, however numerous they may be, are subjected one after another to a single person, this seems to me only a case of master and slaves, not of a nation and its chief; they form, if you will, an aggregation, but not an association, for they have neither public property nor a body politic. Such a man, had he enslaved half the world, is never anything but an individual; his interest, separated from that of the rest, is never anything but a private interest, If he dies, his empire after him is left disconnected and disunited, as an oak dissolves and becomes a heap of ashes after the fire has consumed it.

A nation, says Grotius, can give itself to a king. According to Grotius, then, a nation is a nation before it gives itself to a king. This gift itself is a civil act, and presupposes a public resolution. Consequently, before examining the act by which a nation elects a king, it would be proper to examine the act by which a nation becomes a nation; for this act, being necessarily anterior to the other, is the real foundation of the society.

In fact, if there were no anterior convention, where, unless the election were unanimous, would be the obligation upon the minority to submit to the decision of the majority? And whence do the hundred who desire a master derive the right to vote on behalf of ten who do not desire one? The law of the plurality of votes is itself established by convention, and presupposes unanimity once at least.

CHAPTER 6
The Social Pact

I assume that men have reached a point at which the obstacles that endanger their preservation in the state of nature overcome, by their resistance, the forces which each individual can exert with a view to maintaining himself in that state. Then this primitive condition can no longer subsist, and the human race would perish unless it changed its mode of existence.

Now, as men cannot create any new forces, but only combine and direct those that exist, they have no other means of self-preservation than to form by aggregation a sum of forces which may overcome the resistance, to put them in action by a single motive power, and to make them work in concert.

This sum of forces can be produced only by the combination of many; but the strength and freedom of each man being the chief instruments of his preservation, how can he pledge them without injuring himself, and without neglecting the cares which he owes to himself? This difficulty, applied to my subject, may be expressed in these terms:

"To find a form of association which may defend and protect with the whole force of the community the person and property of every associate, and by means of which each, coalescing with all, may nevertheless obey only himself, and remain as free as before." Such is the fundamental problem of which the social contract furnishes the solution.

The clauses of this contract are so determined by the nature of the act that the slightest modification would render them vain and ineffectual; so that, although they have never perhaps been formally enunciated, they are everywhere the same, everywhere tacitly admitted and recognised, until, the social pact being violated, each man regains his original rights and recovers his natural liberty, whilst losing the conventional liberty for which he renounced it.

These clauses, rightly understood, are reducible to one only, viz. the total alienation to the whole community of each associate with all his rights; for, in the first place, since each gives himself up entirely, the conditions are equal for all; and, the conditions being equal for all, no one has any interest in making them burdensome to others.

Further, the alienation being made without reserve, the union is as perfect as it can be, and an individual associate can no longer claim anything; for, if any rights were left to individuals, since there would be no common superior who could judge between them and the public, each, being on some point his own judge, would soon claim to be so on all; the state of nature would still subsist, and the association would necessarily become tyrannical or useless.

In short, each giving himself to all, gives himself to nobody; and as there is not one associate over whom we do not acquire the same rights which we concede to him over ourselves, we gain the equivalent of all that we lose, and more power to preserve what we have.

If, then, we set aside what is not of the essence of the social contract, we shall find

社会契约论
The Social Contract

that it is reducible to the following terms: "Each of us puts in common his person and his whole power under the supreme direction of the general will; and in return we receive every member as an indivisible part of the whole."

Forthwith, instead of the individual personalities of all the contracting parties, this act of association produces a moral and collective body, which is composed of as many members as the assembly has voices, and which receives from this same act its unity, its common identity, its life, and its will. This public person, which is thus formed by the union of all the individual members, formerly took the name of city, ① and now takes that of republic or body politic, which is called by its members state when it is passive, sovereign when it is active, power when it is compared to similar bodies. With regard to the associates, they take collectively the name of people, and are called individually dozens, as participating in the sovereign power, and subjects, as subjected to the laws of the state. But these terms are often confused and are mistaken one for another; it is sufficient to know how to distinguish them when they are used with complete precision.

---

① The real meaning of this word has been almost completely effaced among the moderns; the majority take a town for a city, and a burgess for a citizen. They do not know that houses make the town, and that citizens make the city. This very mistake cost the Carthaginians dear. I have never read of the title citizens (cives) being given to the subjects of a prince, not even in ancient times to the Macedonians, nor, in our days, to the English, although nearer liberty than all the rest. The French alone employ familiarly this name citizen, because they have no true idea of it, as we can see from their dictionaries; but for this fact, they would, by assuming it, commit the crime of high treason. The name, among them, expresses a virtue, not a right. When Bodin wanted to give an account of our citizens and burgesses he made a gross blunder, mistaking the one for the other. M. d'Alembert has not erred in this, and, in his article Geneva, has clearly distinguished the four orders of men (even five, counting mere foreigners) which exist in our town, and of which two only compose the republic. No other French author that I know of has understood the real meaning of the word citizen.

CHAPTER 7
The Sovereign

We see from this formula that the act of association contains a reciprocal engagement between the public and individuals, and that every individual, contracting so to speak with himself, is engaged in a double relation, viz. as a member of the sovereign towards individuals, and as a member of the state towards the sovereign. But we cannot apply here the maxim of civil law that no one is bound by engagements made with himself; for there is a great difference between being bound to oneself and to a whole of which one forms part.

We must further observe that the public resolution which can bind all subjects to the sovereign in consequence of the two different relations under which each of them is regarded cannot, for a contrary reason, bind the sovereign to itself; and that accordingly it is contrary to the nature of the body politic for the sovereign to impose on itself a law which it cannot transgress. As it can only be considered under one and the same relation, it is in the position of an individual contracting with himself; whence we see that there is not, nor can be, any kind of fundamental law binding upon the body of the people, not even the social contract. This does not imply that such a body cannot perfectly well enter into engagements with others in what does not derogate from this contract; for, with regard to foreigners, it becomes a simple being, an individual.

But the body politic or sovereign, deriving its existence only from the sanctity of the contract, can never bind itself, even to others, in anything that derogates from the original act, such as alienation of some portion of itself, or submission to another sovereign. To violate the act by which it exists would be to annihilate itself; and what is nothing produces nothing.

So soon as the multitude is thus united in one body, it is impossible to injure one of the members without attacking the body, still less to injure the body without the members feeling the effects. Thus duty and interest alike oblige the two contracting parties to give mutual assistance; and the men themselves should seek to combine in this twofold relationship all the advantages which are attendant on it.

Now, the sovereign, being formed only of the individuals that compose it, neither has nor can have any interest contrary to theirs; consequently the sovereign power needs no guarantee towards its subjects, because it is impossible that the body should wish to injure all its members; and we shall see hereafter that it can injure no one as an individual. The sovereign, for the simple reason that it is so, is always everything that it ought to be.

But this is not the case as regards the relation of subjects to the sovereign, which, notwithstanding the common interest, would have no security for the performance of their engagements, unless it found means to ensure their fidelity.

Indeed, every individual may, as a man, have a particular will contrary to, or divergent from, the general will which he has as a citizen; his private interest may prompt him quite differently from the common interest; his absolute and naturally independent existence may make him regard what he owes to the common cause as a gratuitous contribution, the loss of which will be less harmful to others than the payment of it will be burdensome to him; and, regarding the moral person that constitutes the state as an imaginary being because it is not a man, he would be willing to enjoy the rights of a citizen without being willing to fulfil the duties of a subject. The progress of such injustice would bring about the ruin of the body politic.

In order, then, that the social pact may not be a vain formulary, it tacitly includes this engagement, which can alone give force to the others, that whoever refuses to obey the general will shall be constrained to do so by the whole body; which means nothing else than that he shall be forced to be free; for such is the condition which, uniting every citizen to his native land, guarantees him from all personal dependence, a condition that ensures the control and working of the political machine, and alone renders legitimate civil engagements, which, without it, would be absurd and tyrannical, and subject to the most enormous abuses.

CHAPTER 8
The Civil State

The passage from the state of nature to the civil state produces in man a very remarkable change, by substituting in his conduct justice for instinct, and by giving his actions the moral quality that they previously lacked. It is only when the voice of duty succeeds physical impulse, and law succeeds appetite, that man, who till then had regarded only himself, sees that he is obliged to act on other principles, and to consult his reason before listening to his inclinations. Although, in this state, he is deprived of many advantages that he derives from nature, he acquires equally great ones in return; his faculties are exercised and developed; his ideas are expanded; his feelings are ennobled; his whole soul is exalted to such a degree that, if the abuses of this new condition did not often degrade him below that from which he has emerged, he ought to bless without ceasing the happy moment that released him from it for ever, and transformed him from a stupid and ignorant animal into an intelligent being and a man.

Let us reduce this whole balance to terms easy to compare. What man loses by the social contract is his natural liberty and an unlimited right to anything which tempts him and which he is able to attain; what he gains is civil liberty and property in all that he possesses. In order that we may not be mistaken about these compensations, we must clearly distinguish natural liberty, which is limited only by the powers of the individual, from civil liberty, which is limited by the general will; and possession, which is nothing but the result of force or the right of first occupancy, from property, which can be based only on a positive tide.

Besides the preceding, we might add to the acquisitions of the civil state moral freedom, which alone renders man truly master of himself; for the impulse of mere appetite is slavery, while obedience to a self-prescribed law is liberty. But I have already said too much on this head, and the philosophical meaning of the term liberty does not belong to my present subject.

CHAPTER 9
Real Property

Every member of the community at the moment of its formation gives himself up to it, just as he actually is, himself and all his powers, of which the property that he possesses forms part. By this act, possession does not change its nature when it changes hands, and become property in those of the sovereign; but, as the powers of the state (cite) are incomparably greater than those of an individual, public possession is also, in fact, more secure and more irrevocable, without being more legitimate, at least in respect of foreigners; for the state, with regard to its members, is owner of all their property by the social contract, which, in the state, serves as the basis of all rights; but with regard to other powers, it is owner only by the right of first occupancy which it derives from individuals.

The right of first occupancy, although more real than that of the strongest, becomes a true right only after the establishment of that of property. Every man has by nature a right to all that is necessary to him; but the positive act which makes him proprietor of certain property excludes him from all the residue. His portion having been allotted, he ought to confine himself to it, and he has no further right to the undivided property. That is why the right of first occupancy, so weak in the state of nature, is respected by every member of a state. In this right men regard not so much what belongs to others as what does not belong to themselves.

In order to legalise the right of first occupancy over any domain whatsoever, the following conditions are, in general, necessary: first, the land must not yet be inhabited by anyone; secondly, a man must occupy only the area required for his subsistence; thirdly, he must take possession of it, not by an empty ceremony, but by labour and cultivation, the only mark of ownership which, in default of legal title, ought to be respected by others.

Indeed, if we accord the right of first occupancy to necessity and labour, do we not extend it as far as it can go? Is it impossible to assign limits to this light? Will the mere setting foot on common ground be sufficient to give an immediate claim to the ownership of it? Will the power of driving away other men from it for a moment suffice to deprive them for ever of the right of returning to it? How can a man or a people take possession of an immense territory and rob the whole human race of it except by a punishable usurpation, since other men are deprived of the place of residence and the sustenance which nature gives to them in common? When Nunez Balbao on the sea-shore took possession of the Pacific Ocean and of the whole of South America in the name of the crown of Castille, was this sufficient to dispossess all the inhabitants, and exclude from it all the princes in the world? On this supposition, such ceremonies might have been multiplied vainly enough; and the Catholic king in his cabinet might, by a single stroke, have taken possession of the whole world, only cutting off afterwards from his empire what was previously occupied by other princes.

We perceive how the lands of individuals, united and contiguous, become public territory, and how the right of sovereignty, extending itself from the subjects to the land which they occupy, becomes at once real and personal; which places the possessors in greater dependence, and makes their own powers a guarantee for their fidelity an advantage which ancient monarchs do not appear to have clearly perceived, for, calling themselves only kings of the Persians or Scythians or Macedonians, they seem to have regarded themselves as chiefs of men rather than as owners of countries. Monarchs of today call themselves more cleverly kings of France, Spain, England, etc.; in thus holding the land they are quite sure of holding its inhabitants.

The peculiarity of this alienation is that the community, in receiving the property of individuals, so far from robbing them of it, only assures them lawful possession, and changes usurpation into true right, enjoyment into ownership. Also, the possessors being considered as depositaries of the public property, and their rights being respected by all the members of the state, as well as maintained by all its power against foreigners, they have, as it were, by a transfer advantageous to the public and still more to themselves, acquired all that they have given up a paradox which is easily explained by distinguishing between the rights which the sovereign and the proprietor have over the same property, as we shall see hereafter.

It may also happen that men begin to unite before they possess anything, and that afterwards occupying territory sufficient for all, they enjoy it in common, or share it among themselves, either equally or in proportions fixed by the sovereign: In whatever way this acquisition is made, the right which every individual has over his own property is always subordinate to the right which the community has over all; otherwise there would be no stability in the social union, and no real force in the exercise of sovereignty.

I shall close this chapter and this book with a remark which ought to serve as a basis for the whole social system; it is that instead of destroying natural equality, the fundamental pact, on the contrary, substitutes a moral and lawful equality for the physical inequality which nature imposed upon men, so that, although unequal in strength or intellect, they all become equal by convention and legal right.[①]

BOOK ONE

① Under bad governments this equality is only apparent and illusory; it serves only to keep the poor in their misery and the rich in their usurpations. In fact, laws are always useful to those who possess and injurious to those that have nothing; whence it follows that the social state is advantageous to men only so far as they all have something, and none of them has too much.

BOOK TWO

With regard to the right of conquest, it has no other foundation than the law of the strongest. If war does not confer on the victor the right of slaying the vanquished, this right, which he does not possess, cannot be the foundation of a right to enslave them. If we have a right to slay an enemy only when it is impossible to enslave him, the right to enslave him is not derived from the right to kill him; it is, therefore, an iniquitous bargain to make him purchase his life, over which the victor has no right, at the cost of his liberty. In establishing the right of life and death upon the right of slavery, and the right of slavery upon the right of life and death, is it not manifest that one falls into a vicious circle?

Jean-Jacques Rousseau

BOOK TWO

CHAPTER 1
That Sovereignty is Inalienable

The first and most important consequence of the principles above established is that the general will alone can direct the forces of the state according to the object of its institution, which is the common good; for if the opposition of private interests has rendered necessary the establishment of societies, the agreement of these same interests has rendered it possible. That which is common to these different interests forms the social bond; and unless there were some point in which all interests agree, no society could exist. Now, it is solely with regard to this common interest that the society should be governed.

I say, then, that sovereignty, being nothing but the exercise of the general will, can never be alienated, and that the sovereign power, which is only a collective being, can be represented by itself alone; power indeed can be transmitted, but not will.

In fact, if it is not impossible that a particular will should agree on some point with the general will, it is at least impossible that this agreement should be lasting and constant; for the particular will naturally tends to preferences, and the general will to equality. It is still more impossible to have a security for this agreement; even though it should always exist, it would not be a result of art, but of chance. The sovereign may indeed say: 'I will now what a certain man wills, or at least what he says that he wills'; but he cannot say: 'What that man wills tomorrow, I shall also will', since it is absurd that the will should bind itself as regards the future, and since it is not incumbent on any will to consent to anything contrary to the welfare of the being that wills. If, then, the nation simply promises to obey, it dissolves itself by that act and loses its character as a people; the moment there is a master, there is no longer a sovereign, and forthwith the body politic is destroyed.

This does not imply that the orders of the chiefs cannot pass for decisions of the general will, so long as the sovereign, free to oppose them, refrains from doing so. In such a case the consent of the people should be inferred from the universal silence. This will be explained at greater length.

CHAPTER 2
That Sovereignty is Indivisible

For the same reason that sovereignty is inalienable it is indivisible; for the will is either general, ① or it is not; it is either that of the body of the people, or that of only a portion. In the first case, this declared will is an act of sovereignty and constitutes law; in the second case, it is only a particular will, or an act of magistracy it is at most a decree.

But our publicists, being unable to divide sovereignty in its principle, divide it in its object. They divide it into force and will, into legislative power and executive power; into rights of taxation, of justice, and of war; into internal administration and power of treating with foreigners sometimes confounding all these departments, and sometimes separating them. They make the sovereign a fantastic being, formed of connected parts; it is as if they composed a man of several bodies, one with eyes, another with arms, another with feet, and nothing else. The Japanese conjurers, it is said, cut up a child before the eyes of the spectators; then, throwing all its limbs into the air, they make the child come down again alive and whole. Such almost are the jugglers' tricks of our publicists; after dismembering the social body, by a deception worthy of the fair, they recombine its parts, nobody knows how.

This error arises from their not having formed exact notions about the sovereign authority, and from their taking as parts of this authority what are only emanations from it. Thus, for example, the acts of declaring war and making peace have been regarded as acts of sovereignty, which is not the case, since neither of them is a law, but only an application of the law, a particular act which determines the case of the law, as will be clearly seen when the idea attached to the word law is fixed. but only an application of the law, a particular act which determines the case of the law, as will be clearly seen when the idea attached to the word law is fixed.

By following out the other divisions in the same way, it would be found that, whenever the sovereignty appears divided, we are mistaken in our supposition; and that the rights which are taken as parts of that sovereignty are all subordinate to it, and always suppose supreme wills of which these rights are merely executive.

It would be impossible to describe the great obscurity in which this want of precision has involved the conclusions of writers on the subject of political right when they have endeavoured to decide upon the respective rights of kings and peoples on the principles that they had established. Everyone can see, in chapters III and IV of the first book of Grotius, how that learned man and his translator Barbeyrac become entangled and embarrassed in their sophisms, for fear of saying too much or not saying enough according to their views, and so offending the interests that they had to conciliate. Grotius, having taken refuge in France through discontent with his own country, and wishing to pay court to Louis XIII, to whom his book is dedicated, spares no pains to despoil the people of all their rights and, in the most artful manner, bestow them on kings. This also would clearly have been the inclination of Barbeyrac, who dedicated his translation to the king of England, George I. But unfortunately the expulsion of James II, which he calls an abdication, forced him to be reserved and to equivocate and evade, in order not to make William appear a usurper. If these two writers had adopted true principles, all difficulties would have been removed, and they would have been always consistent; but they would have spoken the truth with regret, and would have paid court only to the people. Truth, however, does not lead to fortune, and the people confer neither embassies, nor professorships, nor pensions.

① That a will may be general, it is not always necessary that it should be unanimous, but it is necessary that all votes should be counted; any formal exclusion destroys the generality.

CHAPTER 3
Whether the General Will Can Err

It follows from what precedes that the general will is always right and always tends to the public advantage; but it does not follow that the resolutions of the people have

BOOK TWO

always the same rectitude. Men always desire their own good, but do not always discern it; the people are never corrupted, though often deceived, and it is only then that they seem to will what is evil.

There is often a great deal of difference between the will of all and the general will; the latter regards only the common interest, while the former has regard to private interests, and is merely a sum of particular wills; but take away from these same wills the pluses and minuses which cancel one another, ① and the general will remains as the sum of the differences.

If the people came to a resolution when adequately informed and without any communication among the citizens, the general will would always result from the great number of slight differences, and the resolution would always be good. But when factions, partial associations, are formed to the detriment of the whole society, the will of each of these associations becomes general with reference to its members, and particular with reference to the state; it may then be said that there are no longer as many voters as there are men, but only as many voters as there are associations. The differences become less numerous and yield a less general result. Lastly, when one of these associations becomes so great that it predominates over all the rest, you no longer have as the result a sum of small differences, but a single difference; there is then no longer a general will, and the opinion which prevails is only a particular opinion.

It is important, then, in order to have a clear declaration of the general will, that there should be no partial association in the state, and that every citizen should express only his own opinion. ②Such was the unique and sublime institution of the great Lycurgus. But if there are partial associations, it is necessary to multiply their number and prevent inequality, as Solon, Numa, and Servius did. These are the only proper precautions for ensuring that the general will may always be enlightened, and that the people may not be deceived.

① "Every interest," says the Marquis d'Argenson, "has different principles. The accord of two particular interests is formed by opposition to that of a third." He might have added that the accord of all interests is formed by opposition to that of each. Unless there were different interests, the common interest would scarcely be felt and would never meet with any obstacle; everything would go of itself, and politics would cease to be an art.

②"It is true," says Machiavelli, "that some divisions injure the state, while some are beneficial to it; those are injurious to it which are accompanied by cabals and factions; those assist it which are maintained without cabals, without factions. Since, therefore, no founder of a state can provide against enmities in it, he ought at least to provide that there shall be no cabals." (History of Florence, Book VII)

CHAPTER 4
The Limits of the Sovereign Power

If the state or city is nothing but a moral person, the life of which consists in the union of its members, and if the most important of its cares is that of self-preservation, it needs a universal and compulsive force to move and dispose every part in the manner most expedient for the whole. As nature gives every man an absolute power over all his limbs, the social pact gives the body politic an absolute power over all its members; and it is this same power which, when directed by the general will, bears, as I said, the name of sovereignty.

But besides the public person, we have to consider the private persons who compose it, and whose life and liberty are naturally independent of it. The question, then, is to distinguish clearly between the respective rights of the citizens and of the sovereign, ① as well as between the duties which the former have to fulfil in their capacity as subjects and the natural rights which they ought to enjoy in their character as men.

It is admitted that whatever part of his power, property, and liberty each one alienates by the social compact is only that part of the whole of which the use is important to the community, but we must also admit that the sovereign alone is judge of what is important.

All the services that a citizen can render to the state he owes to it as soon as the sovereign demands them; but the sovereign, on its part, cannot impose on its subjects any burden which is useless to the community; it cannot even wish to do so, for, by the law of reason, just as by the law of nature, nothing is done without a cause.

The engagements which bind us to the social body are obligatory only because they are mutual; and their nature is such that in fulfilling them we cannot work for others without also working for ourselves. Why is the general will always right, and why do all invariably desire the prosperity of each, unless it is because there is no one but appropriates to himself this word each and thinks of himself in voting on behalf of all? This proves that equality of rights and the notion of justice that it produces are derived from the preference which each gives to himself, and consequently from man's nature; that the general will, to be truly such, should be so in its object as well as in its essence; that it ought to proceed from all in order to be applicable to all; and that it loses its natural rectitude when it tends to some individual and determinate object, because in that case, judging of what is unknown to us, we have no true principle of equity to guide us.

Indeed, so soon as a particular fact or right is in question with regard to a point which has not been regulated by an anterior general convention, the matter becomes contentious; it is a process in which the private persons interested are one of the parties and the public the other, but in which I perceive neither the law which must be followed, nor the judge who should decide. It would be ridiculous in such a case to wish to refer the matter for an express decision of the general will, which can be nothing but the decision of one of the parties, and which, consequently, is for the other party only a will that is foreign, partial, and inclined on such an occasion to injustice as well as liable to error. Therefore, just as a particular will cannot represent the general will, the general will in turn changes its nature when it has a particular end, arid cannot, as general, decide about either a person or a fact. When the people of Athens, for instance, elected or deposed their chiefs, decreed honours to one, imposed penalties on another, and by multitudes of particular decrees exercised indiscriminately all the functions of government, the people no longer had any general will properly so called; they no longer acted as a sovereign power, but as magistrates. This will appear contrary to common ideas, but I must be allowed time to expound my own.

From this we must understand that what generalises the will is not so much the number of voices as the common interest which unites them; for, under this system, each necessarily submits to the conditions which he imposes on others an admirable union of interest and justice, which gives to the deliberations of the community a spirit of equity that seems to disappear in the discussion of any private affair, for want of a common interest to unite and identify the ruling principle of the judge with that of the party.

By whatever path we return to our principle we always arrive at the same conclusion, viz. that the social compact establishes among the citizens such an equality that they all pledge themselves under the same conditions and ought all to enjoy the same rights. Thus, by the nature of the compact, every act of sovereignty, that is, every authentic act of the general will, binds or favours equally all the citizens; so that the sovereign knows only the body of the nation, and distinguishes none of those that compose it.

What, then, is an act of sovereignty properly so called? It is not an agreement between a superior and an inferior, but an agreement of the body with each of its members; a lawful agreement, because it has the social contract as its foundation; equitable, because it is common to all; useful, because it can have no other object than the general welfare; and stable, because it has the public force and the supreme power as a guarantee. So long as the subjects submit only to such conventions, they obey no one, but simply their own will; and to ask how far the respective rights of the sovereign and citizens extend is to ask up to what point the latter can make engagements among themselves, each with all and all with each.

BOOK TWO

Thus we see that the sovereign power, wholly absolute, wholly sacred, and wholly inviolable as it is, does not, and cannot, pass the limits of general conventions, and that every man can fully dispose of what is left to him of his property and liberty by these conventions; so that the sovereign never has a right to burden one subject more than another, because then the matter becomes particular and his power is no longer competent.

These distinctions once admitted, so untrue is it that in the social contract there is on the part of individuals any real renunciation, that their situation, as a result of this contract, is in reality preferable to what it was before, and that, instead of an alienation, they have only made an advantageous exchange of an uncertain and precarious mode of existence for a better and more assured one, of natural independence for liberty, of the power to injure others for their own safety, and of their strength, which others might overcome, for a right which the social union renders inviolable. Their lives, also, which they have devoted to the state, are continually protected by it; and in exposing their lives for its defence, what do they do but restore what they have received from it? What do they do but what they would do more frequently and with more risk in the state of nature, when, engaging in inevitable struggles, they would defend at the peril of their lives their means of preservation? All have to fight for their country in case of need, it is true; but then no one ever has to fight for himself Do we not gain, moreover, by incurring, for what ensures our safety, a part of the risks that we should have to incur for ourselves individually, as soon as we were deprived of it?

① Attentive readers, do not, I beg you, hastily charge me with contradiction here. I could not avoid it in terms owing to the poverty of the language, but wait.

社会契约论
The Social Contract

CHAPTER 5
The Right of Life and Death

It may be asked how individuals who have no right to dispose of their own lives can transmit to the sovereign that right which they do not possess. The question appears hard to solve only because it is badly stated. Every man has a right to risk his own life in order to preserve it. Has it ever been said that one who throws himself out of a window to escape from a fire is guilty of suicide? Has the crime, indeed, ever been imputed to a man who perishes in a storm, although, on embarking, he was not ignorant of the danger?

The social treaty has as its end the preservation of the contracting parties. He who desires the end desires also the means, and some risks, even some losses, are inseparable from these means. He who is willing to preserve his life at the expense of others ought also to give it up or them when necessary. Now, the citizen is not a judge of the peril to which the law requires that he should expose himself; and when the prince has said to him: "It is expedient for the state that you should die", he ought to die, since it is only on this condition that he has lived in security up to that time, and since his life is no longer merely a gift of nature, but a conditional gift of the state.

The penalty of death inflicted on criminals may be regarded almost from the same point of view; it is in order not to be the victim of an assassin that a man consents to die if he becomes one. In this treaty, far from disposing of his own life, he thinks only of securing it, and it is not supposed that any of the contracting parties contemplates at the time being hanged.

Moreover, every evil-doer who attacks social rights becomes by his crimes a rebel and a traitor to his country; by violating its laws he ceases to be a member of it, and even

第二卷
BOOK TWO

makes war upon it. Then the preservation of the state is incompatible with his own one of the two must perish; and when a guilty man is executed, it is less as a citizen than as an enemy. The proceedings and the judgment are the proofs and the declaration that he has broken the social treaty, and consequently that he is no longer a member of the state. Now, as he has acknowledged himself to be such, at least by his residence, he ought to be cut off from it by exile as a violator of the compact, or by death as a public enemy; for such an enemy is not a moral person, he is simply a man; and this is a case in which the right of war is to slay the vanquished.

But, it will be said, the condemnation of a criminal is a particular act. I admit it; but this condemnation does not belong to the sovereign; it is a right which that power can confer, though itself unable to exercise it. All my ideas are connected, but I could not expound them all at once.

Again, the frequency of capital punishments is always a sign of weakness or indolence in the government. There is no man so worthless that he cannot be made good for something. We have a right to kill, even for example's sake, only those who cannot be preserved without danger.

As regards the right to pardon or to exempt a guilty man from the penalty imposed by the law and inflicted by the judge, it belongs only to a power which is above both the judge and the law, that is to say, the sovereign; still its right in this is not very plain, and the occasions for exercising it are very rare. In a well-governed state there are few punishments, not because many pardons are granted, but because there are few criminals; the multitude of crimes ensures impunity when the state is decaying. Under the Roman Republic neither the Senate nor the consuls attempted to grant pardons; the people even did not grant any, although they sometimes revoked their own judgments. Frequent pardons proclaim that crimes will soon need them no longer, and everyone sees to what that leads. But I feel my heart murmuring and restraining my pen; let us leave these questions to be discussed by the just man who has not erred and who never needed pardon himself.

CHAPTER 6
The Law

By the social compact we have given existence and life to the body politic the question now is to endow it with movement and will by legislation. For the original act by which this body is formed and consolidated determines nothing in addition as to what it must do for its own preservation.

What is right and conformable to order is such by the nature of things, and independently of human conventions. All justice comes from God, he alone is the source of it; but could we receive it direct from so lofty a source, we should need neither government nor laws. Without doubt there is a universal justice emanating from reason alone; but this justice, in order to be admitted among us, should be reciprocal. Regarding things from a human standpoint, the laws of justice are inoperative among men for want of a natural sanction; they only bring good to the wicked and evil to the just when the latter observe them with everyone, and no one observes them in return. Conventions and laws, then, are necessary to couple rights with duties and apply justice to its object. In the state of nature, where everything is in common, I owe nothing to those to whom I have promised nothing; I recognise as belonging to others only what is useless to me. This is not the case in the civil state, in which all rights are determined by law.

But then, finally, what is a law? So long as men are content to attach to this word only metaphysical ideas, they will continue to argue without being understood; and when they have stated what a law of nature is, they will know no better what a law of the state is.

I have already said that there is no general will with reference to a particular object. In fact, this particular object is either in the state or outside of it. If it is outside the state, a will which is foreign to it is not general in relation to it; and if it is within the state, it forms part of it; then there is formed between the whole and its part a relation which makes of it two separate beings, of which the part is one, and the whole, less this same part, is the other. But the whole less one part is not the whole, and so long as the relation subsists, there is no longer any whole, but two unequal parts; whence it follows that the will of the one is no longer general in relation to the other.

But when the whole people decree concerning the whole people, they consider themselves alone; and if a relation is then constituted, it is between the whole object under one point of view and the whole object under another point of view, without any division at all. Then the matter respecting which they decree is general like the will that decrees. It is this act that I call a law.

When I say that the object of the laws is always general, I mean that the law considers subjects collectively, and actions as abstract, never a man as an individual nor a particular action. Thus the law may indeed decree that there shall be privileges, but cannot confer them on any person by name; the law can create several classes of citizens, and even assign the qualifications which shall entitle them to rank in these classes, but it cannot nominate such and such persons to be admitted to them; it can establish a royal government and a hereditary succession, but cannot elect a king or appoint a royal family; in a word, no function which has reference to an individual object appertains to the legislative power.

From this standpoint we see immediately that it is no longer necessary to ask whose office it is to make laws, since they are acts of the general will; nor whether the prince is above the laws, since he is a member of the state; nor whether the law can be unjust, since no one is unjust to himself; nor how we are free and yet subject to the laws, since the laws are only registers of our wills.

We see, further, that since the law combines the universality of the will with the universality of the object, whatever any man prescribes on his own authority is not a law; and whatever the sovereign itself prescribes respecting a particular object is not a law, but a decree, not an act of sovereignty, but of magistracy.

I therefore call any state a republic which is governed by laws, under whatever form of administration it may be; for then only does the public interest predominate and the commonwealth count for something. Every legitimate government is republican;① 1 will explain hereafter what government is.

Laws are properly only the conditions of civil association. The people, being subjected to the laws, should be the authors of them; it concerns only the associates to determine the conditions of association. But how will they be determined? Will it be by a common agreement, by a sudden inspiration? Has the body politic an organ for expressing its will? Who will give it the foresight necessary to frame its acts and publish them at the outset? Or how shall it declare them in the hour of need? How would a blind multitude, which often knows not what it wishes because it rarely knows what is good for it, execute of itself an enterprise so great, so difficult, as a system of legislation? Of themselves, the people always desire what is good, but do not always discern it. The general will is always right, but the judgment which guides it is not always enlightened. It must be made to see objects as they are, sometimes as they ought to appear; it must be shown the good path that it is seeking, and guarded from the seduction of private interests; it must be made to observe closely times and places, and to balance the attraction of immediate and palpable advantages against the danger of remote and concealed evils. Individuals see the good which they reject; the public desire the good which they do not see. All alike have need of guides. The former must be compelled to conform their wills to their reason; the people must be taught to know what they require. Then from the public enlightenment results the union of the understanding and the will in the social body; and from that the close co-operation of the parts, and, lastly, the maximum power of the whole. Hence arises the need of a legislator.

① I do not mean by this word an aristocracy or democracy only, but in general any government directed by the general will, which is the law. To be legitimate, the government must not be combined with the sovereign power, but must be its minister; then monarchy itself is a republic. This will be made clear in the next book.

CHAPTER 7
The Legislator

In order to discover the rules of association that are most suitable to nations, a superior intelligence would be necessary who could see all the passions of men without experiencing any of them; who would have no affinity with our nature and yet know it thoroughly; whose happiness would not depend on us, and who would nevertheless be quite willing to interest himself in ours; and, lastly, one who, storing up for himself with the progress of time a far-off glory in the future, could labour in one age and enjoy in another. ① Gods would be necessary to give laws to men.

The same argument that Caligula adduced as to fact, Plato put forward with regard to right, in order to give an idea of the civil or royal man whom he is in quest of in his work the Statesman. But if it is true that a great prince is a rare man, what will a great legislator be? The first has only to follow the model which the other has to frame. The latter is the mechanician who invents the machine, the former is only the workman who puts it in readiness and works it. "In the birth of societies," says Montesquieu, "it is the chiefs of the republics who frame the institutions, and afterwards .it is the institutions which mould the chiefs of the republics."

He who dares undertake to give institutions to a nation ought to feel himself capable, as it were, of changing human nature; of transforming every individual, who in himself is a complete and independent whole, into part of a greater whole from which he receives in some manner his life and his being; of altering man's constitution in order to strengthen it; of substituting a social and moral existence for the independent and physical existence which we have all received from nature. In a word, it is necessary to deprive man of his native powers in order to endow him with some which are alien to him, and of which he cannot make use without the aid of other people. The more thoroughly those natural powers are deadened and destroyed, the greater and more durable are the acquired powers, the more solid and perfect also are the institutions; so that if every citizen is nothing, and can be nothing, except in combination with all the rest, and if the force acquired by the whole be equal or superior to the sum of the natural forces of all the individuals, we may say that legislation is at the highest point of perfection which it can attain.

The legislator is in all respects an extraordinary man in the state. If he ought to be so by his genius, he is not less so by his office. It is not magistracy nor sovereignty. This office, which constitutes the republic, does not enter into its constitution; it is a special and superior office, having nothing in common with human government; for, if he who rules men ought not to control legislation, he who controls legislation ought not to rule men; otherwise his laws, being ministers of his passions, would often serve only to perpetuate his acts of injustice; he would never be able to prevent private interests from corrupting the sacredness of his work.

When Lycurgus gave laws to his country, he began by abdicating his royalty. It was the practice of the majority of the Greek towns to entrust to foreigners the framing of their laws. The modern republics of Italy often imitated this usage; that of Geneva did the same and found it advantageous.② Rome, at her most glorious epoch, saw all the crimes of tyranny spring up in her bosom, and saw herself on the verge of destruction, through uniting in the same hands legislative authority and sovereign power.

Yet the Decemvirs themselves never arrogated the right to pass any law on their sole authority. Nothing that we propose to you, they said to the people, can pass into law without your consent. Romans, be yourselves the authors of the laws which are to secure

BOOK TWO

your happiness.

He who frames laws, then, has, or ought to have, no legislative right, and the people themselves cannot, even if they wished, divest themselves of this incommunicable right, because, according to the fundamental compact, it is only the general will that binds individuals, and we can never be sure that a particular will is conformable to the general will until it has been submitted to the free votes of the people. I have said this already, but it is not useless to repeat it.

Thus we find simultaneously in the work of legislation two things that seem incompatible an enterprise surpassing human powers, and, to execute it, an authority that is a mere nothing.

Another difficulty deserves attention. Wise men who want to speak to the vulgar in their own language instead of in a popular way will not be understood. Now, there are a thousand kinds of ideas which it is impossible to translate into the language of the people. Views very general and objects very remote are alike beyond its reach; and each individual, approving of no other plan of government than that which promotes his own interests, does not readily perceive the benefits that he is to derive from the continual deprivations which good laws impose. In order that a newly formed nation might approve sound maxims of politics and observe the fundamental rules of state policy, it would be necessary that the effect should become the cause; that the social spirit, which should be the work of the institution, should preside over the institution itself, and that men should be, prior to the laws, what they ought to become by means of them. Since, then, the legislator cannot employ either force or reasoning, he must needs have recourse to an authority of a different order, which can compel without violence and persuade without convincing.

It is this which in all ages has constrained the founders of nations to resort to the intervention of heaven, and to give the gods the credit for their own wisdom, in order that the nations subjected to the laws of the state as to those of nature, and recognising the same power in the formation of man and in that of the state, might obey willingly, and

社会契约论
The Social Contract

bear submissively the yoke of the public welfare.

The legislator puts into the mouths of the immortals that sublime reason which soars beyond the reach of common men, in order that he may win over by divine authority those whom human prudence could not move. ③ But it does not belong to every man to make the gods his oracles, nor to be believed when he proclaims himself their interpreter. The great soul of the legislator is the real miracle which must give proof of his mission. Any man can engrave tables of stone, or bribe an oracle, or pretend secret intercourse with some divinity, or train a bird to speak in his ear, or find some other clumsy means to impose on the people. He who is acquainted with such means only will perchance be able to assemble a crowd of foolish persons; but he will never found an empire, and his extravagant work will speedily perish with him. Empty deceptions form but a transient bond; it is only wisdom that makes it lasting. The Jewish law, which still endures, and that of the child of Ishmael, which for ten centuries has ruled half the world, still bear witness today to the great men who dictated them; and whilst proud philosophy or blind party spirit sees in them nothing but fortunate impostors, the true statesman admires in their systems the great and powerful genius which directs durable institutions.

It is not necessary from all this to infer with Warburton that politics and religion have among us a common aim, but only that, in the origin of nations, one serves as an instrument of the other.

① A nation becomes famous only when its legislation is beginning to decline. We are ignorant during how many centuries the institutions of Lycurgus conferred happiness on the Spartans before they were known in the rest of Greece.

②Those who consider Calvin only as a theologian are but little acquainted with the extent of his genius. The preparation of our wise edicts, in which he had a large share, does him as much credit as his Institutes. Whatever revolution time may bring about in our religion, so long as love of country and of liberty is not extinct among us, the memory of that great man will not cease to be revered.

③ "It is true," says Machiavelli, "there never was in a nation any promulgator of extraordinary laws who had not recourse to God, because otherwise they would not have been accepted; for there are many advantages recognised by a wise man which are not so self-evident that they can convince others." (Discourses on Titus Livius, Book I, chapter 11.)

CHAPTER 8
The People

As an architect, before erecting a large edifice, examines and tests the soil in order to see whether it can support the weight, so a wise lawgiver does not begin by drawing up laws that are good in themselves, but considers first whether the people for whom he designs them are fit to endure them. It is on this account that Plato refused to legislate for the Arcadians and Cyrenians, knowing that these two peoples were rich and could not tolerate equality; and it is on this account that good laws and worthless men were to be found in Crete, for Minos had only disciplined a people steeped in vice.

A thousand nations that have flourished on the earth could never have borne good laws; and even those that might have done so could have succeeded for only a very short period of their whole duration. The majority of nations, as well as of men, are tractable only in their youth; they become incorrigible as they grow old. When once customs are established and prejudices have taken root, it is a perilous and futile enterprise to try and reform them; for the people cannot even endure that their evils should be touched with a view to their removal, like those stupid and cowardly patients that shudder at the sight of a physician.

But just as some diseases unhinge men's minds and deprive them of all remembrance of the past, so we sometimes find, during the existence of states, epochs of violence, in which revolutions produce an influence upon nations such as certain crises produce upon individuals, in which horror of the past supplies the place of forgetfulness, and in which the state, inflamed by civil wars, springs forth so to speak from its ashes, and regains the vigour of youth in issuing from the arms of death. Such was Sparta in the time of Lycurgus, such was Rome after the Tarquins, and such among us moderns were Holland and Switzerland after the expulsion of their tyrants.

But these events are rare; they are exceptions, the explanation of which is always found in the particular constitution of the excepted state. They could not even happen twice with the same nation; for it may render itself free so long as it is merely barbarous, but can no longer do so when the resources of the state are exhausted. Then commotions may destroy it without revolutions being able to restore it, and as soon as its chains are broken, it falls in pieces and ceases to exist; henceforward it requires a master and not a deliverer. Free nations, remember this maxim: "Liberty may be acquired but never recovered."

Youth is not infancy. There is for nations as for men a period of youth, or, if you will, of maturity, which they must await before they are subjected to laws; but it is not always easy to discern when a people is mature, and if the time is anticipated, the labour is abortive. One nation is governable from its origin, another is not so at the end of ten centuries. The Russians will never be really civilised, because they have been civilised too early. Peter had an imitative genius; he had not the true genius that creates and produces anything from nothing. Some of his measures were beneficial, but the majority were ill-timed. He saw that his people were barbarous, but he did not see that they were unripe for civilisation; he wished to civilise them, when it was necessary only to discipline them. He wished to produce at once Germans or Englishmen, when he should have begun by making Russians; he prevented his subjects from ever becoming what they might have been, by persuading them that they were what they were not. It is in this way that a French tutor trains his pupil to shine for a moment in childhood, and then to be for ever a nonentity. The Russian Empire will desire to subjugate Europe, and will itself be subjugated. The Tartars, its subjects or neighbours, will become its masters and ours. This revolution appears to me inevitable. All the kings of Europe are working in concert to accelerate it.

CHAPTER 9
The People(continued)

As nature has set limits to the stature of a properly formed man, outside which it produces only giants and dwarfs; so likewise, with regard to the best constitution of a state, there are limits to its possible extent so that it may be neither too great to enable it to be well governed, nor too small to enable it to maintain itself single-handed. There is in every body politic a maximum of force which it cannot exceed, and which is often diminished as the state is aggrandised. The more the social bond is extended, the more it is weakened; and, in general, a small state is proportionally stronger than a large one.

A thousand reasons demonstrate the truth of this maxim. In the first place, administration becomes more difficult at great distances, as a weight becomes heavier at the end of a longer lever. It also becomes more burdensome in proportion as its parts are multiplied; for every town has first its own administration, for which the people pay; every district has its administration, still paid for by the people; next, every province, then the superior governments, the satrapies, the vice-royalties, which must be paid for more dearly as we ascend, and always at the cost of the unfortunate people; lastly comes the supreme administration, which overwhelms everything. So many additional burdens perpetually exhaust the subjects; and far from being better governed by all these different orders, they are much worse governed than if they had but a single superior. Meanwhile, hardly any resources remain for cases of emergency; and when it is necessary to have recourse to them the state trembles on the brink of ruin.

Nor is this all; not only has the government less vigour and activity in enforcing observance of the laws, in putting a stop to vexations, in reforming abuses, and in forestalling seditious enterprises which may be entered upon in distant places; but the people have less affection for their chiefs whom they never see, for their country, which is in their eyes like the world, and for their fellow-citizens, most of whom are strangers to them. The same laws cannot be suitable to so many different provinces, which have different customs and different climates, and cannot tolerate the same form of government. Different laws beget only trouble and confusion among the nations which, living under the same chiefs and in constant communication, mingle or intermarry with one another, and, when subjected to other usages, never know whether their patrimony is really theirs. Talents are hidden, virtues ignored, vices unpunished, in that multitude of men, unknown to one another, whom the seat of the supreme administration gathers together in one place. The chiefs, overwhelmed with business, see nothing themselves; clerks rule the state. In a word, the measures that must be taken to maintain the general authority, which so many officers at a distance wish to evade or impose upon, absorb all the public attention; no regard for the welfare of the people remains, and scarcely any for their defence in time of need; and thus a body too huge for its constitution sinks and perishes, crushed by its own weight.

On the other hand, the state must secure a certain foundation, that it may possess stability and resist the shocks which it will infallibly experience, as well as sustain the efforts which it will be forced to make in order to maintain itself; for all nations have a kind of centrifugal force, by which they continually act one against another, and tend to aggrandise themselves at the expense of their neighbours, like the vortices of Descartes. Thus the weak are in danger of being quickly swallowed up, and none can preserve itself long except by putting itself in a kind of equilibrium with all, which renders the compression almost equal everywhere.

Hence we see that there are reasons for expansion and reasons for contraction; and it is not the least of a statesman's talents to find the proportion between the two which is most advantageous for the preservation of the state. We may say, in general, that the former, being only external and relative, ought to be subordinated to the others, which are internal and absolute. A healthy and strong constitution is the first thing to be sought; and we should rely more on the vigour that springs from a good government than on the resources furnished by an extensive territory.

States have, however, been constituted in such a way that the necessity of making conquests entered into their very constitution, and in order to maintain themselves they were forced to enlarge themselves continually. Perhaps they rejoiced greatly at this happy necessity, which nevertheless revealed to them, with the limit of their greatness, the inevitable moment of their fall.

CHAPTER 10
The People(continued)

A body politic may be measured in two ways, viz, by the extent of its territory, and by the number of its people; and there is between these two modes of measurement a suitable relation according to which the state may be assigned its true dimensions. It is the men that constitute the state, and it is the soil that sustains the men; the due relation, then, is that the land should suffice for the maintenance of its inhabitants, and that there should be as many inhabitants as the land can sustain. In this proportion is found the maximum power of a given number of people; for if there is too much land, the care of it is burdensome, the cultivation inadequate, and the produce superfluous, and this is the proximate cause of defensive wars. If there is not enough land, the state is at the mercy of its neighbours for the additional quantity; and this is the proximate cause of offensive wars. Any nation which has, by its position, only the alternative between commerce and war is weak in itself; it is dependent on its neighbours and on events; it has only a short and precarious existence. It conquers and changes its situation, or it is conquered and reduced to nothing. It can preserve its freedom only by virtue of being small or great.

It is impossible to express numerically a fixed ratio between the extent of land and the number of men which are reciprocally sufficient, on account of the differences that are found in the quality of the soil, in its degrees of fertility, in the nature of its products, and in the influence of climate, as well as on account of those which we observe in the constitutions of the inhabitants, of whom some consume little in a fertile country, while others consume much on an unfruitful soil. Further, attention must be paid to the greater or less fecundity of the women, to the conditions of the country, whether more or less favourable to population, and to the numbers which the legislator may hope to draw thither by his institutions; so that an opinion should be based not on what is seen, but on what is foreseen, while the actual state of the people should be less observed than that which it ought naturally to attain. In short, there are a thousand occasions on which the particular accidents of situation require or permit that more territory than appears necessary should be taken up. Thus men will spread out a good deal in a mountainous country, where the natural productions, viz, woods and pastures, require less labour, where experience teaches that women are more fecund than in the plains, and where with an extensive inclined surface there is only a small horizontal base, which alone should count for vegetation. On the other hand, people may inhabit a smaller space on the seashore, even among rocks and sands that are almost barren, because fishing can, in great measure, supply the deficiency in the productions of the earth, because men ought to be more concentrated in order to repel pirates, and because, further, it is easier to relieve the country, by means of colonies, of the inhabitants with which it is overburdened.

In order to establish a nation, it is necessary to add to these conditions one which cannot supply the place of any other, but without which they are all useless it is that the people should enjoy abundance and peace; for the time of a state's formation is, like that of forming soldiers in a square, the time when the body is least capable of resistance and most easy to destroy. Resistance would be greater in a state of absolute disorder than at a moment of fermentation, when each is occupied with his own position and not with the common danger. Should a war, a famine, or a sedition supervene at this critical period, the state is inevitably overthrown.

Many governments, indeed, may be established during such storms, but then it is these very governments that destroy the state. Usurpers always bring about or select troublous times for passing, under cover of the public agitation, destructive laws which the people would never adopt when sober-minded. The choice of the moment for the establishment of a government is one of the surest marks for distinguishing the work of the legislator from that of the tyrant.

What nation, then, is adapted for legislation? That which is already united, by some bond of interest, origin, or convention, but has not yet borne the real yoke of the laws; that which has no fear of being overwhelmed by a sudden invasion, but which, without entering into the disputes of its neighbours, can single-handed resist either of them, or aid one in repelling the other; that in which every member can be known by all, and in which there is no necessity to lay on a man a greater burden than a man can bear; that which can subsist without other nations, and without which every other nation can subsist;[①] that which is neither rich nor poor and is self-sufficing; lastly, that which combines the stability of an old nation with the docility of a new one. The work of legislation is rendered arduous not so much by what must be established as by what must be destroyed; and that which makes success so rare is the impossibility of finding the simplicity of nature conjoined with the necessities of society. All these conditions, it is true, are with difficulty combined; hence few well-constituted states are seen.

There is still one country in Europe capable of legislation; it is the island of Corsica. The courage and firmness which that brave nation has exhibited in recovering and defending its freedom would well deserve that some wise man should teach it how to preserve it. I have some presentiment that this small island will one day astonish Europe.

① If of two neighbouring nations one could not subsist without the other, it would be a very hard situation for the first, and a very dangerous one for the second. Every wise nation in such a case will endeavour very quickly to free the other from this dependence. The republic of Thlascala, enclosed in the empire of Mexico, preferred to do without salt rather than buy it of the Mexicans or even accept it gratuitously. The wise Thlascalans saw a trap hidden beneath this generosity. They kept themselves free; and this small state, enclosed in that great empire, was at last the instrument of its downfall.

CHAPTER 11
The Different of Legislation

If we ask precisely wherein consists the greatest good of all, which ought to be the aim of every system of legislation, we shall find that it is summed up in two principal objects, liberty and equality liberty, because any individual dependence is so much force with-drawn from the body of the state; equality, because liberty cannot subsist without it.

I have already said what civil liberty is. With regard to equality, we must not understand by this word that the degrees of power and wealth should be absolutely the same; but that, as to power, it should fall short of all violence, and never be exercised except by virtue of station and of the laws; while, as to wealth, no citizen should be rich enough to be able to buy another, and none poor enough to be forced to sell himself, ① which supposes, on the part of the great, moderation in property and influence, and, on the part of ordinary citizens, repression of avarice and covetousness.

It is said that this equality is a chimera of speculation which cannot exist in practical affairs. But if the abuse is inevitable, does it follow that it is unnecessary even to regulate it? It is precisely because the force of circumstances is ever tending to destroy equality that the force of legislation should always tend to maintain it.

But these general objects of every good institution ought to be modified in each country by the relations which arise both from the local situation and from the character of the inhabitants; and it is with reference to these relations that we must assign to each nation a particular system of institutions, which shall be the best, not perhaps in itself, but for the state for which it is designed. For instance, if the soil is unfruitful and barren, or the country too confined for its inhabitants, turn your attention to arts and manufactures, and exchange their products for the provisions that you require. On the other hand, if you occupy rich plains and fertile slopes, if, in a productive region, you are in need of inhabitants, bestow all your cares on agriculture, which multiplies men, and drive out the arts, which would only end in depopulating the country by gathering together in a few spots the few inhabitants that the land possesses.② If you occupy extensive and convenient coasts, cover the sea with vessels and foster commerce and navigation; you will have a short and brilliant existence. If the sea on your coasts bathes only rocks that are almost inaccessible, remain fish-eating barbarians; you will lead more peaceful, perhaps better, and certainly happier lives. In a word, besides the maxims common to all, each nation contains within itself some cause which influences it in a particular way, and renders its legislation suitable for it alone. Thus the Hebrews in ancient times, and the Arabs more recently, had religion as their chief object, the Athenians literature, Carthage and Tyre commerce, Rhodes navigation, Sparta war, Rome valour. The author of the Spirit of the Laws has shown in a multitude of instances by what arts the legislator directs his institutions towards each of these objects.

What renders the constitution of a state really solid and durable is the observance of expediency in such a way that natural relations and the laws always coincide, the latter only serving, as it were, to secure, support, and rectify the former. But if the legislator, mistaken in his object, takes a principle different from that which springs from the nature of things; if the one tends to servitude, the other to liberty, the one to riches, the other to population, the one to peace, the other to conquests, we shall see the laws imperceptibly weakened and the constitution impaired; and the state will be ceaselessly agitated until it is destroyed or changed, and invincible nature has resumed her sway.

①If, then, you wish to give stability to the state, bring the two extremes as near together as possible; tolerate neither rich people nor beggars. These two conditions, naturally inseparable, are equally fatal to the general welfare; from the one class spring tyrants, from the other, the supporters of tyranny it is always between these that the traffic in public liberty is carried on; the one buys and the other sells.

②Any branch of foreign commerce, says the Marquis d' Argenson, diffuses merely a deceptive utility through the kingdom generally; it may enrich a few individuals, even a few towns, but the nation as a whole gains nothing, and the people are none the better for it.

CHAPTER 12
Division of the Laws

In order that everything may be duly regulated and the best possible form given to the commonwealth, there are various relations to be considered. First, the action of the whole body acting on itself, that is, the relation of the whole to the whole, or of the sovereign to the state; and this relation is composed of that of the intermediate terms, as we shall see hereafter.

The laws governing this relation bear the name of political laws, and are also called fundamental laws, not without some reason if they are wise ones; for, if in every state there is only one good method of regulating it, the people which has discovered it ought to adhere to it; but if the established order is bad, why should we regard as fundamental laws which prevent it from being good? Besides, in any case, a nation is always at liberty to change its laws, even the best; for if it likes to injure itself, who has a right to prevent it from doing so?

The second relation is that of the members with one another, or with the body as a whole; and this relation should, in respect of the first, be as small, and, in respect of the second, as great as possible; so that every citizen may be perfectly independent of all the rest, and in absolute dependence on the state. And this is always effected by the same means; for it is only the power of the state that secures the freedom of its members. It is from this second relation that civil laws arise.

We may consider a third kind of relation between the individual man and the law, viz, that of punishable disobedience; and this gives rise to the establishment of criminal laws, which at bottom are not so much a particular species of laws as the sanction of all the others.

To these three kinds of laws is added a fourth, the most important of all, which is graven neither on marble nor on brass, but in the hearts of the Citizens; a law which creates the real constitution of the state, which acquires new strength daily, which, when other laws grow obsolete or pass away, revives them or supplies their place, preserves a people in the spirit of their institutions, and imperceptibly substitutes the force of habit for that of authority. I speak of manners, customs, and above all of opinion a province unknown to our politicians, but one on which the success of all the rest depends; a province with which the great legislator is occupied in private, while he appears to confine himself to particular regulations, that are merely the arching of the vault, of which manners, slow to develop, form at length the immovable keystone.

Of these different classes, political laws, which constitute the form of government, alone relate to my subject.

Jean-Jacques Rousseau

BOOK THREE

With regard to the right of conquest, it has no other foundation than the law of the strongest. If war does not confer on the victor the right of slaying the vanquished, this right, which he does not possess, cannot be the foundation of a right to enslave them. If we have a right to slay an enemy only when it is impossible to enslave him, the right to enslave him is not derived from the right to kill him, it is, therefore, an iniquitous bargain to make him purchase his life, over which the victor has no right, at the cost of his liberty. In establishing the right of life and death upon the right of slavery, and the right of slavery upon the right of life and death, is it not manifest that one falls into a vicious circle?

Before speaking of the different forms of government, let us try to fix the precise meaning of that word, which has not yet been very clearly explained.

第三卷
BOOK THREE

CHAPTER 1
Government in General

I warn the reader that this chapter must be read carefully, and that I do not know the art of making myself intelligible to those that will not be attentive.

Every free action has two causes concurring to produce it; the one moral, viz, the will which determines the act; the other physical, viz, the power which executes it. When I walk towards an object, I must first will to go to it; in the second place, my feet must carry me to it. Should a paralytic wish to run, or an active man not wish to do so, both will remain where they are. The body politic has the same motive powers; in it, likewise, force and will are distinguished, the latter under the name of legislative power, the former under the name of executive power. Nothing is, or ought to be, done in it without their co-operation.

We have seen that the legislative power belongs to the people and can belong to it alone. On the other hand, it is easy to see from the principles already established, that the executive power cannot belong to the people generally as legislative or sovereign, because that power is exerted only in particular acts, which are not within the province of the law, nor consequently within that of the sovereign, all the acts of which must be laws.

The public force, then, requires a suitable agent to concentrate it and put it in action according to the directions of the general will, to serve as a means of communication between the state and the sovereign, to effect in some manner in the public person what the union of soul and body effects in a man. This is, in the state, the function of the government, improperly confounded with the sovereign of which it is only the minister.

What, then, is the government? An intermediate body established between the subjects and the sovereign for their mutual correspondence, charged with the execution of the laws and with the maintenance of liberty both civil and political.

The members of this body are called magistrates or kings, that is, governors; and the body as a whole bears the name of Prince. [1] Those therefore who maintain that the act by which a people submits to its chiefs is not a contract are quite right. It is absolutely nothing but a commission, an employment, in which, as simple officers of the sovereign, they exercise in its name the power of which it has made them depositaries, and which it can limit, modify, and resume when it pleases. The alienation of such a right, being incompatible with the nature of the social body, is contrary to the object of the association.

Consequently, I give the name government or supreme administration to the legitimate exercise of the executive power, and that of Prince or magistrate to the man or body charged with that administration.

It is in the government that are found the intermediate powers, the relations of which constitute the relation of the whole to the whole, or of the sovereign to the state. This last relation can be represented by that of the extremes of a continued proportion, of which the mean proportional is the government. The government receives from the sovereign the commands which it gives to the people; and in order that the state may be in stable equilibrium, it is necessary, everything being balanced, that there should be equality between the product or the power of the government taken by itself, and the product or the power of the citizens, who are sovereign in the one aspect and subjects in the other.

Further, we could not alter any of the three terms without at once destroying the proportion. If the sovereign wishes to govern, or if the magistrate wishes to legislate, or if the subjects refuse to obey, disorder succeeds order, force and will no longer act in concert, and the state being dissolved falls into despotism or anarchy. Lastly, as there is but one mean proportional between each relation, there is only one good government possible in a state; but as a thousand events may change the relations of a people, not only may different governments be good for different peoples, but for the same people at different times.

To try and give an idea of the different relations that may exist between these two extremes, I will take for an example the number of the people, as a relation most easy to express.

Let us suppose that the state is composed of ten thousand citizens. The sovereign can only be considered collectively and as a body; but every private person, in his capacity of subject, is considered as an individual; therefore the sovereign is to the subject as ten thousand is to one, that is, each member of the state has as his share only one ten-thousandth part of the sovereign authority, although he is entirely subjected to it.

If the nation consists of a hundred thousand men, the position of the subjects does not change, and each alike is subjected to the whole authority of the laws, whilst his vote, reduced to one hundred-thousandth, has ten times less influence in their enactment. The subject, then, always remaining a unit, the proportional power of the sovereign increases in the ratio of the number of the citizens. Whence it follows that the more the state is enlarged, the more does liberty diminish.

When I say that the proportional power increases, I mean that it is farther removed from equality. Therefore, the greater the ratio is in the geometrical sense, the less is the ratio in the common acceptation; in the former, the ratio, considered according to quantity, is measured by the exponent, and in the other, considered according to identity, it is estimated by the similarity.

Now, the less the particular wills correspond with the general will, that is, customs with laws, the more should the repressive power be increased. The government, then, in order to be effective, should be relatively stronger in proportion as the people are more numerous.

On the other hand, as the aggrandisement of the state gives the depositaries of the public authority more temptations and more opportunities to abuse their power, the more force should the government have to restrain the people, and the more should the sovereign have in its turn to restrain the government. I do not speak here of absolute force, but of the relative force of the different parts of the state.

It follows from this double ratio that the continued proportion between the sovereign, the Prince, and the people is not an arbitrary idea, but a necessary consequence of the nature of the body politic. It follows, further, that one of the extremes, viz. the people, as subject, being fixed and represented by unity, whenever the double ratio increases or diminishes, the single ratio increases or diminishes in like manner, and consequently the middle term is changed. This shows that there is no unique and absolute constitution of government, but that there may be as many governments different in nature as there are states different in size.

If, for the sake of turning this system to ridicule, it should be said that, in order to find this mean proportional and form the body of the government, it is, according to me, only necessary to take the square root of the number of the people, I should answer that I take that number here only as an example; that the ratios of which I speak are not measured only by the number of men, but in general by the quantity of action, which

BOOK THREE

results from the combination of multitudes of causes; that, moreover, if for the purpose of expressing myself in fewer words, I borrow for a moment geometrical terms, I am nevertheless aware that geometrical precision has no place in moral quantities.

The government is on a small scale what the body politic which includes it is on a large scale. It is a moral person endowed with certain faculties, active like the sovereign, passive like the state, and it can be resolved into other similar relations; from which arises as a consequence a new proportion, and yet another within this, according to the order of the magistracies, until we come to an indivisible middle term, that is, to a single chief or supreme magistrate, who may be represented, in the middle of this progression, as unity between the series of fractions and that of the whole numbers.

Without embarrassing ourselves with this multiplication of terms, let us be content to consider the government as a new body in the state, distinct from the people and from the sovereign, and intermediate between the two.

There is this essential difference between those two bodies, that the state exists by itself, while the government exists only through the sovereign. Thus the dominant will of the Prince is, or ought to be, only the general will, or the law; its force is only the public force concentrated in itself; so soon as it wishes to perform of itself some absolute and independent act, the connection of the whole begins to be relaxed. If, lastly, the Prince should chance to have a particular will more active than that of the sovereign, and if, to enforce obedience to this particular will, it should employ the public force which is in its hands, in such a manner that there would be so to speak two sovereigns, the one de jure and the other de facto, the social union would immediately disappear, and the body politic would be dissolved.

Further, in order that the body of the government may have an existence, a real life, to distinguish it from the body of the state; in order that all its members may be able to act in concert and fulfil the object for which it is instituted, a particular personality is necessary to it, a feeling common to its members, a force, a will of its own tending to its preservation. This individual existence supposes assemblies, councils, a power of deliberating and resolving, rights, titles, and privileges which belong to the Prince exclusively, and which render the position of the magistrate more honourable in proportion as it is more arduous. The difficulty lies in the method of disposing, within the whole, this subordinate whole, in such a way that it may not weaken the general constitution in strengthening its own; that its particular force, intended for its own preservation, may always be kept distinct from the public force, designed for the preservation of the state; and, in a word, that it may always be ready to sacrifice the government to the people, and not the people to the government.

Moreover, although the artificial body of the government is the work of another artificial body, and has in some respects only a derivative and subordinate existence, that does not prevent it from acting with more or less vigour or celerity, from enjoying, so to speak, more or less robust health. Lastly, without directly departing from the object for which it was instituted, it may deviate from it more or less, according to the manner in which it is constituted.

From all these differences arise the different relations which the government must have with the body of the state, so as to accord with the accidental and particular relations by which the state itself is modified. For often the government that is best in itself will become the most vicious, unless its relations are changed so as to meet the defects of the body politic to which it belongs.

① It is for this reason that at Venice the title of Most Serene Prince is given to the College, even when the Doge does not attend it.

BOOK THREE

CHAPTER 2
The Principle which Constitutes the Different Forms of Government

To explain the general cause of these differences, I must here distinguish the Prince from the government, as I before distinguished the state from the sovereign.

The body of the magistracy may be composed of a greater or less number of members. We said that the ratio of the sovereign to the subjects was so much greater as the people were more numerous; and, by an evident analogy, we can say the same of the government with regard to the magistrates.

Now, the total force of the government, being always that of the state, does not vary: whence it follows that the more it employs this force on its own members, the less remains for operating upon the whole people.

Consequently, the more numerous the magistrates are, the weaker is the government. As this maxim is fundamental, let us endeavour to explain it more clearly.

We can distinguish in the person of the magistrate three wills essentially different: first, the will peculiar to the individual, which tends only to his personal advantage; secondly, the common will of the magistrates, which has reference solely to the advantage of the Prince, and which may be called the corporate will, being general in relation to the government, and particular in relation to the state of which the government forms part; in the third place, the will of the people, or the sovereign will, which is general both in relation to the state considered as the whole, and in relation to the government considered as part of the whole.

In a perfect system of legislation the particular or individual will should be inoperative; the corporate will proper to the government quite subordinate; and consequently the general or sovereign will always dominant, and the sole rule of all the rest.

On the other hand, according to the natural order, these different wills become more active in proportion as they are concentrated. Thus the general will is always the weakest, the corporate will has the second rank, and the particular will the first of all; so that in the government each member is, firstly, himself, next a magistrate, and then a citizen a gradation directly opposed to that which the social order requires.

But suppose that the whole government is in the hands of a single man, then the particular will and the corporate will are perfectly united, and consequently the latter is in the highest possible degree of intensity. Now, as it is on the degree of will that the exertion of force depends, and as the absolute power of the government does not vary, it follows that the most active government is that of a single person.

On the other hand, let us unite the government with the legislative authority let us make the sovereign the Prince, and all the citizens magistrates; then the corporate will, confounded with the general will, will have no more activity than the latter, and will leave the particular will in all its force. Thus the government, always with the same absolute force, will be at its minimum of relative force or activity.

These relations are incontestable, and other considerations serve still further to confirm them. We see, for example, that each magistrate is more active in his body than each citizen is in his, and that consequently the particular will has much more influence in the acts of government than in those of the sovereign; for every magistrate is almost always charged with some function of government, whereas each citizen, taken by himself, has no function of sovereignty. Besides, the more a state extends, the more is its real force increased, although it does not increase in proportion to its extent; but, while the state remains the same, it is useless to multiply magistrates, for the government acquires no greater real force, inasmuch as this force is that of the state, the quantity of which is always uniform. Thus the relative force or activity of the government diminishes without its absolute or real force being able to increase.

It is certain, moreover, that the despatch of business is retarded in proportion as more people are charged with it; that, in laying too much stress on prudence, we leave too little to fortune; that opportunities are allowed to pass by, and that owing to excessive deliberation the fruits of deliberation are often lost.

BOOK THREE

I have just shown that the government is weakened in proportion to the multiplication of magistrates, and I have before demonstrated that the more numerous the people is, the more ought the repressive force to be increased. Whence it follows that the ratio between the magistrates and the government ought to be inversely as the ratio between the subjects and the sovereign; that is, the more the state is enlarged, the more should the government contract; so that the number of chiefs should diminish in proportion as the number of the people is increased.

But I speak here only of the relative force of the government, and not of its rectitude; for, on the other hand, the more numerous the magistracy is, the more does the corporate will approach the general will; whereas, under a single magistrate, this same corporate will is, as I have said, only a particular will. Thus, what is lost on one side can be gained on the other, and the art of the legislator consists in knowing how to fix the point where the force and will of the government, always in reciprocal proportion, are combined in the ratio most advantageous to the state.

CHAPTER 3
Classification of Governments

We have seen in the previous chapter why the different kinds or forms of government are distinguished by the number of members that compose them; it remains to be seen in the present chapter how this division is made.

The sovereign may, in the first place, commit the charge of the government to the whole people, or to the greater part of the people, in such a way that there may be more citizens who are magistrates than simple individual citizens. We call this form of government a democracy.

Or it may confine the government to a small number, so that there may be more ordinary citizens than magistrates; and this form bears the name of aristocracy.

Lastly, it may concentrate the whole government in the hands of a single magistrate from whom all the rest derive their power. This third form is the most common, and is called monarchy, or royal government.

We should remark that all these forms, or at least the first two, admit of degrees, and may indeed have a considerable range; for democracy may embrace the whole people, or be limited to a half. Aristocracy, in its turn, may restrict itself from a half of the people to the smallest number indeterminately. Royalty even is susceptible of some division. Sparta by its constitution always had two kings; and in the Roman Empire there were as many as eight Emperors at once without its being possible to say that the Empire was divided. Thus there is a point at which each form of government blends with the next; and we see that, under three denominations only, the government is really susceptible of as many different forms as the state has citizens.

What is more, this same government being in certain respects capable of subdivision into other parts, one administered in one way, another in another, there may result from combinations of these three forms a multitude of mixed forms, each of which can be multiplied by all the simple forms.

In all ages there has been much discussion about the best form of government, without consideration of the fact that each of them is the best in certain cases, and the worst in others.

If, in the different states, the number of the supreme magistrates should be in inverse ratio to that of the citizens, it follows that, in general, democratic government is suitable to small states, aristocracy to those of moderate size, and monarchy to large ones. This rule follows immediately from the principle. But how is it possible to estimate the multitude of circumstances which may furnish exceptions?

BOOK THREE

CHAPTER 4
Democracy

He that makes the law knows better than anyone how it should be executed and interpreted. It would seem, then, that there could be no better constitution than one in which the executive power is united with the legislative; but it is that very circumstance which makes a democratic government inadequate in certain respects, because things which ought to be distinguished are not, and because the Prince and the sovereign, being the same person, only form as it were a government without government.

It is not expedient that he who makes the laws should execute them, nor that the body of the people should divert its attention from general considerations in order to bestow it on particular objects. Nothing is more dangerous than the influence of his private interests on public affairs; and the abuse of the laws by the government is a less evil than the corruption of the legislator, which is the infallible result of the pursuit of private interests. For when the state is changed in its substance all reform becomes impossible. A people which would never abuse the government would likewise never abuse its independence; a people which always governed well would not need to be governed.

Taking the term in its strict sense, there never has existed, and never will exist, any true democracy. It is contrary to the natural order that the majority should govern and that the minority should be governed. It is impossible to imagine that the people should remain in perpetual assembly to attend to public affairs, and it is easily apparent that commissions could not be established for that purpose without the form of administration being changed.

In fact, I think I can lay down as a principle that when the functions of government are shared among several magistracies, the least numerous acquire, sooner or later, the greatest authority, if only on account of the facility in transacting business which naturally leads them on to that.

Moreover, how many things difficult to combine does not this government presuppose! First, a very small state, in which the people may be readily assembled and in which every citizen can easily know all the rest; secondly, great simplicity of manners, which prevents a multiplicity of affairs and thorny discussions; next, considerable equality in rank and fortune, without which equality in rights and authority could not long subsist; lastly, little or no luxury, for luxury is either the effect of wealth or renders it necessary; it corrupts both the rich and the poor, the former by possession, the latter by covetousness; it betrays the country to effeminacy and vanity; it deprives the state of all its citizens in order to subject them one to another, and all to opinion.

That is why a famous author has assigned virtue as the principle of a republic, for all these conditions could not subsist without virtue; but, through not making the necessary distinctions, this brilliant genius has often lacked precision and sometimes clearness, and has not seen that the sovereign authority being everywhere the same, the same principle ought to have a place in every well-constituted state, in a greater or less degree, it is true, according to the form of government.

Let us add that there is no government so subject to civil wars and internal agitations as the democratic or popular, because there is none which tends so strongly and so constantly to change its form, none which demands more vigilance and courage to be maintained in its own form. It is especially in this constitution that the citizen should arm himself with strength and steadfastness, and say every day of his life from the bottom of his heart what a virtuous Palatine① said in the Diet of Poland: Malo periculosam libertatem quam quietum servitium.②

If there were a nation of gods, it would be governed democratically. So perfect a government is unsuited to men.

---

① The Palatine of Posnania, father of the King of Poland, Duke of Lorraine.
②("I prefer a perilous freedom to a peaceful slavery.")

BOOK THREE

CHAPTER 5
Aristocracy

We have here two moral persons quite distinct, viz, the government and the sovereign; and consequently two general wills, the one having reference to all the citizens, the other only to the members of the administration. Thus, although the government can regulate its internal policy as it pleases, it can never speak to the people except in the name of the sovereign, that is, in the name of the people themselves. This must never be forgotten.

The earliest societies were aristocratic ally governed. The heads of families deliberated among themselves about public affairs. The young men yielded readily to the authority of experience. Hence the names priests, elders, senate, gerontes. The savages of North America are still governed in this way at the present time, and are very well governed.

But in proportion as the inequality due to institutions prevailed over natural inequality, wealth or power[①] was preferred to age, and aristocracy became elective. Finally, the power transmitted with the father's property to the children, rendering the families patrician, made the government hereditary, and there were senators only twenty years old.

There are, then, three kinds of aristocracy—natural, elective and hereditary. The first is only suitable for simple nations; the third is the worst of all governments. The second is the best; it is aristocracy properly so-called.

Besides the advantage of the distinction between the two powers, aristocracy has that of the choice of its members; for in a popular government all the citizens are born magistrates; but this one limits them to a small number, and they become magistrates by election only;[②] a method by which probity, intelligence, experience, and all other grounds of preference and public esteem are so many fresh guarantees that men will be wisely governed.

Further, assemblies are more easily convoked; affairs are better discussed and are despatched with greater order and diligence; while the credit of the state is better maintained abroad by venerable senators, than by an unknown or despised multitude.

In a word, it is the best and most natural order of things that the wisest should govern the multitude, when we are sure that they will govern it for its advantage and not for their own. We should not uselessly multiply means, nor do with twenty thousand men what a hundred chosen men can do still better. But we must observe that the corporate interest begins here to direct the public force in a less degree according to the rule of the general will, and that another inevitable propensity deprives the laws of a part of the executive power.

With regard to special expediencies, a state must not be so small, nor a people so simple and upright, that the execution of the laws should follow immediately upon the public will, as in a good democracy. Nor again must a nation be so large that the chief men, who are dispersed in order to govern it, can set up as sovereigns, each in his own province, and begin by making themselves independent so as at last to become masters.

But if aristocracy requires a few virtues less than popular government, it requires also others that are peculiarly its own, such as moderation among the rich and contentment among the poor; for a rigorous equality would seem to be out of place in it, and was not even observed in Sparta.

Besides, if this form of government comports with a certain inequality of fortune, it is expedient in general that the administration of public affairs should be entrusted to those that are best able to devote their whole time to it, but not, as Aristotle maintains, that the rich should always be preferred. On the contrary, it is important that an opposite choice should sometimes teach the people that there are, in men's personal merits, reasons for preference more important than wealth.

① It is clear that the word optimates among the ancients did not mean the best, but the most powerful.

② It is very important to regulate by law the form of election of magistrates; for, in leaving it to the will of the Prince, it is impossible to avoid falling into hereditary aristocracy, as happened in the republics of Venice and Berne. In consequence, the first has long been a decaying state, but the second is maintained by the extreme wisdom of its Senate; it is a very honourable and a very dangerous exception.

CHAPTER 6
Monarchy

We have hitherto considered the Prince as a moral and collective person united by the force of the laws, and as the depositary of the executive power in the state. We have now to consider this power concentrated in the hands of a natural person, of a real man, who alone has a right to dispose of it according to the laws. He is what is called a monarch or a king.

Quite the reverse of the other forms of administration, in which a collective being represents an individual, in this one an individual represents a collective being: so that the moral unity that constitutes it is at the same time a physical unity, in which all the powers that the law combines in the other with so much effort are combined naturally.

Thus the will of the people, the will of the Prince, the public force of the state, and the particular force of the government, all obey the same motive power; all the springs of the machine are in the same hand, everything works for the same end; there are no opposite movements that counteract one another, and no kind of constitution can be imagined in which a more considerable action is produced with less effort. Archimedes, quietly seated on the shore, and launching without difficulty a large vessel, represents to me a skilful monarch, governing from his cabinet his vast states, and, while he appears motionless, setting everything in motion.

But if there is no government which has more vigour, there is none in which the particular will has more sway and more easily governs others. Everything works for the same end, it is true; but this end is not the public welfare, and the very power of the administration turns continually to the prejudice of the state.

Kings wish to be absolute, and from afar men cry to them that the best way to become so is to make themselves beloved by their people. This maxim is very fine, and also very true in certain respects; unfortunately it will always be ridiculed in courts. Power which springs from the affections of the people is doubtless the greatest, but it is precarious and conditional; princes will never be satisfied with it. The best kings wish to have the power of being wicked if they please, without ceasing to be masters. A political preacher will tell them in vain that, the strength of the people being their own, it is their greatest interest that the people should be flourishing, numerous, and formidable; they know very well that that is not true. Their personal interest is, in the first place, that the people should be weak and miserable, and should never be able to resist them. Supposing all the subjects always perfectly submissive, I admit that it would then be the prince's interest that the people should be powerful, in order that this power, being his own, might render him formidable to his neighbours; but as this interest is only secondary and subordinate, and as the two suppositions are incompatible, it is natural that princes should always give preference to the maxim which is most immediately useful to them. It is this that Samuel strongly represented to the Hebrews; it is this that Machiavelli clearly demonstrated. While pretending to give lessons to kings, he gave great ones to peoples. The Prince of Machiavelli is the book of republicans. ①

We have found, by general considerations, that monarchy is suited only to large states; and we shall find this again by examining monarchy itself The more numerous the public administrative body is, the more does the ratio of the Prince to the subjects diminish and approach equality, so that this ratio is unity or equality, even in a

BOOK THREE

democracy. This same ratio increases in proportion as the government contracts, and is at its maximum when the government is in the hands of a single person. Then the distance between the Prince and the people is too great, and the state lacks cohesion. In order to unify it, then, intermediate orders, princes, grandees, and nobles, are required to fill them. Now, nothing at all of this kind is proper for a small state, which would be ruined by all these orders.

But if it is difficult for a great state to be well governed, it is much more so for it to be well governed by a single man; and everyone knows what happens when the king appoints deputies.

One essential and inevitable defect, which will always render a monarchical government inferior to a republican one, is that in the latter the public voice hardly ever raises to the highest posts any but enlightened and capable men, who fill them honourably; whereas those who succeed in monarchies are most frequently only petty mischief-makers, petty knaves, petty intriguers, whose petty talents, which enable them to attain high posts in courts, only serve to show the public their ineptitude as soon as they have attained them. The people are much less mistaken about their choice than the prince is; and a man of real merit is almost as rare in a royal ministry as a fool at the head of a republican government. Therefore, when by some fortunate chance one of these born rulers takes the helm of affairs in a monarchy almost wrecked by such a fine set of ministers, it is quite astonishing what resources he finds, and his accession to power forms an epoch in a country.

In order that a monarchical state might be well governed, it would be necessary that its greatness or extent should be proportioned to the abilities of him that governs. It is easier to conquer than to rule. With a sufficient lever, the world may be moved by a finger; but to support it the shoulders of Hercules are required. However small a state may be, the prince is almost always too small for it. When, on the contrary, it happens that the state is too small for its chief, which is very rare, it is still badly governed, because the chief, always pursuing his own great designs, forgets the interests of the people, and renders them no less unhappy by the abuse of his transcendent abilities, than an inferior chief by his lack of talent. It would be necessary, so to speak, that a kingdom should be enlarged or contracted in every reign, according to the capacity of the prince; whereas, the talents of a senate having more definite limits, the state may have permanent boundaries, and the administration prosper equally well.

The most obvious inconvenience of the government of a single person is the lack of that uninterrupted succession which forms in the two others a continuous connection. One king being dead, another is necessary; elections leave dangerous intervals; they are stormy; and unless the citizens are of a disinterestedness, an integrity, which this government hardly admits of, intrigue and corruption intermingle with it. It would be hard for a man to whom the state has been sold not to sell it in his turn, and indemnify himself out of the helpless for the money which the powerful have extorted from him. Sooner or later everything becomes venal under such an administration, and the peace which is then enjoyed under a king is worse than the disorder of an interregnum.

What has been done to prevent these evils? Crowns have been made hereditary in certain families; and an order of succession has been established which prevents any dispute on the demise of kings; that is to say, the inconvenience of regencies being substituted for that of elections, an appearance of tranquillity has been preferred to a wise administration, and men have preferred to risk having as their chiefs children, monsters, and imbeciles, rather than have a dispute about the choice of good kings. They have not considered that in thus exposing themselves to the risk of this alternative, they put almost all the chances against themselves. That was a very sensible answer of Dionysius the younger, to whom his father, in reproaching him with a dishonourable action, said: "Have I set you the example in this?" "Ah!" replied the son, "your father was not a king."

All things conspire to deprive of justice and reason a man brought up to govern others. Much trouble is taken, so it is said, to teach young princes the art of reigning; this education does not appear to profit them. It would be better to begin by teaching them the art of obeying. The greatest kings that history has celebrated were not trained to rule; that

BOOK THREE

is a science which men are never less masters of than after excessive study of it, and it is better acquired by obeying than by ruling. Nam utilissimus idem ac brevissimus bonarum malarumque rerum delectus, cogitare quid aut nolueris sub alio principe, aut volueris.[②]

A result of this want of cohesion is the instability of royal government, which, being regulated sometimes on one plan, sometimes on another, according to the character of the reigning prince or that of the persons who reign for him, cannot long pursue a fixed aim or a consistent course of conduct, a variableness which always makes the state fluctuate between maxim and maxim, project and project, and which does not exist in other governments, where the Prince is always the same. So we see that, in general, if there is more cunning in a court, there is more wisdom in a senate, and that republics pursue their ends by more steadfast and regular methods; whereas every revolution in a royal ministry produces one in the state, the maxim common to all ministers, and to almost all kings, being to reverse in every respect the acts of their predecessors.

From this same want of cohesion is obtained the solution of a sophism very familiar to royal politicians; this is not only to compare civil government with domestic government, and the prince with the father of a family, an error already refuted, but, further, to ascribe freely to this magistrate all the virtues which he might have occasion for, and always to suppose that the prince is what he ought to be on which supposition royal government is manifestly preferable to every other, because it is incontestably the strongest, and because it only lacks a corporate will more conformable to the general will to be also the best.

But if, according to Plato, a king by nature is so rare a personage, how many times will nature and fortune conspire to crown him? And if the royal education necessarily corrupts those who receive it, what should be expected from a succession of men trained to rule? It is, then, voluntary self-deception to confuse royal government with that of a good king. To see what this government is in itself; we must consider it under incapable or wicked princes; for such will come to the throne, or the throne will make them such.

These difficulties have not escaped our authors, but they have not been embarrassed by them. The remedy, they say, is to obey without murmuring; God gives bad kings in his wrath, and we must endure them as chastisements of heaven. Such talk is doubtless edifying, but I am inclined to think it would be more appropriate in a pulpit than in a book on politics. What should we say of a physician who promises miracles, and whose whole art consists in exhorting the sick man to be patient? We know well that when we have a bad government it must be endured; the question is to find a good one.

① Machiavelli was an honourable man and a good citizen; but, attached to the house of the Medici, he was forced, during the oppression of his country, to conceal his love for liberty. The mere choice of his execrable hero sufficiently manifests his secret intention; and the opposition between the maxims of his book the Prince and those of his Discourses on Titus Livius and his History of Florence shows that this profound politician has had hitherto only superficial or corrupt readers. The court of Rame has strictly prohibited his book; I certainly believe it, for it is that court which he most clearly depicts.

②["For the quickest and most useful way of choosing between things that are good and evil is to consider what, under another emperor, you would have approved or disapproved." Tacitus, Histories I, 16]

CHAPTER 7
Mixed Governments

Properly speaking, there is no simple government. A single chief must have subordinate magistrates; a popular government must have a head. Thus, in the partition of the executive power there is always a gradation from the greater number to the less, with this difference, that sometimes the majority depends on the minority, and sometimes the minority on the majority.

Sometimes there is an equal division, either when the constituent parts are in mutual dependence, as in the government of England; or when the authority of each part is independent, but imperfect, as in Poland. This latter form is bad, because there is no unity in the government, and the state lacks cohesion.

Is a simple or a mixed government the better? A question much debated among publicists, and one to which the same answer must be made that I have before made about every form of government.

The simple government is the better in itself, for the reason that it is simple. But when the executive power is not sufficiently dependent on the legislative, that is, when there is a greater proportion between the Prince and the sovereign than between the people and the Prince, this want of proportion must be remedied by dividing the government; for then all its parts have no less authority over the subjects, and their division renders them all together less strong against the sovereign.

The same inconvenience is also provided against by the establishment of intermediate magistrates, who, leaving the government in its entirety, only serve to balance the two powers and maintain their respective rights. Then the government is not mixed, but temperate.

The opposite inconvenience can be remedied by similar means, and, when the government is too lax, tribunals may be erected to concentrate it. That is customary in all democracies. In the first case the government is divided in order to weaken it, and in the second in order to strengthen it; for the maximum of strength and also of weakness is found in simple governments, while the mixed forms give a medium strength.

CHAPTER 8
That Every Form of Government Is Not Fit for Every Country

Liberty, not being a fruit of all climates, is not within the reach of all peoples. The more we consider this principle established by Montesquieu, the more do we perceive its truth; the more it is contested, the greater opportunity is given to establish it by new proofs.

In all the governments of the world, the public person consumes, but produces nothing. Whence, then, comes the substance it consumes? From the labour of its members. It is the superfluity of individuals that supplies the necessaries of the public. Hence it follows that the civil state can subsist only so long as men's labour produces more than they need.

Now this excess is not the same in all countries of the world. In several it is considerable, in others moderate, in others nothing, in others a minus quantity. This proportion depends on the fertility due to climate, on the kind of labour which the soil requires, on the nature of its products, on the physical strength of its inhabitants, on the greater or less consumption that is necessary to them, and on several other like proportions of which it is composed.

On the other hand, all governments are not of the same nature; there are some more or less wasteful; and the differences are based on this other principle, that the further the public contributions are removed from their source, the more burdensome they are. We must not measure this burden by the amount of the imposts, but by the distance they have to traverse in order to return to the hands from which they have come. When this circulation is prompt and well-established, it matters not whether little or much is paid; the people are always rich, and the finances are always prosperous. On the other hand, however little the people may contribute, if this little does not revert to them, they are soon exhausted by constantly giving; the state is never rich and the people are always in beggary.

It follows from this that the more the distance between the people and the government is increased, the more burdensome do the tributes become; therefore, in a democracy the people are least encumbered, in an aristocracy they are more so, and in a monarchy they bear the greatest weight. Monarchy, then, is suited only to wealthy nations; aristocracy, to states moderate both in wealth and size; democracy, to small and poor states.

BOOK THREE

Indeed, the more we reflect on it, the more do we find in this the difference between free and monarchical states. In the first, everything is used for the common advantage; In the others, public and private resources are reciprocal, and the former are increased by the diminution of the latter; lastly, instead of governing subjects in order to make them happy, despotism renders them miserable in order to govern them.

There are, then, in every climate natural causes by which we can assign the form of government which is adapted to the nature of the climate, and even say what kind of inhabitants the country should have.

Unfruitful and barren places, where the produce does not repay the labour, ought to remain uncultivated and deserted, or should only be peopled by savages; places where men's toil yields only bare necessaries ought to be inhabited by barbarous nations; in them any polity would be an impossibility. Places where the excess of the produce over the labour is moderate are suitable for free nations; those in which abundant and fertile soil yields much produce for little labour are willing to be governed monarchically, in order that the superfluity of the subjects may be consumed by the luxuries of the Prince; for it is better that this excess should be absorbed by the government than squandered by private persons. There are exceptions, I know; but these exceptions themselves confirm the rule, in that, sooner or later, they produce revolutions which restore things to their natural order.

We should always distinguish general laws from the particular causes which may modify their effects. If the whole south should be covered with republics, and the whole north with despotic states, it would not be less true that, through the influence of climate, despotism is suitable to warm countries, barbarism to cold countries, and a good polity to intermediate regions. I see, however, that while the principle is admitted, its application may be disputed; it will be said that some cold countries are very fertile, and some southern ones very unfruitful. But this is a difficulty only for those who do not examine the matter in all its relations. It is necessary, as I have already said, to reckon those connected with labour, resources, consumption, etc.

Let us suppose that the produce of two districts equal in area is in the ratio of five to ten. If the inhabitants of the former consume four and those of the latter nine parts, the surplus produce of the first will be one-fifth, and that of the second one-tenth. The ratio between these two surpluses being then inversely as that of the produce of each, the district which yields only five will give a surplus double that of the district which produces ten.

But it is not a question of double produce, and I do not think that anyone dare, in general, place the fertility of cold countries even on an equality with that of warm countries. Let us, however, assume this equality; let us, if you will, put England in the scales with Sicily, and Poland with Egypt; more to the south we shall have Africa and India; more to the north we shall have nothing. For this equality in produce what a difference in the cultivation! In Sicily it is only necessary to scratch the soil, in England what care is needed to till it! But where more exertion is required to yield the same produce, the surplus must necessarily be very small.

Consider, besides this, that the same number of men consume much less in warm countries. The climate demands that people should be temperate in order to be healthy; Europeans who want to live as at home all die of dysentery and dyspepsia. "We are," says Chardin, "carnivorous beasts, wolves, in comparison with Asiatics. Some attribute the temperance of the Persians to the fact that their country is scantily cultivated; I believe, on the contrary, that their country is not very abundant in provisions because the inhabitants need very little. If their frugality," he continues, "resulted from the poverty of the country, it would be only the poor who would eat little, whereas it is the people generally; and more or less would be consumed in each province according to the fertility of the country, whereas the same abstemiousness is found throughout the kingdom. They pride themselves greatly on their mode of living, saying that it is only necessary to look at their complexions, to see how much superior they are to those of Christians. Indeed, the complexions of the Persians are smooth; they have beautiful skins, delicate and clear; while the complexions of their subjects, the Armenians, who live in European fashion, are rough and blotched, and their bodies are coarse and heavy."

The nearer we approach to the Equator, the less do the people live upon. They eat scarcely any meat; rice, maize, couscous, millet, cassava, are their ordinary foods. There are in India millions of men whose diet does not cost a halfpenny a day. We see even in Europe palpable differences in appetite between northern and southern nations. A Spaniard will live for eight days on a German's dinner. In countries where men are most voracious luxury is directed to matters of consumption; in England it is displayed in a table loaded with meats; in Italy you are regaled with sugar and flowers.

Again, luxury in dress presents similar differences. In climates where the changes of the seasons are sudden and violent, garments are better and simpler; in those where people dress only for ornament, splendour is more sought after than utility, for clothes themselves are a luxury. At Naples you will see men every day walking to Posilippo with gold-embroidered coats, and no stockings. It is the same with regard to buildings; everything is sacrificed to magnificence when there is nothing to fear from injury by the atmosphere. In Paris and in London people must be warmly and comfortably housed; in Madrid they have superb drawing-rooms, but no windows that shut, while they sleep in mere closets.

The foods are much more substantial and nutritious in warm countries; this is a third difference which cannot fail to influence the second. Why do people eat so many vegetables in Italy? Because they are good, nourishing, and of excellent flavour. In France, where they are grown only on water, they are not nourishing and count almost for nothing on the table; they do not, however, occupy less ground, and they cost at least as much labour to cultivate. It is found by experience that the wheats of Barbary, inferior in other respects to those of France, yield much more flour, and that those of France, in their turn, yield more than the wheats of the north. Whence we may infer that a similar gradation is observable generally, in the same direction, from the Equator to the Pole. Now is it not a manifest disadvantage to have in an equal quantity of produce a smaller quantity of nutriment?

To all these different considerations I may add one which springs from, and strengthens, them; it is that warm countries have less need of inhabitants than cold countries, but would be able to maintain a greater number; hence a double surplus is produced, always to the advantage of despotism. The greater the surface occupied by the same number of inhabitants, the more difficult do rebellions become, because measures cannot be concerted promptly and secretly, and because it is always easy for the government to discover the plans and cut off communications. But the more closely packed a numerous population is, the less power has a government to usurp the sovereignty; the chiefs deliberate as securely in their cabinets as the prince in his council, and the multitude assemble in the squares as quickly as the troops in their quarters. The advantage, then, of a tyrannical government lies in this, that it acts at great distances. By help of the points of support which it procures, its power increases with the distance, like that of levers. ① That of the people, on the other hand, acts only when concentrated; it evaporates and disappears as it extends, like the effect of powder scattered on the ground, which takes fire only grain by grain. The least populous countries are thus the best adapted for tyranny; wild beasts reign only in deserts.

① This does not contradict what I said before (II, 9) on the inconveniences of large states; for there it was a question of the authority of the government over its members, and here it is a question of its power against its subjects. Its scattered members serve as points of support to it for operating at a distance upon the people, but it has no point of support for acting on its members themselves. Thus, the length of the lever is the cause of its weakness in the one case, and of its strength in the other.

CHAPTER 9
The Marks of a Good Government

When, then, it is asked absolutely which is the best government, an insoluble and likewise indeterminate question is propounded; or, if you will, it has as many correct solutions as there are possible combinations in the absolute and relative positions of the nations.

But if it were asked by what sign it can be known whether a given people is well or ill governed, that would be a different matter, and the question of fact might be determined.

It is, however, not settled, because everyone wishes to decide it in his own way. Subjects extol the public tranquillity, citizens the liberty of individuals; the former prefer security of possessions, the latter, that of persons; the former are of opinion that the best government is the most severe, the latter maintain that it is the mildest; the one party wish that crimes should be punished and the other that they should be prevented; the one party think it well to be feared by their neighbours, the other party prefer to be unacquainted with them; the one party are satisfied when money circulates, the other party demand that the people should have bread. Even though there should be agreement on these and other similar points, would further progress be made? Since moral quantities lack a precise mode of measurement, even if people were in accord about the sign, how could they be so about the valuation of it?

For my part, I am always astonished that people fail to recognise a sign so simple, or that they should have the insincerity not to agree about it. What is the object of political association? It is the preservation and prosperity of its members. And what is the surest sign that they are preserved and prosperous? It is their number and population. Do not, then, go and seek elsewhere for this sign so much discussed. All other things being equal, the government under which, without external aids, without naturalisations, and without colonies, the citizens increase and multiply most, is infallibly the best. That under which a people diminishes and decays is the worst. Statisticians, it is now your business; reckon, measure, compare.①

社会契约论
The Social Contract

① On the same principle must be judged the centuries which deserve preference in respect of the prosperity of the human race. Those in which literature and art were seen to flourish have been too much admired, without the secret object of their cultivation being penetrated, without their fatal consequences being considered: Idque apud imperitos humanitas vocabatur, quum pars servitutis esset. ["And this was called civilisation by the ignorant, when it was only part of their slavery." Tacitus, Agricola, xxi.] Shall we never detect in the maxims of books the gross self-interest which makes the authors speak? No, whatever they may say, when, notwithstanding its brilliancy, a country is being depopulated, it is untrue that all goes well, and it is not enough that a poet should have an income of 100,000 livres for his epoch to be the best of all. The apparent repose and tranquillity of the chief men must be regarded less than the welfare of nations as a whole, and especially that of the most populous states. Hail lays waste a few cantons, but it rarely causes scarcity. Riots and civil wars greatly startle the chief men; but they do not produce the real misfortunes of nations, which may even be abated, while it is being disputed who shall tyrannise over them. It is from their permanent condition that their real prosperity or calamities spring; when all is left crushed under the yoke, it is then that everything perishes; it is then that the chief men, destroying them at their leisure, ubi solitudinem faciunt, pacem appellant. ["while they are creating a desert, they call it peace." Tacitus, Agricola, xxx.] When the broils of the great agitated the kingdom of France, and the coadjutor of Paris carried a poniard in his pocket to the Parlement, that did not prevent the French nation from living happily and harmoniously in free and honourable ease. Greece of old flourished in the midst of the most cruel wars; blood flowed there in streams, and the whole country was covered with men. It seemed, said Machiavelli, that amid murders proscriptions, and civil wars, our republic became more powerful; the virtues of its citizens, their manners, their independence, were more effectual in strengthening it than all its dissensions had been in weakening it. A little agitation gives energy to men's minds, and what makes the race truly prosperous is not so much peace as liberty.

BOOK THREE

第三卷

CHAPTER 10
The Abuse of the Government and Its Tendency to Degenerate

As the particular will acts incessantly against the general will, so the government makes a continual effort against the sovereignty. The more this effort is increased, the more is the constitution altered; and as there is here no other corporate will which, by resisting that of the Prince, may produce equilibrium with it, it must happen sooner or later that the Prince at length oppresses the sovereign and violates the social treaty. Therein is the inherent and inevitable vice which, from the birth of the body politic, tends without intermission to destroy it, just as old age and death at length destroy the human body.

There are two general ways by which a government degenerates, viz, when it contracts, or when the state is dissolved.

The government contracts when it passes from the majority to the minority, that is, from democracy to aristocracy, and from aristocracy to royalty. That is its natural tendency.① If it retrograded from the minority to the majority, it might be said to relax; but this inverse progress is impossible.

In reality, the government never changes its form except when its exhausted energy leaves it too weak to preserve itself; and if it becomes still more relaxed as it extends, its force will be annihilated, and it will no longer subsist. We must therefore concentrate the energy as it dwindles; otherwise the state which it sustains will fall into ruin.

The dissolution of the state may occur in two ways.

Firstly, when the Prince no longer administers the state in accordance with the laws; and, secondly, when he usurps the sovereign power. Then a remarkable change takes place the state, and not the government, contracts; I mean that the state dissolves, and that another is formed within it, which is composed only of the members of the government, and which is to the rest of the people nothing more than their master and their tyrant.

社会契约论
The Social Contract

So that as soon as the government usurps the sovereignty, the social compact is broken, and all the ordinary citizens, rightfully regaining their natural liberty, are forced, but not morally bound, to obey.

The same thing occurs also when the members of the government usurp separately. the power which they ought to exercise only collectively; which is no less a violation of the laws, and occasions still greater disorder. Then there are, so to speak, as many Princes as magistrates; and the state, not less divided than the government, perishes or changes its form.

When the state is broken up, the abuse of the government, whatever it may be, takes the common name of anarchy. To distinguish, democracy degenerates into ochlocracy, aristocracy into oligarchy; I should add that royalty degenerates into tyranny; but this last word is equivocal and requires explanation.

In the vulgar sense a tyrant is a king who governs with violence and without regard to justice and the laws. In the strict sense, a tyrant is a private person who arrogates to himself the royal authority without having a right to it. It is in this sense that the Greeks understood the word tyrant; they bestowed it indifferently on good and bad princes whose authority was not legitimate.② Thus tyrant and usurper are two words perfectly synonymous.

To give different names to different things, I call the usurper of royal authority a tyrant, and the usurper of sovereign power a despot. The tyrant is he who, contrary to the laws, takes upon himself to govern according to the laws; the despot is he who sets himself above the laws themselves. Thus the tyrant cannot be a despot, but the despot is always a tyrant.

①The slow formation and the progress of Venice in her lagoons present a notable example of this succession; it is indeed astonishing that, after more than twelve hundred years, the Venetians seem to be still only in the second stage, which began with the Serrar di Consiglio in 1198. As for the ancient Doges, with whom they are reproached, whatever the Squittillio della libertà veneta

第三卷
BOOK THREE

may say, it is proved that they were not their sovereigns.

People will not fail to bring forward as an objection to my views the Roman Republic, which followed, it will be said, a course quite contrary, passing from monarchy to aristocracy, and from aristocracy to democracy. I am very far from regarding it in this way.

The first institution of Romulus was a mixed government, which speedily degenerated into despotism. From peculiar causes the state perished before its time, as we see a new-born babe die before attaining manhood. The expulsion of the Tarquins was the real epoch of the birth of the Republic. But it did not at first assume a regular form, because, through not abolishing the patrician order, only a half of the work was done. For, in this way, the hereditary aristocracy, which is the worst of legitimate administrations, remaining in conflict with the democracy, the form of the government, always uncertain and fluctuating, was fixed, as Machiavelli has shown, only on the institution of the tribunes; not till then was there a real government and a true democracy. Indeed, the people then were not only sovereign, but also magistrates and judges; the Senate was only a subordinate tribunal for moderating and concentrating the government; and the consuls themselves, although patricians, although chief magistrates, although generals with absolute authority in war, were in Rome only the presidents of the people.

From that time, moreover, the government seemed to follow its natural inclination, and tend strongly to aristocracy. The patriciate abolishing itself as it were, the aristocracy was no longer in the body of patricians as it is at Venice and Genoa, but in the body of the Senate, composed of patricians and plebeians, and also in the body of tribunes when they began to usurp an active power; for words make no difference in things, and when a nation has chiefs to govern for them, whatever name those chiefs bear, they always form an aristocracy.

From the abuses of aristocracy sprang the civil wars and the triumvirate. Sulla, Julius Caesar, Augustus, became in fact real monarchs; and at length, under the despotism of Tiberius, the state was broken up. Roman history, then, does not belie my principle, but confirms it.

②Omnes enim et habentur et dicuntur tyranni, qui potestate utuntur perpetua in ea civitate quae libertate usa est. ["For the reputation and name of tyrant belongs to all who exercise perpetual power in a state which has enjoyed freedom."] (Corn. Nep., in Miltiad., viii.) It is true that Aristotle (Nic. Eth., VIII, x) distinguishes the tyrant from the king, by the circumstance that the former governs for his own benefit, and the latter only for the benefit of his subjects, but besides the fact that, in general, all the Greek authors have taken the word tyrant in a different sense, as appears especially from Xenophon's

Hiero, it would follow from Aristotle's distinction that, since the beginning of the world, not a single king has yet existed.

CHAPTER 11
The Dissolution of the Body Politic

Such is the natural and inevitable tendency of the best constituted governments. If Sparta and Rome have perished, what state can hope to endure for ever? If we wish to form a durable constitution, let us, then, not dream of making it eternal. In order to succeed we must not attempt the impossible, nor flatter ourselves that we are giving to the work of men a stability which human things do not admit of.

The body politic, as well as the human body, begins to die from its birth, and bears in itself the causes of its own destruction. But both may have a constitution more or less robust, and fitted to preserve them a longer or shorter time. The constitution of man is the work of nature; that of the state is the work of art. It does not rest with men to prolong their lives; it does rest with them to prolong that of the state as far as possible by giving it the best constitution practicable. The best constituted will come to an end, but not so soon as another, unless some unforeseen accident brings about its premature destruction.

The principle of political life is in the sovereign authority. The legislative power is the heart of the state; the executive power is its brain, giving movement to all the parts. The brain may be paralysed and yet the individual may live. A man remains an imbecile and lives; but so soon as the heart ceases its functions, the animal dies.

It is not by laws that the state subsists, but by the legislative power. The law of yesterday is not binding today; but tacit consent is presumed from silence, and the sovereign is supposed to confirm continually the laws which it does not abrogate when able to do so. Whatever it has once declared that it wills, it wills always, unless the declaration is revoked.

Why, then, do people show so much respect for ancient laws? It is on account of their antiquity. We must believe that it is only the excellence of the ancient laws which has enabled them to be so long preserved; unless the sovereign had recognised them as constantly salutary, it would have revoked them a thousand times. That is why, far from being weakened, the laws are ever acquiring fresh vigour in every well-constituted state; the prejudice in favour of antiquity renders them more venerable every day; while, wherever laws are weakened as they grow old, this fact proves that there is no longer any legislative power, and that the state no longer lives.

CHAPTER 12
How the Sovereign Authority Is Maintained

The sovereign, having no other force than the legislative power, acts only through the laws; and the laws being nothing but authentic acts of the general will, the sovereign can act only when the people are assembled. The people assembled, it will be said: what a chimera! It is a chimera today; but it was not so two thousand years ago. Have men changed their nature?

The limits of the possible in moral things are less narrow than we think; it is our weaknesses, our vices, our prejudices, that contract them. Sordid souls do not believe in great men; vile slaves smile with a mocking air at the word liberty.

From what has been done let us consider what can be done. I shall not speak of the ancient republics of Greece; but the Roman Republic was, it seems to me, a great state, and the city of Rome a great city. The last census in Rome showed that there were 400,000 citizens bearing arms, and the last enumeration of the Empire showed more than 4,000,000 citizens, without reckoning subjects, foreigners, women, children, and slaves.

What a difficulty, we might suppose, there would be in assembling frequently the enormous population of the capital and its environs. Yet few weeks passed without the Roman people being assembled, even several times. Not only did they exercise the rights of sovereignty, but a part of the functions of government. They discussed certain affairs and judged certain causes, and in the public assembly the whole people were almost as often magistrates as citizens.

By going back to the early times of nations, we should find that the majority of the ancient governments, even monarchical ones like those of the Macedonians and the Franks, had similar councils. Be that as it may, this single incontestable fact solves all difficulties; inference from the actual to the possible appears to me sound.

CHAPTER 13
How the Sovereign Authority Is Maintained (continued)

It is not sufficient that the assembled people should have once fixed the constitution of the state by giving their sanction to a body of laws; it is not sufficient that they should have established a perpetual government, or that they should have once for all provided for the election of magistrates. Besides the extraordinary assemblies which unforeseen events may require, it is necessary that there should be fixed and periodical ones which nothing can abolish or prorogue; so that, on the appointed day, the people are rightfully convoked by the law, without needing for that purpose any formal summons.

But, excepting these assemblies which are lawful by their date alone, every assembly of the people that has not been convoked by the magistrates appointed for that duty and according to the prescribed forms, ought to be regarded as unlawful and all that is done in it as invalid, because even the order to assemble ought to emanate from the law.

As for the more or less frequent meetings of the lawful assemblies, they depend on so many considerations that no precise rules can be given about them. Only it may be said generally that the more force a government has, the more frequently should the sovereign display itself.

This, I shall be told, may be good for a single city; but what is to be done when the state comprises many cities? Will the sovereign authority be divided? Or must it be concentrated in a single city and render subject all the rest?

I answer that neither alternative is necessary. In the first place, the sovereign authority is simple and undivided, and we cannot divide it without destroying it. In the second place, a city, no more than a nation, can be lawfully subject to another, because the essence of the body politic consists in the union of obedience and liberty, and these words, subject and sovereign, are correlatives, the notion underlying them being expressed in the one word citizen.

I answer, further, that it is always an evil to combine several towns into a single state, and in desiring to effect such a union we must not flatter ourselves that we shall avoid the natural inconveniences of it. The abuses of great states cannot be brought as an objection against a man who only desires small ones. But how can small states be endowed with sufficient force to resist great ones? Just in the same way as when the Greek towns of old resisted the Great King, and as more recently Holland and Switzerland have resisted the House of Austria.

If, however, the state cannot be reduced to proper limits, one resource still remains; it is not to allow any capital, but to make the government sit alternately in each town, and also to assemble in them by turns the estates of the country.

People the territory uniformly, extend the same rights everywhere, spread everywhere abundance and life: in this way the state will become at once the strongest and the best governed that may be possible. Remember that the walls of the towns are formed solely of the remains of houses in the country. For every palace that I see rising in the capital, I seem to see a whole rural district laid in ruins.

CHAPTER 14
How the Sovereign Authority Is Maintained (continued)

So soon as the people are lawfully assembled as a sovereign body, the whole jurisdiction of the government ceases, the executive power is suspended, and the person of the meanest citizen is as sacred and inviolable as that of the first magistrate, because where the represented are, there is no longer any representative. Most of the tumults that arose in Rome in the comitia proceeded from ignorance or neglect of this rule. The consuls were then only presidents of the people and the tribunes simple orators;① the Senate had no power at all.

These intervals of suspension, in which the Prince recognises or ought to recognise the presence of a superior, have always been dreaded by that power; and these assemblies of the people, which are the shield of the body politic and the curb of the government, have in all ages been the terror of the chief men; hence such men are never wanting in solicitude, objections, obstacles, and' promises, in the endeavour to make the citizens disgusted with the assemblies. When the latter are avaricious, cowardly, pusillanimous, and more desirous of repose than of freedom, they do not long hold out against the repeated efforts of the government; and thus, as the resisting force constantly increases, the sovereign authority at last disappears, and most of the states decay and perish before their time.

But between the sovereign authority and an arbitrary government there is sometimes introduced an intermediate power of which I must speak.

---

① Almost in the sense given to this term in the Parliament of England. The resemblance between their offices would have set the consuls and tribunes in conflict, even if all jurisdiction had been suspended,

BOOK THREE

CHAPTER 15
Deputies or Representatives

So soon as the service of the state ceases to be the principal business of the citizens, and they prefer to render aid with their purses rather than their persons, the state is already on the brink of ruin. Is it necessary to march to battle, they pay troops and remain at home; is it necessary to go to the council, they elect deputies and remain at home. As a result of indolence and wealth, they at length have soldiers to enslave their country and representatives to sell it.

It is the bustle of commerce and of the arts, it is the greedy pursuit of gain, it is effeminacy and love of comforts, that commute personal services for money. Men sacrifice a portion of their profit in order to increase it at their ease. Give money and soon you will have chains. That word finance is a slave's word; it is unknown among citizens. In a country that is really free, the citizens do everything with their hands and nothing with money; far from paying for exemption from their duties, they would pay to perform them themselves. I am far removed from ordinary ideas; I believe that statute-labour (ies corvees) is less repugnant to liberty than taxation is.

The better constituted a state is, the more do public affairs outweigh private ones in the minds of the citizens. There is, indeed, a much smaller number of private affairs, because the amount of the general prosperity furnishes a more considerable portion to that of each individual, and less remains to be sought by individual exertions. In a well-conducted city-state everyone hastens to the assemblies; while under a bad government no one cares to move a step in order to attend them, because no one takes an interest in the proceedings, since it is foreseen that the general will will not prevail; and so at last private concerns become all absorbing. Good laws pave the way for better ones; bad laws lead to won;e ones. As soon as anyone says of the affairs of the state, "Of what importance are they to me?" we must consider that the state is lost.

The decline of patriotism, the active pursuit of private interests, the vast size of states, conquests, and the abuses of government, have suggested the plan of deputies or representatives of the people in the assemblies of the nation. It is this which-in certain countries they dare to call the third estate. Thus the private interest of two orders; is put in the first and second rank, the public interest only in the third.

Sovereignty cannot be represented for the same reason that it cannot be alienated; it consists essentially in the general will, and the will cannot be represented; it is the same or it is different; there is no medium. The deputies of the people, then, are not and cannot be its representatives; they are only its commissioners and can conclude nothing definitely. Every law which the people in person have not ratified is invalid; it is not a law. The English nation thinks that it is free, but is greatly mistaken, for it is so only during the election of members of Parliament; as soon as they are elected, it is enslaved and counts for nothing. The use which it makes of the brief moments of freedom renders the loss of liberty well-deserved.

The idea of representatives is modern; it comes to us from feudal government that absurd and iniquitous government, under which mankind is degraded and the name of man dishonoured. In the republics, and even in the monarchies, of antiquity, the people never had representatives; they did not know the word. It is very singular that in Rome, where the tribunes were so sacred, it was not even imagined that they could usurp the functions of the people, and in the midst of so great a multitude, they never attempted to pass of their own accord a single plebiscitum. We may judge, however, of the embarrassment which the crowd sometimes caused from what occurred in the time of the Gracchi, when a part of the citizens gave their votes on the house-tops. But where right and liberty are all in all, inconveniences are nothing. In that wise nation everything was estimated at a true value; it allowed the lictors to do what the tribunes had not dared to do, and was not afraid that the lictors would want to represent it.

第三卷
BOOK THREE

To explain, however, in what manner the tribunes sometimes represented it, it is sufficient to understand how the government represents the sovereign. The law being nothing but the declaration of the general will, it is clear that in their legislative capacity the people cannot be represented; but they can and should be represented in the executive power, which is only force applied to law. This shows that very few nations would, upon careful examination, be found to have laws. Be that as it may, it is certain that the tribunes, having no share in the executive power, could never represent the Roman people by right of their office, but only by encroaching on the rights of the Senate.

Among the Greeks, whatever the people had to do, they did themselves; they were constantly assembled in the public place. They lived in a mild climate and they were not avaricious; slaves performed the manual labour; the people's great business was liberty. Not having the same advantages, how are you to preserve the same rights? Your more rigorous climates give you more wants;① for six months in a year the public place is untenable, and your hoarse voices cannot be heard in the open air. You care more for gain than for liberty, and you fear slavery far less than you do misery.

What! is liberty maintained only with the help of slavery? Perhaps; extremes meet. Everything which is not according to nature has its inconveniences, and civil society more than all the rest. There are circumstances so unfortunate that people can preserve their freedom only at the expense of that of others, and the citizen cannot be completely free except when the slave is enslaved to the utmost. Such was the position of Sparta. As for you, modem nations, you have no slaves, but you are slaves; you pay for their freedom with your own. In vain do you boast of this preference; I find in it more of cowardice than of humanity.

I do not mean by all this that slaves are necessary and that the right of slavery is lawful, since I have proved the contrary; I only mention the reasons why modem nations who believe themselves free have representatives, and why ancient nations had none. Be that as it may, as soon as a nation appoints representatives, it is no longer free; it no longer exists.

After very careful consideration I do not see that it is possible henceforward for the sovereign to preserve among us the exercise of its rights unless the state is very small. But if it is very small will it not be subjugated? No; I shall show hereafter② how the external power of a great nation can be combined with the convenient polity and good order of a small state.

① To adopt in cold countries the effeminacy and luxuriousness of Orientals is to be willing to assume their chains, and to submit to them even more necessarily than they do.

② It is this which I had intended to do in the sequel to this work, when, in treating of external relations, I came to confederations - a wholly new subject, the principles of which have yet to be established.

CHAPTER 16
That the Institution of the Government Is Not a Contract

The legislative power being once well established, the question is to establish also the executive power; for this latter, which operates only by particular acts, not being of the essence of the other, is naturally separated from it. If it were possible that the sovereign, considered as such, should have the executive power, law and fact would be so confounded that it could no longer be known what is law and what is not; and the body politic, thus perverted, would soon become a prey to the violence against which it was instituted.

The citizens being all equal by the social contract, all can prescribe what all ought to do, while no one has a right to demand that another should do what he will not do himself Now, it is properly this right, indispensable to make the body politic live and move, which the sovereign gives to the Prince in establishing the government.

Several have pretended that the instrument in this establishment is a contract between the people and the chiefs whom they set over themselves a contract by which it is stipulated between the two parties on what conditions the one binds itself to rule, the other to obey. It will be agreed, I am sure, that this is a strange method of contracting. But let us see whether such a position is tenable.

First, the supreme authority can no more be modified than alienated; to limit it is to destroy it. It is absurd and contradictory that the sovereign should acknowledge a superior; to bind itself to obey a master is to regain full liberty.

Further, it is evident that this contract of the people with such or such persons is a particular act; whence it follows that the contract cannot be a law nor an act of sovereignty, and that consequently it is unlawful.

Moreover, we see that the contracting parties themselves would be under the law of nature alone, and without any security for the performance of their reciprocal engagements, which is in every way repugnant to the civil state. He who possesses the power being always capable of executing it, we might as well give the name contract to the act of a man who should say to another: "I give you all my property, on condition that you restore me what you please."

There is but one contract in the state that of association; and this of itself excludes any other. No public contract can be conceived which would not be a violation of the first.

CHAPTER 17
The Institution of the Government

Under what general notion, then must be included the act by which the government is instituted? I shall observe first that this act is complex, or composed of two others, viz, the establishment of the law and the execution of the law.

By the first, the sovereign determines that there shall be a governing body established in such or such a form; and it is clear that this act is a law.

By the second, the people nominate the chiefs who will be entrusted with the government when established. Now, this nomination, being a particular act, is not a second law, but only a consequence of the first, and a function of the government.

The difficulty is to understand how there can be an act of government before the government exists, and how the people, who are only sovereign or subjects, can, in certain circumstances, become the Prince or the magistrates.

Here, however, is disclosed one of those astonishing properties of the body politic, by which it reconciles operations apparently contradictory; for this is effected by a sudden conversion of sovereignty into democracy in such a manner that, without any perceptible change, and merely by a new relation of all to all, the citizens, having become magistrates, pass from general acts to particular acts, and from the law to the execution of it.

This change of relation is not a subtlety of speculation without example in practice; it occurs every day in the Parliament of England, in which the Lower House on certain occasions resolves itself into Grand Committee in order to discuss business better, and thus becomes a simple commission instead of the sovereign court that it was the moment before. In this way it afterwards reports to itself, as the House of Commons, what it has just decided in Grand Committee.

Such is the advantage peculiar to a democratic government, that it can be established in fact by a simple act of the general will; and after this, the provisional government remains in power, should that be the form adopted, or establishes in the name of the sovereign the government prescribed by the law; and thus everything is according to rule. It is impossible to institute the government in any other way that is legitimate without renouncing the principles heretofore established.

CHAPTER 18
Means of Preventing Usurpations of the Government

From these explanations it follows, in confirmation of chapter 16, that the act which institutes the government is not a contract, but a law; that the depositaries of the executive power are not the masters of the people, but its officers; that the people can appoint them and dismiss them at pleasure; that for them it is not a question of contracting, but of obeying, and that in undertaking the functions which the state imposes on them, they simply fulfil their duty as citizens, without having in any way a right to discuss the conditions.

When, therefore, it happens that the people institute a hereditary government, whether monarchical in a family or aristocratic in one order of citizens, it is not an engagement that they make, but a provisional form which they give to the administration, until they please to regulate it differently.

It is true that such changes are always dangerous, and that the established government must never be touched except when it becomes incompatible with the public good; but this circumspection is a maxim of policy, not a rule of right; and the state is no more bound to leave the civil authority to its chief men than the military authority to its generals.

Moreover, it is true that in such a case all the formalities requisite to distinguish a regular and lawful act from a seditious tumult, and the will of a whole people from the clamours of a faction, cannot be too carefully observed. It is especially in this case that only such concessions should be made as cannot in strict justice be refused; and from this obligation also the Prince derives a great advantage in preserving its power in spite of the people, without their being able to say that it has usurped the power; for while appearing to exercise nothing but its rights, it may very easily extend them, and, under pretext of maintaining the public peace, obstruct the assemblies designed to re-establish good order; so that it takes advantage of a

社会契约论
The Social Contract

silence which it prevents from being broken, or of irregularities which it causes to be committed, so as to assume in its favour the approbation of those whom fear renders silent and punish those that dare to speak. It is in this way that the Decemvirs, having at first been elected for one year, and then kept in office for another year, attempted to retain their power in perpetuity by no longer permitting the comitia to assemble; and it is by this easy method that all the governments in the world, when once invested with the public force, usurp sooner or later the sovereign authority.

The periodical assemblies of which I have spoken before are fitted to prevent or postpone this evil, especially when they need no formal convocation; for then the Prince cannot interfere with them, without openly proclaiming itself a violator of the laws and an enemy of the state.

These assemblies, which have as their object the maintenance of the social treaty, ought always to be opened with two propositions, which no one should be able to suppress, and which should pass separately by vote.

The first: "Whether it pleases the sovereign to maintain the present form of government."

The second: "Whether it pleases the people to leave the administration to those at present entrusted with it."

I presuppose here what I believe that I have proved, viz, that there is in the state no fundamental law which cannot be revoked, not even the social compact; for if all the citizens assembled in order to break this compact by a solemn agreement, no one can doubt that it would be quite legitimately broken. Grotius even thinks that each man can renounce the state of which he is a member, and regain his natural freedom and his property by quitting the country. [1]Now it would be absurd if all the citizens combined should be unable to do what each of them can do separately.

第三卷
BOOK THREE

① It must be clearly understood that no one should leave in order to evade his duty and relieve himself from serving his country at a moment when it needs him. Flight in that case would be criminal and punishable; it would no longer be retirement, but desertion.

BOOK FOUR

With regard to the rights of conquest, it has no other foundation than the law of the strongest. If war does not confer on the victor the right of slaying the vanquished, this right, which he does not possess, cannot be the foundation of a right to enslave them. If we have a right to slay an enemy only when it is impossible to enslave him, the right to enslave him is not derived from the right to kill him. It is therefore an iniquitous bargain to make him purchase his life, over which the victor has no right, at the cost of his liberty. In establishing the right of life and death upon the right of slavery, and the right of slavery upon the right of life and death, is it not manifest that one falls into a vicious circle?

Jean-Jacques Rousseau

第四卷
BOOK FOUR

CHAPTER 1
That the General Will Is Indestructible

So long as a number of men in combination are considered as a single body, they have but one will, which relates to the common preservation and to the general well-being. In such a case all the forces of the state are vigorous and simple, and its principles are clear and luminous; it has no confused and conflicting interests, the common good is everywhere plainly manifest and only good sense is required to perceive it. Peace, union, and equality are foes to political subtleties. Upright and simple-minded men are hard to deceive because of their simplicity; allurements and refined pretexts do not impose upon them; they are not even cunning enough to be dupes. When, in the happiest nation in the world, we see troops of peasants regulating the affairs of the state under an oak and always acting wisely, can we refrain from despising the refinements of other nations, who make themselves illustrious and wretched with so much art and mystery?

A state thus governed needs very few laws; and in so far as it becomes necessary to promulgate new ones, this necessity is universally recognised. The first man to propose them only gives expression to what all have previously felt, and neither factions nor eloquence will be needed to pass into law what everyone has already resolved to do, so soon as he is sure that the rest will act as he does.

What deceives reasoners is that, seeing only states that are illconstituted from the beginning, they are impressed with the impossibility of maintaining such a policy in those states; they laugh to think of all the follies to which a cunning knave, an insinuating speaker, can persuade the people of Paris or London. They know not that Cromwell would have been put in irons by the people of Berne, and the Duke of Beaufort imprisoned by the Genevese.

But when the social bond begins to be relaxed and the state weakened, when private interests begin to make themselves felt and small associations to exercise influence on the state, the common interest is injuriously affected and finds adversaries; unanimity no longer reigns in the voting; the general will is no longer the will of all; opposition and disputes arise, and the best counsel does not pass uncontested.

Lastly, when the state, on the verge of ruin, no longer subsists except in a vain and illusory form, when the social bond is broken in all hearts, when the basest interest shelters itself impudently under the sacred name of the public welfare, the general will becomes dumb; all, under the guidance of secret motives, no more express their opinions as citizens than if the state had never existed; and, under the name of laws, they deceitfully pass unjust decrees which have only private interest as their end.

Does it follow from this that the general will is destroyed or corrupted? No; it is always constant, unalterable, and pure; but it is subordinated to others which get the better of it. Each detaching his own interest from the common interest, sees clearly that he cannot completely separate it; but his share in the injury done to the state appears to him as nothing in comparison with the exclusive advantage which he aims at appropriating to himself This particular advantage being excepted, he desires the general welfare for his own interests quite as strongly as any other. Even in selling his vote for money, he does not extinguish in himself the general will, but eludes it. The fault that he commits is to change the state of the question, and to answer something different from what he was asked; so that, instead of saying by a vote: "It is beneficial to the state," he says: "It is beneficial to a certain man or a certain party that such or such a motion should pass." Thus the law of public order in assemblies is not so much to maintain in them the general will as to ensure that it shall always be consulted and always respond.

I might in this place make many reflections on the simple right of voting in every act of sovereignty a right which nothing can take away from the citizens and on that of speaking, proposing, dividing, and discussing, which the government is always very careful to leave to its members only; but this important matter would require a separate treatise, and I cannot say everything in this one.

CHAPTER 2
Voting

We see from the previous chapter that the manner in which public affairs are managed may give a sufficiently trustworthy indication of the character and health of the body politic. The more that harmony reigns in the assemblies, that is, the more the voting approaches unanimity, the more also is the general will predominant; but long discussions, dissensions, and uproar proclaim the ascendency of private interests and the decline of the state.

This is not so clearly apparent when two or more orders enter into its constitution, as, in Rome, the patricians and plebeians, whose quarrels often disturbed the comitia, even in the palmiest days of the Republic; but this exception is more apparent than real, for, at that time, by a vice inherent in the body politic, there were, so to speak, two states in one; what is not true of the two together is true of each separately. And, indeed, even in the most stormy times, the plebiscita of the people, when the Senate did not interfere with them, always passed peaceably and by a large majority of votes; the citizens having but one interest, the people had but one will.

At the other extremity of the circle unanimity returns; that is, when the citizens, fallen into slavery, have no longer either liberty or will. Then fear and flattery change votes into acclamations; men no longer deliberate, but adore or curse. Such was the disgraceful mode of speaking in the Senate under the Emperors. Sometimes it was done with ridiculous precautions. Tacitus observes that under Otho the senators, in overwhelming Vitellius with execrations, affected to make at the same time a frightful noise, in order that, if he happened to become master, he might not know what each of them had said.

From these different considerations are deduced the principles by which we should regulate the method of counting votes and of comparing opinions, according as the general will is more or less easy to ascertain and the state more or less degenerate.

There is but one law which by its nature requires unanimous consent, that is, the social compact; for civil association is the most voluntary act in the world; every man being born free and master of himself, no one can, under any pretext whatever, enslave him without his assent. To decide that the son of a slave is born a slave is to decide that he is not born a man.

If, then, at the time of the social compact, there are opponents of it, their opposition does not invalidate the contract, but only prevents them from being included in it; they

第四卷
BOOK FOUR

are foreigners among citizens. When the state is established, consent lies in residence; to dwell in the territory is to submit to the sovereignty.①

Excepting this original contract, the vote of the majority always binds all the rest, this being a result of the contract itself But it will be asked how a man can be free and yet forced to conform to wills which are not his own. How are opponents free and yet subject to laws they have not consented to?

I reply that the question is wrongly put. The citizen consents to all the laws, even to those which are passed in spite of him and even to those which puriish him when he dares to violate any of them. The unvarying will of all the members of the state is the general will; it is through that that they are citizens and free.② When a law is proposed in the assembly of the people, what is asked of them is not exactly whether they approve the proposition or reject it, but whether it is conformable or not to the general will, which is their own; each one in giving his vote expresses his opinion thereupon; and from the counting of the votes is obtained the declaration of the general will. When, therefore; the opinion opposed to my own prevails, that simply shows that I was mistaken, and that what I considered to be the general will was not so. Had my private opinion prevailed, I should have done something other than I wished; and in that case I should not have been free.

This supposes, it is true, that all the marks of the general will are still in the majority; when they cease to be so, whatever side we take, there is no longer any liberty.

In showing before how particular wills were substituted for general wills in public resolutions, I have sufficiently indicated the means practicable for preventing this abuse; I will speak of it again hereafter. With regard to the proportional number of votes for declaring this will, I have also laid down the principles according to which it may be determined. The difference of a single vote destroys unanimity; but between unanimity and equality there are many unequal divisions, at each of which this number can be fixed according to the condition and requirements of the body politic.

Two general principles may serve to regulate these proportions: the one, that the more important and weighty the resolutions, the nearer should the opinion which prevails approach unanimity; the other, that the greater the despatch requisite in the matter under discussion, the more should we restrict the prescribed difference in the division of opinions; in resolutions which must be come to immediately the majority of a single vote should suffice. The first of these principles appears more suitable to laws, the second to affairs. Be that as it may, it is by their combination that are established the best proportions which can be assigned for the decision of a majority.

① This must always be understood to relate to a free state, for otherwise family, property, want of an asylum, necessity, or violence, may detain an inhabitant in a country against his will; and then his residence alone no longer supposes his consent to the contract or to the violation of it.

②At Genoa we read in front of the prisons and on the fetters of the galley slaves the word, Libertas. This employment of the device is becoming and just. In reality, it is only the malefactors in all states who prevent the citizen from being free. In a country where all such people are in the galleys the most perfect liberty will be enjoyed.

CHAPTER 3
Elections

With regard to the elections of the Prince and the magistrates which are, as I have said, complex acts, there are two modes of procedure, viz. choice and lot. Both have been employed in different republics, and a very complicated mixture of the two is seen even now in the election of the Doge of Venice.

"Election by lot," says Montesquieu, "is of the nature of democracy." I agree, but how is it so? "The lot," he continues, "is a mode of election which mortifies no one; it leaves every citizen a reasonable hope of serving his country." But these are not the reasons.

If we are mindful that the election of the chiefs is a function of government and not of sovereignty, we shall see why the method of election by lot is more in the nature of democracy, in which the administration is by so much the better as its acts are less multiplied.

In every true democracy, the magistracy is not a boon but an onerous charge, which cannot fairly be imposed on one individual rather than on another. The law alone can impose this burden on the person upon whom the lot falls. For then, the conditions being equal for all, and the choice not being dependent on any human will, there is no particular application to alter the universality of the law.

In an aristocracy the Prince chooses the Prince, the government is maintained by itself, and voting is rightly established.

The instance of the election of the Doge of Venice, far from destroying this distinction, confirms it; this composite form is suitable in a mixed government. For it is an error to take the government of Venice as a true aristocracy. If the people have no share in the government, the nobles themselves are numerous. A multitude of poor Barnabotes never come near any magistracy, and have for their nobility only the empty title of Excellency and the right to attend the Great Council. This Great Council being as numerous as our General Council at Geneva, its illustrious members have no more privileges than our simple citizens (citoyens). It is certain that, setting aside the extreme disparity of the two Republics, the burgesses (la bourgeoisie) of Geneva exactly correspond to the Venetian order of patricians; our natives (natifs) and residents (habitants) represent the citizens and people of Venice; our peasants (paysans) represent the subjects of the mainland; in short, in whatever way we consider this Republic apart from its size, its government is no more aristocratic than ours. The whole difference is that, having no chief for life, we have not the same need for election by lot.

Elections by lot would have few drawbacks in a true democracy, in which, all being equal as well in character and ability as in sentiments and fortune, the choice would become almost indifferent. But I have already said that there is no true democracy.

When choice and lot are combined, the first should be employed to fill the posts that require peculiar talents, such as military appointments; the other is suitable for those in which good sense, justice, and integrity are sufficient, such as judicial offices, because, in a well-constituted state, these qualities are common to all the citizens.

Neither lot nor voting has any place in a monarchical government. The monarch being by right sole Prince and sole magistrate, the choice of his lieutenants belongs to him alone. When the Abbe de Saint-Pierre proposed to multiply the councils of the King of France and to elect the members of them by ballot, he did not see that he was proposing to change the form of government.

It would remain for me to speak of the method for recording and collecting votes in the assembly of the people; but perhaps the history of the Roman policy in that respect will explain more clearly all the principles which I might be able to establish. It is not unworthy of a judicious reader to see in some detail how public and private affairs were dealt with in a council of 200,000 men.

CHAPTER 4
The Roman Comitia

We have no very trustworthy records of the early times of Rome: there is even great probability that most of the things which have been handed down are fables,① and, in general, the most instructive part of the annals of nations, which is the history of their institution, is the most defective. Experience every day teaches us from what causes spring the revolutions of empires, but, as nations are no longer in process of formation, we have scarcely anything but conjectures to explain how they have been formed.

The customs which are found established at least testify that these customs had a beginning. Of the traditions that go back to these origins, those which the greatest authorities countenance, and which the strongest reasons confirm, ought to pass as the

BOOK FOUR

most undoubted. These are the principles which I have tried to follow in enquiring how the freest and most powerful nation in the world exercised its supreme power.

After the foundation of Rome, the growing republic, that is, the army of the founder, composed of Albans, Sabines, and foreigners, was divided into three classes, which, from this division, took the name of tribes. Each of these tribes was subdivided into ten curiae, and each curia into decuriae, at the head of which were placed curiones and decurianes.

Besides this, a body of one hundred horsemen or knights, called a centuria, was drawn from each tribe, whence we see that tHese divisions, not very necessary in a town, were at first only military. But it seems that an instinct of greatness induced the little town of Rome from the first to adopt a polity suitable to the capital of the world.

From this first division an inconvenience soon resulted; the tribe of the Albans[②] and that of the Sabines[③] remaining always in the same condition, while that of the foreigners[④] increased continually through perpetual accessions, the last soon outnumbered the two others. The remedy which Servius found for this dangerous abuse was to change the mode of division, and for the division by races, which he abolished, to substitute another derived from the districts of the city occupied by each tribe. Instead of three tribes he made four, each of which occupied one of the hills of Rome and bore its name. Thus, in remedying the existing inequality, he also prevented it for the future; and in order that this might be a division, not only of localities, but of men, he prohibited the inhabitants of one quarter from removing into another, which prevented the races from being mingled.

He also doubled the three old centuriae of cavalry and added twelve others to them, but still under the old names a simple and judicious means by which he effected a distinction between the body of knights and that of the people, without making the latter murmur.

To these four urban tribes Servius added fifteen others, called rural tribes, because they were formed of inhabitants of the country, divided into so many cantons. Afterwards as many new ones were formed; and the Roman people were at length divided into thirty-five tribes, a number which remained fixed until the close of the Republic.

From this distinction between the urban and the rural tribes resulted an effect worthy of notice, because there is no other instance of it, and because Rome owed to it both the preservation of her manners and the growth of her empire. It might be supposed that the urban tribes soon arrogated to themselves the power and the honours, and were ready to disparage the rural tribes. It was quite the reverse. We know the taste of the old Romans for a country life. This taste they derived from their wise founder, who united with liberty rural and military works, and relegated, so to speak, to the towns arts, trades, intrigue, wealth, and slavery.

Thus every eminent man that Rome had being a dweller in the fields and a tiller of the soil, it was customary to seek in the country only for the defenders of the Republic. This condition, being that of the worthiest patricians, was honoured by everyone: the simple and laborious life of villagers was preferred to the lax and indolent life of the burgesses of Rome; and many who would have been only wretched proletarians in the city became, as labourers in the fields, respected citizens. It is not without reason, said Varro, that our high-minded ancestors established in the village the nursery of those hardy and valiant men who defended them in time of war and sustained them in time of peace. Pliny says positively that the rural tribes were honoured because of the men that composed them, while the worthless whom it was desired to disgrace were transferred as a mark of ignominy into the urban tribes. The Sabine Appius Claudius, having come to settle in Rome, was there loaded with honours and enrolled in a rural tribe, which afterwards took the name of his family. Lastly, all the freedmen entered the urban tribes, never the rural; and during the whole of the Republic there is not a single example of any of these freedmen attaining a magistracy, although they had become citizens.

This maxim was excellent, but was pushed so far that at length a change, and certainly an abuse, in government, resulted from it.

First, the censors, after having long arrogated the right of transferring citizens arbitrarily from one tribe to another, allowed the majority to be enrolled in whichever

BOOK FOUR

they pleased - a permission which certainly was in no way advantageous, and took away one of the great resources of the censorship. Further, since the great and powerful all enrolled themselves in the rural tribes, while the freedmen who had become citizens remained with the populace in the urban ones, the tribes in general had no longer any district or territory, but all were so intermingled that it was impossible to distinguish the members of each except by the registers; so that the idea of the word tribe passed thus from the real to the personal, or rather became almost a chimera.

Moreover, it came about that the urban tribes, being close at hand, were often the most powerful in the comitia, and sold the state to those who stooped to buy the votes of the mob of which they were composed.

With regard to the curiae, the founder having formed ten in each tribe, the whole Roman people, at that time enclosed in the walls of the city, consisted of thirty curiae, each of which had its temples, its gods, its officers, its priests, and its festivals called compitalia, resembling the paganalia which the rural tribes had afterwards.

In the new division of Servius, the number thirty being incapable of equal distribution into four tribes, he was unwilling to touch them; and the curiae, being independent of the tribes, became another division of the inhabitants of Rome. But there was no question of curiae either in the rural tribes or in the people composing them, because the tribes having become a purely civil institution, and another mode of levying troops having been introduced, the military divisions of Romulus were found superfluous. Thus, although every citizen was enrolled in a tribe, it was far from being the case that each was enrolled in a curia.

Servius made yet a third division, which had no relation to the two preceding, but became by its effects the most important of all. He distributed the whole Roman people into six classes, which he distinguished, not by the place of residence, nor by the men, but by property; so that the first classes were filled with rich men, the last with poor men, and the intermediate ones with those who enjoyed a moderate fortune. These six classes were subdivided into one hundred and ninety-three other bodies called centuriae, and these bodies were so distributed that the first class alone comprised more than a half and the last formed only one. It thus happened that the class least numerous in men had most centuriae, and that the last entire class was counted as only one subdivision, although it alone contained more than a half of the inhabitants of Rome.

In order that the people might not so clearly discern the consequences of this last form, Servius affected to give it a military aspect. He introduced in the second class two centuriae of armourers, and two of makers of instruments of war in the fourth; in each class, except the last, he distinguished the young and the old, that is to say, those who were obliged to bear arms, and those who were exempted by law on account of age a distinction which, more than that of property, gave rise to the necessity of frequently repeating the census or enumeration; finally, he required that the assembly should be held in the Campus Martius, and that all who were qualified for service by age should gather there with their arms.

The reason why he did not follow in the last class this same division into seniors and juniors is, that the honour of bearing arms for their country was not granted to the populace of which it was composed; it was necessary to have homes in order to obtain the right of defending them; and out of those innumerable troops of beggars with which the armies of kings nowadays glitter, there is perhaps not one but would have been driven with scorn from a Roman cohort when soldiers were defenders of liberty.

Yet again, there was in the last class a distinction between the proletarii and those who were called capite censi. The former, not altogether destitute, at least supplied citizens to the state, sometimes even soldiers in pressing need. As for those who had nothing at all and could only be counted by heads, they were regarded as altogether unimportant, and Marius was the first who condescended to enrol them.

Without deciding here whether this third enumeration was good or bad in itself, I think I may affirm that nothing but the simple manners of the early Romans their disinterestedness, their taste for agriculture, their contempt for commerce and for the ardent pursuit of gain could have rendered it practicable. In what modern nation would rapacious greed, restlessness of spirit, intrigue, continual changes of residence, and the perpetual revolutions of fortune have allowed such an institution to endure for twenty years without the whole state being subverted? It is, indeed, necessary to observe carefully that morality and the censorship, more powerful than this institution, corrected its imperfections in Rome, and that many a rich man was relegated to the class of the poor for making too much display of his wealth.

From all this we may easily understand why mention is scarcely ever made of more than five classes, although there were really six. The sixth, which furnished neither soldiers to the army, nor voters to the Campus Martius,[5] and which was almost useless in the Republic, rarely counted as anything.

Such were the different divisions of the Roman people. Let us see now what effect they produced in the assemblies. These assemblies, lawfully convened, were called comitia; they were usually held in the Forum of Rome or in the Campus Martius, and were distinguished as comitia curiata, comitia centuriata, and comitia trihuta, in accordance with that one of the three forms by which they were regulated. The comitia curiata were founded by Romulus, the comitia centuriata by Servius, and the comitia trihuta by the tribunes of the people. No law received sanction, no magistrate was elected, except in the comitia; and as there was no citizen who was not enrolled in a curia, in a centuria, or in a tribe, it follows that no citizen was excluded from the right of voting, and that the Roman people were truly sovereign de jure and de facto.

In order that the comitia might be lawfully assembled, and that what was done in them might have the force of law, three conditions were necessary: the first, that the body or magistrate which convoked them should be invested with the necessary authority for that purpose; the second, that the assembly should be held on one of the days permitted by law; the third, that the auguries should be favourable.

The reason for the first regulation need not be explained; the second is a matter of administration; thus it was not permitted to hold the comitia on feast days and market days, when the country people, coming to Rome on business, had no leisure to pass the day in the place of assembly. By the third, the Senate kept in check a proud and turbulent people, and seasonably tempered the ardour of seditious tribunes; but the latter found more than one means of freeing themselves from this constraint.

Laws and the election of chiefs were not the only points submitted for the decision of the comitia; the Roman people having usurped the most important functions of government, the fate of Europe may be said to have been determined in their assemblies. This variety of subjects gave scope for the different forms which these assemblies took according to the matters which had to be decided.

To judge of these different forms, it is sufficient to compare them. Romulus, in instituting the curiae, desired to restrain the Senate by means of the people, and the people by means of the Senate, while ruling equally over all. He therefore gave the people by this form all the authority of numbers in order to balance that of power and wealth, which he left to the patricians. But, according to the spirit of a monarchy, he left still more advantage to the patricians through the influence of their clients in securing a plurality of votes. This admirable institution of patrons and clients was a masterpiece of policy and humanity, without which the patrician order, so opposed to the spirit of a republic, could not have subsisted. Rome alone has had the honour of giving to the world such a fine institution, from which there never resulted any abuse, and which notwithstanding has never been followed.

Since the form of the assembly of the curiae subsisted under the kings down to Servius, and since the reign of the last Tarquin is not considered legitimate, the royal laws were on this account generally distinguished by the name of leges curiatae.

Under the Republic the assembly of the curiae, always limited to the four urban tribes, and containing only the Roman populace, did not correspond either with the Senate, which was at the head of the patricians, or with the tribunes, who, although plebeians, were at the head of the middle-class citizens. It therefore fell into disrepute; and its degradation was such that its thirty assembled lictors did what the comitia curiata ought to have done.

The comitia centuriata was so favourable to the aristocracy that we do not at first see why the Senate did not always prevail in the comitia which bore that name, and by which the consuls, censors, and other curule magistrates were elected. Indeed, of the one hundred and ninety-three centuriae which formed the six classes of the whole Roman people, the first class comprising ninety-eight, and the votes being counted only by centuriae, this first class alone outnumbered in votes all the others. When all these centuriae were in agreement, the recording of votes was even discontinued; what the minority had decided passed for a decision of the multitude; and we may say that in the comitia centuriata affairs were regulated rather by the majority of crowns (ecus) than of votes.

But this excessive power was moderated in two ways: first, the tribunes usually, and a great number of plebeians always, being in the class of the rich, balanced the influence of the patricians in this first class. The second means consisted in this, that instead of making the centuriae vote according to their order, which would have caused the first class to begin always, one of them⁶ was drawn by lot and proceeded alone to the election; after which all the centuriae, being summoned on another day according to their rank, renewed the election and usually confirmed it. Thus the power of example was taken away from rank to be given to lot, according to the principle of democracy.

From this practice resulted yet another advantage; the citizens from the country had time, between the two elections, to gain information about the merits of the candidate provisionally chosen, and so record their votes with knowledge of the case. But, under pretence of despatch, this practice came to be abolished and the two elections took place on the same day.

The camilia tributa were properly the council of the Roman people. They were convoked only by the tribunes; in them the tribunes were elected and passed their plebiscita. Not only had the Senate no status in them it had not even a right to attend; and, being compelled to obey laws on which they could not vote, the senators were, in this respect, less free than the meanest citizens. This injustice was altogether impolitic, and alone sufficed to invalidate the decrees of a body to which all the citizens were not admitted. If all the patricians had taken part in these comitia according to the rights which they had as citizens, having become in that case simple individuals, they would have scarcely influenced a form in which votes were counted by the head, and in which the meanest proletarian had as much power as the Chief of the Senate.

We see, then, that besides the order which resulted from these different divisions for the collection of the votes of so great a people, these divisions were not reduced to forms immaterial in themselves, but that each had results corresponding with the purposes for which it was chosen.

Without entering upon this in greater detail, it follows from the preceding explanations that the camitia tributa were more favourable to popular government, and the camitia centuriata to aristocracy. With regard to the comitia curiata, in which the Roman populace alone formed the majority, as they served only to favour tyranny and evil designs, they deserved to fall into discredit, the seditious themselves refraining from a means which would too plainly reveal their projects. It is certain that the full majesty of the Roman people was found only in the comitia centuriata, which were alone complete, seeing that the rural tribes were absent from the comitia curiata and the Senate and the patricians from the comitia tributa.

The mode of collecting the votes among the early Romans was as simple as their manners, although still less simple than in Sparta. Each gave his vote with a loud voice, and a recording officer duly registered it; a majority of votes in each tribe determined the suffrage of the tribe; a majority of votes among the tribes determined the suffrage of the people; and so with the curiae and centuriae. This was a good practice so long as probity prevailed among the citizens and everyone was ashamed to record his vote publicly for an unjust measure or an unworthy man; but when the people were corrupted and votes were bought, it was expedient that they should be given secretly in order to restrain purchasers by distrust and give knaves an opportunity of not being traitors.

I know that Cicero blames this change and attributes to it in part the fall of the Republic. But although I feel the weight which Cicero's authority ought to have in this matter, I cannot adopt his opinion; on the contrary, I think that through not making sufficient changes of this kind, the downfall of the state was hastened. As the regimen of healthy persons is unfit for invalids, so we should not desire to govern a corrupt people by the laws which suit a good nation. Nothing supports this maxim better than the duration of the republic of Venice, only the semblance of which now exists, solely because its laws are suitable to none but worthless men.

Tablets, therefore, were distributed to the citizens In means of which each could vote without his decision being known; new formalities were also established for the collection of tablets, the counting of votes, the comparison of numbers, etc.; but this did not prevent suspicions as to the fidelity of the officers① charged with these duties. At length edicts were framed, the multitude of which proves their uselessness.

Towards the closing years, they were often compelled to resort to extraordinary expedients in order to supply the defects of the laws. Sometimes prodigies were feigned; but this method, which might impose on the people, did not impose on those who governed them. Sometimes an assembly was hastily summoned before the candidates had had time to canvass. Sometimes a whole sitting was consumed in talking when it was seen that the people having been won over were ready to pass a bad resolution. But at last ambition evaded everything; and it seems incredible that in the midst of so many abuses, this great nation, by favour of its ancient institutions, did not cease to elect magistrates, to pass laws, to judge causes, and to despatch public and private affairs with almost as much facility as the Senate itself could have done.

① The name of Rome, which is alleged to be derived from Ramulus, is Greek and means force; the name of Numa is also Greek and means law. What likelihood is there that the first two kings of that city should have borne at the outset names so clearly related to what they did?
② Ramnenses.
③ Tatientes.
④ Luceres.
⑤ I say 'to the Campus Martius', because it was there that the comitia

centuriata assembled; in the two other forms the people assembled in the Forum or elsewhere; and then the capite censi had as much influence and authority as the chief citizens.

⑥ This centuria, thus chosen by lot, was called praerogativa, because its suffrage was demanded first; hence came the word prerogative.

⑦ Custodes,diribitores,rogatores suffragiorum.

CHAPTER 5
The Tribuneship

When an exact relation cannot be established among the constituent parts of the state, or when indestructible causes are incessantly changing their relations, a special magistracy is instituted, which is not incorporated with the others, but which replaces each term in its true relation, forming a connection or middle term either between the Prince and the people, or between the Prince and the sovereign, or if necessary between both at once.

This body, which I shall call the tribuneship, is the guardian of the laws and of the legislative power. It sometimes serves to protect the sovereign against the government, as the tribunes of the people did in Rome; sometimes to support the government against the people, as the Council of Ten now does in Venice; and sometimes to maintain an equilibrium among all parts, as the ephors did in Sparta.

The tribuneship is not a constituent part of the state, and should have no share in the legislative or in the executive power; but it is in this very circumstance that its own power is greatest; for, while unable to do anything, it can prevent everything. It is,more sacred and more venerated, as defender of the laws, than the Prince that executes them and the sovereign that enacts them. This was very clearly seen in Rome, when those proud patricians, who always despised the people as a whole, were forced to bow before a simple officer of the people, who had neither auspices nor jurisdiction.

The tribuneship, wisely moderated, is the strongest support of a good constitution; but if its power be ever so little in excess, it overthrows everything. Weakness is not natural to it; and provided it has some power, it is never less than it should be.

It degenerates into tyranny when it usurps the executive power, of which it is only the moderator, and when it wishes to make the laws which it should only defend. The enormous power of the ephors, which was without danger so long as Sparta preserved her morality, accelerated the corruption when it had begun. The blood of Agis, slain by these tyrants, was avenged by his successor; but the crime and the punishment of the ephors alike hastened the fall of the republic, and, after Cleomenes, Sparta was no longer of any account. Rome, again, perished in the same way; and the excessive power of the tribunes, usurped by degrees, served at last, with the aid of laws framed on behalf of liberty, as a shield for the emperors who destroyed her. As for the Council of Ten in Venice, it is a tribunal of blood, horrible both to the patricians and to the people; and, far from resolutely defending the laws, it has only served since their degradation for striking secret blows which men dare not remark.

The tribuneship, like the government, is weakened by the multiplication of its members. When the tribunes of the Roman people, at first two in number and afterwards five, wished to double this number, the Senate allowed them to do so, being quite sure of controlling some by means of others, which did not fail to happen.

The best means of preventing the usurpations of such a formidable body, a means of which no government has hitherto availed itself, would be, not to make this body permanent, but to fix intervals during which it should remain suspended. These intervals, which should not be long enough to allow abuses time to become established, can be fixed by law in such a manner that it may be easy to shorten them in case of need by means of extraordinary commissions.

This method appears to me free from objection, because, as I have said, the tribuneship, forming no part of the constitution, can be removed without detriment; and it seems to me efficacious, because a magistrate newly established does not start with the power that his predecessor had, but with that which the law gives him.

CHAPTER 6
The Dictatorship

The inflexibility of the laws, which prevents them from being adapted to emergencies, may in certain cases render them pernicious, and thereby cause the ruin of the state in a time of crisis. The order and tardiness of the forms require a space of time which circumstances sometimes do not allow. A thousand cases may arise for which the legislator has not provided, and to perceive that everything cannot be foreseen is a very needful kind of foresight.

We must therefore not desire to establish political institutions so firmly as to take away the power of suspending their effects. Even Sparta allowed her laws to sleep.

But only the greatest dangers can outweigh that of changing the public order, and the sacred power of the laws should never be interfered with except when the safety of the country is at stake. In these rare and obvious cases, the public security is provided for by a special act, which entrusts the care of it to the most worthy man. This commission can be conferred in two ways, according to the nature of the danger.

If an increase in the activity of the government suffices to remedy this evil, we may concentrate it in one or two of its members; in that case it is not the authority of the laws which is changed but only the form of their administration. But if the danger is such that the formal process of law is an obstacle to our security, a supreme head is nominated, who may silence all the laws and suspend for a moment the sovereign authority. In such a case the general will is not doubtful, and it is clear that the primary intention of the people is that the state should not perish. In this way the suspension of the legislative power does not involve its abolition; the magistrate who silences it can make it speak; he dominates it without having power to represent it; he can do everything but make laws.

The first method was employed by the Roman Senate when it charged the consuls, by a consecrated formula, to provide for the safety of the Republic. The second was adopted when one of the two consuls nominated a dictator,[①] a usage of which Alba had furnished the precedent to Rome.

At the beginning of the Republic they very often had recourse to the dictatorship, because the state had not yet a sufficiently firm foundation to be able to maintain itself by the vigour of its constitution alone.

Public morality rendering superfluous at that time many precautions that would have been necessary at another time, there was no fear either that a dictator would abuse his authority or that he would attempt to retain it beyond the term. On the contrary, it seemed that so great a power must be a burden to him who was invested with it, such haste did he make to divest himself of it, as if to take the place of the laws were an office too arduous and too dangerous.

Therefore it is the danger, not of its abuse, but of its degradation, that makes me blame the indiscreet use of this supreme magistracy in early times; for whilst it was freely used at elections, at dedications, and in purely formal matters, there was reason to fear that it would become less formidable in case of need, and that the people would grow accustomed to regard as an empty title that which was only employed in empty ceremonies.

Towards the close of the Republic, the Romans, having become more circumspect, used the dictatorship sparingly with as little reason as they had formerly been prodigal of it. It was easy to see that their fear was ill-founded; that the weakness of the capital then constituted its security against the magistrates whom it had within it; that a dictator could, in certain cases, defend the public liberty without ever being able to assail it; and that the chains of Rome would not be forged in Rome itself, but in her armies. The slight resistance which Marius made against Sulla, and Pompey against Caesar, showed clearly what might be looked for from the authority within against the force without.

This error caused them to commit great mistakes; such, for example, was that of not appointing a dictator in the Catiline affair; for as it was only a question of the interior of the city, or at most of some province of Italy, a dictator, with the unlimited authority that the laws gave him, would have easily broken up the conspiracy, which was suppressed only by a combination of happy accidents such as human prudence could not have foreseen.

Instead of that, the Senate was content to entrust all its power to the consuls; whence it happened that Cicero, in order to act effectively, was constrained to exceed his authority in a material point, and that, although the first transports of joy caused his conduct to be approved, he was afterwards justly called to account for the blood of citizens shed contrary to the laws, a reproach which could not have been brought against a dictator. But the consul's eloquence won over everybody; and he himself, although a Roman, preferred his own glory to his country's good, and sought not so much the most certain and legitimate means of saving the state as the way to secure the whole credit of this affair.② Therefore he was justly honoured as the liberator of Rome and justly punished as a violator of the laws. However brilliant his recall may have been, it was certainly a pardon.

Moreover, in whatever way this important commission may be conferred, it is important to fix its duration at a very short term which can never be prolonged. In the crises which cause it to be established, the state is soon destroyed or saved; and, the urgent need having passed away, the dictatorship becomes tyrannical or useless. In Rome the dictators held office for six months only, and the majority abdicated before the end of this term. Had, the term been longer, they would perhaps have been tempted to prolong it still further, as the Decemvirs did their term of one year. The dictator only had time to provide for the necessity which had led to his election; he had no time to think of other projects.

① This nomination was made by night and in secret, as if they were ashamed to set a man above the laws.
② He could not be satisfied about this in proposing a dictator; he dared not nominate himself, and could not feel sure that his colleague would nominate him.

CHAPTER 7
The Censorship

Just as the declaration of the general will is made by the law, the declaration of public opinion is made by the censorship. Public opinion is a kind of law of which the censor is minister, and which he only applies to particular cases in the manner of the Prince.

The censorial tribunal, then, far from being the arbiter of the opinion of the people, only declares it, and so soon as it departs from this position, its decisions are fruitless and ineffectual.

It is useless to distinguish the character of a nation from the objects of its esteem, for all these things depend on the same principle and are necessarily intermixed. In all the nations of the world it is not nature but opinion which decides the choice of their pleasures. Reform men's opinions and their manners will be purified of themselves. People always like what is becoming or what they judge to be so; but it is in this judgment that they make mistakes; the question, then, is to guide their judgment. He who judges of manners judges of honour; and he who judges of honour takes his law from opinion.

The opinions of a nation spring from its constitution. Although the law does not regulate morality, it is legislation that gives it birth, and when legislation becomes impaired, morality degenerates; but then the judgment of the censors will not do what the power of the laws has failed to do.

It follows from this that the censorship may be useful to preserve morality, never to restore it. Institute censors while the laws are vigorous; so soon as they have lost their power all is over. Nothing that is lawful has any force when the laws cease to have any.

The censorship supports morality by preventing opinions from being corrupted, by preserving their integrity through wise applications, sometimes even by fixing them when they are still uncertain. The use of seconds in duels. carried to a mad extreme in the kingdom of France, was abolished by these simple words in an edict of the king: "As for those who have the cowardice to appoint seconds". This judgment, anticipating that of the public, immediately decided it. But when the same edicts wanted to declare that it was also cowardice to fight a duel, which is very true, but contrary to common opinion, the public ridiculed this decision, on which its judgment was already formed.

I have said elsewhere[①] that as public opinion is not subject to constraint, there should be no vestige of this in the tribunal established to represent it. We cannot admire too much the art with which this force, wholly lost among the modems, was set in operation among the Romans and still better among the Lace-daemonians.

A man of bad character having brought forward a good measure in the Council of Sparta, the ephors, without regarding him, caused the same measure to be proposed by a virtuous citizen. What an honour for the one, what a stigma for the other, without praise or blame being given to either! Certain drunkards from Samos[②] defiled the tribunal of the ephors; on the morrow a public edict granted permission to the Samians to be filthy. A real punishment would have been less severe than such impunity. When Sparta pronounced what was or was not honourable, Greece made no appeal from her decisions.

---

① I merely indicate in this chapter what I have treated at greater length in the Letter to M. d'Alembert.

② They were from another island, which the delicacy of our language forbids us to name on this occasion. [The island was Chios.]

BOOK FOUR

CHAPTER 8
Civil Religion

Men had at first no kings except the gods and no government but a theocracy. They reasoned like Caligula, and at that time they reasoned rightly. A long period is needed to change men's sentiments and ideas in order that they may resolve to take a fellow-man as a master and flatter themselves that all will be well.

From the single circumstance that a god was placed at the head of every political society, it followed that there were as many gods as nations. Two nations foreign to each other, and almost always hostile, could not long acknowledge the same master; two armies engaged in battle with each other could not obey the same leader. Thus from national divisions resulted polytheism, and from this, theological and civil intolerance, which are by nature the same, as will be shown hereafter.

The fancy of the Greeks that they recognised their own gods among barbarous nations arose from their regarding themselves as the natural sovereigns of those nations. But in our days that is a very ridiculous kind of erudition which turns on the identity of the gods of different nations, as if Moloch, Saturn, and Chronos could be the same god! As if the Baal of the Phoenicians, the Zeus of the Greeks, and the Jupiter of the Latins could be the same! As if there could be anything in common among imaginary beings bearing different names!

But if it is asked why under paganism, when every state had its worship and its gods, there were no wars of religion, I answer that it was for the same reason that each state, having its peculiar form of worship as well as its own government, did not distinguish its gods from its laws. Political warfare was also religious, the departments of the gods were, so to speak, fixed by the limits of the nations. The god of one nation had no right over other nations. The gods of the pagans were not jealous gods; they shared among them the empire of the world; even Moses and the Hebrew nation sometimes countenanced this idea by speaking of the god of Israel. It is true that they regarded as nought the gods of the Canaanites, proscribed nations, devoted to destruction, whose country they were to occupy; but see how they spoke of the divinities of the neighbouring nations whom they were forbidden to attack: "The possession of what belongs to Chamos your god," said Jephthah to the Ammonites, "is it not lawfully your due? By the same title we possess the lands which our conquering god has acquired."① In this, it seems to me, there was a well-recognised parity between the rights of Chamos and those of the god of Israel.

But when the Jews, subjected to the kings of Babylon, and afterwards to the kings of Syria, obstinately refused to acknowledge any other god than their own, this refusal being regarded as a rebellion against the conqueror, drew upon them the persecutions which we read of in their history, and of which no other instance appears before Christianity.②

Every religion, then, being exclusively attached to the laws of the state which prescribed it, there was no other way of converting a nation than to subdue it, and no other missionaries than conquerors; and the obligation to change their form of worship being the law imposed on the vanquished, it was necessary to begin by conquering before speaking of conversions. Far from men fighting for the gods, it was, as in Homer, the gods who fought for men; each sued for victory from his own god and paid for it with new altars. The Romans, before attacking a place, summoned its gods to abandon it; and when they left to the Tarentines their exasperated gods, it was because they then regarded these gods as subjected to their own and forced to pay them homage. They left the vanquished their gods as they left them their laws. A crown for the Capitoline Jupiter was often the only tribute that they imposed.

At last, the Romans having extended their worship and their laws with their empire, and having themselves often adopted those of the vanquished, the nations of this vast empire, since the light of citizenship was granted to all, found insensibly that they had multitudes of gods and religions, almost the same everywhere; and this is why paganism was at length known in the world as only a single religion.

It was in these circumstances that Jesus came to establish on earth a spiritual kingdom, which, separating the religious from the political system, destroyed the unity of the state, and caused the intestine divisions which have never ceased to agitate Christian nations. Now this new idea of a kingdom in the other world having never been able to enter the minds of the pagans, they always regarded Christians as actual rebels, who, under cover of a hypocritical submission, only sought an opportunity to make themselves independent and supreme, and to usurp by cunning the authority which, in their weakness, they pretended to respect. This was the cause of persecutions.

What the pagans had feared came to pass. Then everything changed its aspect; the humble Christians altered their tone, and soon this pretended kingdom of the other world became, under a visible chief, the most violent despotism in this world.

As, however, there have always been a Prince and civil laws, a perpetual conflict of jurisdiction has resulted from this double power, which has rendered any good polity impossible in Christian states; and no one has ever succeeded in understanding whether he was bound to obey the ruler or the priest.

Many nations, however, even in Europe or on its outskirts, wished to preserve or to re-establish the ancient system, but without success; the spirit of Christianity prevailed over everything. The sacred worship always retained or regained its independence of the sovereign, and without any necessary connection with the body of the state. Muhammad had very sound views; he thoroughly unified his political system; and so long as his form of government subsisted under his successors, the khalifs, the government was quite undivided and in that respect good. But the Arabs having become flourishing, learned, polished, effeminate, and indolent, were subjugated by the barbarians, and then the division between the two powers began again. Although it may be less apparent among the Muhammadans than among the Christians, the division nevertheless exists, especially in the sect of Ali; and there are states, such as Persia, in which it is still seen.

Among us, the kings of England have established themselves as heads of the church, and the Tsars have done the same; but by means of this title they have made themselves its ministers rather than its rulers; they have acquired not so much the right of changing it as the power of maintaining it; they are not its legislators but only its princes. Wherever the clergy form a corporation, ③ they are masters and legislators in their own country. There are, then, two powers, two sovereigns, in England and in Russia, just as elsewhere.

Of all Christian authors, the philosopher Hobbes is the only one who has clearly seen the evil and its remedy, and who has dared to propose a reunion of the heads of the eagle and the complete restoration of political unity, without which no state or government will ever be well constituted. But he ought to have seen that the domineering spirit of Christianity was incompatible with his system, and that the interest of the priest would always be stronger than that of the state. It is not so much what is horrible and false in his political theory as what is just and true that has rendered it odious. ④

I believe that by developing historical facts from this point of view, the opposite opinions of Bayle and Warburton might easily be refuted. The former of these maintains that no religion is useful to the body politic; the latter, on the other hand, asserts that Christianity is its strongest support. To the first it might be proved that no state was ever founded without religion serving as its basis, and to the second, that the Christian law is more injurious than useful to a firm constitution of the state. In order to succeed in making myself understood, I need only give a little more precision to the exceedingly vague ideas about religion in its relation to my subject.

Religion, considered with reference to society, which is either general or particular, may also be divided into two kinds, viz, the religion of the man and that of the citizen. The first, without temples, without altars, without rites, limited to the purely internal worship of the supreme God and to the eternal duties of morality, is the pure and simple religion of the Gospel, the true theism, and what may be called the natural divine law. The other, inscribed in a single country, gives to it its gods, its peculiar and tutelary patrons. It has its dogmas, its rites, its external worship prescribed by the laws; outside the single nation which observes it everything is for it infidel, foreign, and barbarous; it extends the duties and rights of men only as far as its altars. Such were all the religions of early nations, to which may be given the name of divine law, civil or positive.

There is a third and more extravagant kind of religion, which, giving to men two sets of laws, two chiefs, two countries, imposes on them contradictory duties, and prevents them from being at once devout men and citizens. Such is the religion of the Lamas, such is that of the Japanese, such is Roman Christianity. This may be called the religion of the priest. There results from it a kind of mixed and unsocial law which has no name.

Considered politically, these three kinds of religion all have their defects. The third is so evidently bad that it would be a waste of time to stop and prove this. Whatever destroys social unity is good for nothing; all institutions which put a man in contradiction with himself are worthless.

The second is good so far as it combines divine worship with love for the laws, and, by making their country the object of the citizens' adoration, teaches them that to serve the state is to serve the guardian deity. It is a kind of theocracy, in which there ought to be no pontiff but the Prince, no other priests than the magistrates. Then to die for one's country is to suffer martyrdom, to violate the laws is to be impious, and to subject a guilty man to public execration is to devote him to the wrath of the gods: Sacer esto.

But it is evil in so far as being based on error and falsehood, it deceives men, renders them credulous and superstitious, and obscures the true worship of the Deity with vain ceremonial. It is evil, again, when, becoming exclusive and tyrannical, it makes a nation sanguinary and intolerant, so that it thirsts after nothing but murder and massacre, and believes that it is performing a holy action in killing whosoever does not acknowledge its gods. This puts such a nation in a natural state of war with all others, which is very prejudicial to its own safety.

There remains, then, the religion of man or Christianity, not that of today, but that of the Gospel, which is quite different. By this holy, sublime, and pure religion, men, children of the same God, all recognise one another as brethren, and the social bond which unites them is not dissolved even at death.

But this religion, having no particular relation with the body politic, leaves to the laws only the force that they derive from themselves, without adding to them any other; and thereby one of the great bonds of the particular society remains ineffective. What is more, far from attaching the hearts of citizens to the state, it detaches them from it and from all earthly things. I know of nothing more contrary to the social spirit.

We are told that a nation of true Christians would form the most perfect society conceivable. In this supposition I see only one great difficulty that a society of true Christians would be no longer a society of men.

I say even that this supposed society, with all its perfection, would be neither the strongest nor the most durable; by virtue of its perfection it would lack cohesion; its perfection, indeed, would be its destroying vice.

Each man would perform his duty; the people would be obedient to the laws, the chief men would be just and moderate, and the magistrates upright and incorruptible; the soldiers would despise death; there would be neither vanity nor luxury. All this is very good; but let us look further.

Christianity is an entirely spiritual religion, concerned solely with heavenly things; the Christian's country is not of this world. He does his duty, it is true; but he does it with a profound indifference as to the good or ill success of his endeavours. Provided that he has nothing to reproach himself with, it matters little to him whether all goes well or ill here below. If the state is flourishing, he scarcely dares to enjoy the public felicity; he fears to take a pride in the glory of his country. If the state declines, he blesses the hand of God which lies heavy on his people.

In order that the society might be peaceable and harmony maintained, it would be necessary for all citizens without exception to be equally good Christians; but if unfortunately there happens to be in it a single ambitious man, a single hypocrite, a Catiline or a Cromwell for example, such a man will certainly obtain an advantage over his pious compatriots. Christian charity does not suffer men readily to think ill of their neighbours. As soon as a man has found by cunning the art of imposing on them and securing to himself a share in the public authority, he is invested with dignity; God wills that he should be revered. Soon he exercises dominion; God wills that he should be obeyed. The depositary of this power abuses it; this is the rod with which God punishes his children. They would have scruples about driving out the usurper; it would be necessary to disturb the public peace, to employ violence, to shed blood; all this ill accords with the meekness of the Christian, and, after all, does it matter whether they are free or enslaved in this vale of woes? The essential thing is to reach paradise, and resignation is but one means the more towards that.

Some foreign war comes on; the citizens march to battle without anxiety; none of them think of flight. They do their duty, but without an ardent desire for victory; they know better how to die than to conquer. What matters it whether they are the victors or the vanquished? Does not Providence know better than they what is needful for them? Conceive what an advantage a bold, impetuous, enthusiastic enemy can derive from this stoical indifference! Set against them those noble peoples who are consumed with a burning love of glory and of country. Suppose your Christian republic opposed to Sparta or Rome; the pious Christians will be beaten, crushed, destroyed, before they have time to collect themselves, or they will owe their safety only to the contempt which the enemy may conceive for them. To my mind that was a noble oath of the soldiers of Fabius; they did not swear to die or to conquer, they swore to return as conquerors, and kept their oath. Never would Christians have done such a thing; they would have believed that they were tempting God.

But I am mistaken in speaking of a Christian republic; each of these two words excludes the other. Christianity preaches only servitude and dependence. Its spirit is too favourable to tyranny for the latter not to profit by it always. True Christians are made to be slaves; they know it and. are hardly aroused by it. This short life has too little value in their eyes.

Christian troops are excellent, we are told. I deny it; let them show me any that are such. For my part, I know of no Christian troops. The crusades will be cited. Without disputing the valour of the crusaders, I shall observe that, far from being Christians, they were soldiers of the priest, citizens of the Church; they fought for their spiritual country, which the Church had somehow rendered temporal. Properly regarded, this brings us back to paganism; as the Gospel does not establish a national religion, any sacred war is impossible among Christians.

Under the pagan emperors Christian soldiers were brave; all Christian authors affirm it, and I believe it. There was a rivalry of honour against the pagan troops. As soon as the emperors became Christians, this rivalry no longer subsisted; and when the cross had driven out the eagle, all the Roman valour disappeared.

But, setting aside political considerations, let us return to the subject of right and determine principles on this important point. The right which the social pact gives to the sovereign over its subjects does not, as I have said, pass the limits of public utility.[5] Subjects, then., owe no account of their opinions to the sovereign except so far as those opinions are of moment to the community. Now it is very important for the state that every citizen should have a religion which may make him delight in his duties; but the dogmas of this religion concern neither the state nor its members, except so far as they affect morality and the duties which he who professes it is bound to perform towards others. Each may have, in addition, such opinions as he pleases, without its being the business of the sovereign to know them; for as he has no jurisdiction in the other world, the destiny of his subjects in the life to come, whatever it may be, is not his affair, provided they are good citizens in this life.

There is, however, a purely civil profession of faith, the articles of which it is the duty of the sovereign to determine, not exactly as dogmas of religion, but as sentiments of sociability, without which it is impossible to be a good citizen or a faithful subject.[6] Without having power to compel anyone to believe them, the sovereign may banish from the state whoever does not believe them; it may banish him not as impious, but as unsociable, as incapable of sincerely loving law and justice and of sacrificing at need his life to his duty.

BOOK FOUR

But if anyone, after publicly acknowledging these dogmas, behaves like an unbeliever in them, he should be punished with death; he has committed the greatest of crimes, he has lied before the laws.

The dogmas of civil religion ought to be simple, few in number, stated with precision, and without explanations or commentaries. The existence of the Deity, powerful, wise, beneficent, prescient, and bountiful, the life to come, the happiness of the just, the punishment of the wicked, the sanctity of the social contract and of the laws; these are the positive dogmas. As for the negative dogmas, I limit them to one only, that is, intolerance; it belongs to the creeds which we have excluded.

Those who distinguish civil intolerance from theological intolerance are, in my opinion, mistaken. These two kinds of intolerance are inseparable. It is impossible to live at peace with people whom we believe to be damned; to love them would be to hate God who punishes them. It is absolutely necessary to reclaim them or to punish them. Wherever theological intolerance is allowed, it cannot but have some effect in civil life;① and as soon as it has any, the sovereign is no longer sovereign even in secular affairs; from that time the priests are the real masters; the kings are only their officers.

Now that there is, and can be, no longer any exclusive national religion, we should tolerate all those which tolerate others, so far as their dogmas have nothing contrary to the duties of a citizen. But whosoever dares to say, "Outside the Church no salvation", ought to be driven from the state, unless the state be the Church and the Prince be the pontiff. Such a dogma is proper only in a theocratic government; in any other it is pernicious. The reason for which Henry IV is said to have embraced the Romish religion ought to have made any honourable man renounce it, and especially any prince who knew how to reason.

① "Nonne ea quae possidet Chamos deus tuus tibi jure debentur?" (Judges xi, 24). Such is the text of the Vulgate. Pere de Carrieres has translated it thus: "Do you not believe that you have a right to possess what belongs to Chamos your god?" I am ignorant of the force of the Hebrew text, but I see that in the

社会契约论
The Social Contract

Vulgate Jephthah positively acknowledges the right of the god Chamos and that the French translator weakens this acknowledgment by an "according to you" which is not in the Latin.

② There is the strongest evidence that the war of the Phocaeans, called a sacred war, was not a war of religion. Its object was to punish sacrilege, and not to subdue unbelievers.

③ It must, indeed, be remarked that it is not so much the formal assemblies, like those in France, that bind the clergy into one body, as the communion of churches. Communion and excommunication are the social pact of the clergy, a pact by means of which they will always be the masters of nations and kings. All priests who are of the same communion are fellow citizens, though they are as far asunder as the poles. This invention is a masterpiece of policy. There was nothing similar among pagan priests; therefore they never formed a body of clergy.

④ See, among others, in a letter from Grotius to his brother of the 11 th April, 1643, what that learned man approves and what he blames in the book De Cive. It is true that, inclined to indulgence, he appears to pardon the author for the good for the sake of the evil, but everyone is not so merciful.

⑤ 'In the commonwealth,' says the Marquis d'Argenson, 'each is perfectly free in what does not injure others.' That is the unalterable limit; it cannot be more accurately placed. I could not deny myself the pleasure of sometimes quoting this manuscript, although it is not known to the public, in order to do honour to the memory of an illustrious and honourable man, who preserved even in office the heart of a true citizen, and just and sound opinions about the government of his country.

⑥ Caesar, in pleading for Catiline, tried to establish the dogma of the mortality of the soul; Cato and Cicero, to confute him, did not waste time in philosophising; they were content to show that Caesar spoke as a bad citizen and put forward a doctrine pernicious to the state. Indeed, it was that which the Roman Senate had to decide, and not the theological question.

⑦ Marriage, for example, being a civil contract, has civil .consequences, without which it is even impossible for society to subsist. Let us, then, suppose that a clergy should succeed in arrogating to itself the sole right to perform this act, a right which it must necessarily usurp in every intolerant religion; then, is it not clear that in taking the opportunity to strengthen the Church's authority, it will render ineffectual that of the Prince, which will no longer have any subjects except those which the clergy are pleased to give it? Having the option of marrying or not marrying people, according as they hold or do not hold such or such a doctrine, according as they admit or reject such or such a formulary, according as they are more or less devoted to it, is it not clear that by behaving prudently and keeping firm, the Church alone will dispose of inheritances, offices, citizens, and the state itself, which cannot subsist when only composed of bastards? But, it will be said, men will appeal as against abuses; they will summon, issue decrees, and seize on the temporalities. What a pity! The clergy, however little they may have, I do not say of courage, but of good sense, will let this be done and go their way; they will quietly permit appealing, adjourning, decreeing, seizing, and will end by remaining masters. It is not, it seems to me, a great sacrifice to abandon a part, when one is sure of getting possession of the whole.

CHAPTER 9
Conclusion

After laying down the principles of political right and attempting to establish the state on its foundations, it would remain to strengthen it in its external relations; which would comprise the law of nations, commerce, the right of war and conquests, public rights, alliances, negotiations, treaties, etc. But all this forms a new subject too vast for my limited scope. I ought always to have confined myself to a narrower sphere.